Terry Eagleton

A Critical Introduction

James Smith

polity

Key Contemporary Thinkers

Published

Contents

Abbreviations

AG   *Against the Grain* (London: Verso, 1986)

AT   *After Theory* (London: Allen Lane, 2003)

BL   *The Body as Language* (London: Sheed and Ward, 1970)

CI   *Criticism and Ideology* (London: New Left Books, 1976)

CJ   *Crazy John and the Bishop* (Notre Dame: University of Notre Dame Press, 1998)

EE   *Exiles and Émigrés* (London: Chatto and Windus, 1970)

EN   *The English Novel* (Oxford: Blackwell, 2005)

FC   *The Function of Criticism* (London: Verso, 1984)

FD   *Figures of Dissent* (London: Verso, 2003)

G   *The Gatekeeper* (London: Allen Lane, 2001)

HGH   *Heathcliff and the Great Hunger* (London: Verso, 1995)

HRP   *How to Read a Poem* (Oxford: Blackwell, 2007)

HT   *Holy Terror* (Oxford: Oxford University Press, 2005)

I   *Ideology: An Introduction* (London: Verso, 1991)

IA   *The Ideology of the Aesthetic* (Oxford: Blackwell, 1990)

IC   *The Idea of Culture* (Oxford: Blackwell, 2000)

IP   *The Illusions of the Postmodernism* (Oxford: Blackwell, 1996)

LT   *Literary Theory: An Introduction* (Oxford: Blackwell, 1983)

MP   *Myths of Power* (London: Macmillan, 1975)

ML   *The Meaning of Life* (Oxford: Oxford University Press, 2007)

MLC   *Marxism and Literary Criticism* (London: Methuen, 1976)

NLC   *The New Left Church* (London: Sheed and Ward, 1966)

RC   *The Rape of Clarissa* (Oxford: Blackwell 1982)

SO   *Saint Oscar and Other Plays* (Oxford: Blackwell, 1997)

SR   *Scholars and Rebels in Nineteenth-Century Ireland* (Oxford: Blackwell, 1999)

SS   *Shakespeare and Society* (London: Chatto and Windus, 1967)

SSch   *Saints and Scholars* (London: Verso, 1987)

SW   *Sweet Violence* (Oxford: Blackwell, 2003)

WB   *Walter Benjamin* (London: Verso, 1981)

WS   *William Shakespeare* (Oxford: Blackwell, 1986)

Introduction

Terry Eagleton is arguably the most influential contemporary British literary critic and theorist. He is the author of over thirty books and hundreds of articles and essays. For a generation of readers, Eagleton's work has provided both a guide and a provocation in the fields of literary studies, critical theory, and cultural history. His *Literary Theory: An Introduction* served as one of the foundation texts as 'theory' rose to prominence in the higher education curriculum, becoming a staple on reading lists and an academic best-seller, while his writing has influenced and challenged numerous aspects of literary and cultural studies, whether in investigating the possibilities of a Marxist 'science of a text', the history of the aesthetic in modern thought, or the position of tragedy in Western literature, ensuring that Eagleton is one of the most frequently cited and debated figures across the span of literary fields. Equally, Eagleton's influence has extended well beyond the reading lists of literature departments, and he has sought to maintain what he would call a 'public-sphere' of readership and debate. Across a period of time in which the rise of theory has been accused of rendering literary criticism an increasingly specialized and professionalized pursuit, Eagleton's prolific book reviews and articles have regularly appeared in periodicals and newspapers such as the *London Review of Books*, *New Statesman*, the *Guardian*, and even *The Times*, positioning Eagleton as a latter-day man of letters, a public intellectual who is as likely to be explaining the significance of an obscure aspect of literary theory as to be commenting on the discourse of terrorism in contemporary society.

At the same time, Eagleton has achieved this prominence while remaining a political radical. Over an era in which many on the intellectual Left would now more readily identify with strains of post-Marxist thought, Eagleton has been for most of his career a committed Marxist, and his writing has been characterized by critical polemic and political conviction, balanced by his flair for parody and humour. As a result, Eagleton has been a figure who has provoked both admiration and controversy, attracting recognition ranging from being voted, in 2004, one of *Prospect* magazine's 'Top 100' British intellectuals (among whom he was the only literary theorist), to the great Canadian critic Northrop Frye once dubbing him 'that Marxist goof from Linacre College', and Prince Charles (as Eagleton proudly recounts) remarking to Oxford students about 'that dreadful Terry Eagleton'.

Despite this undoubted prominence and prolific critical and fictional output, it is a difficult task to pin a concise critical tag or position on to Eagleton's body of work. To describe Eagleton simply as a 'Marxist literary theorist' would seem too neat a label, and risks effacing the sheer variety and span of Eagleton's critical writing. Similarly, while many critics would speak of the influence that Eagleton's writing has had upon their field, it would be difficult to identify any distinctly 'Eagletonian' critical practice or theory that can be distilled down to a clear methodology, or point to any schools or disciples who would cite Eagleton as their founder, unlike many of the other names who rose to a similar prominence in the wave of literary and cultural theory which swept the academy in the 1970s and 1980s. Instead, Eagleton has occupied a more difficult terrain, with his position constantly adapting, reacting, and evolving throughout his career, his publications frequently situating themselves as polemical interventions in existing debates, displaying an uncanny ability for gauging and anticipating intellectual movements and currents, as well as for fastening upon and opening up areas of acute sensitivity and importance. As one critic assessed, Eagleton's writing can be characterized as being 'lucidly summarial rather than awkwardly pioneering, critically collatory rather than vulnerably visionary',[1] and he has been, as a recent profile in *The Chronicle of Higher Education* suggested, 'a quintessential wanderer', a figure who like 'Zelig or Forrest Gump . . . seems to have been there at all the crucial moments'.[2] To study the span of Eagleton's career is at once to be struck by the sheer variety of seemingly antagonistic positions taken by Eagleton's critical work: the committed socialist who became the first Marxist to hold a professorial chair at Oxford; a literary theorist who rose to prominence as a leading Althussarian 'theoretical anti-humanist', now releasing works unashamedly on *The Meaning of Life*; the political radical whose views on religion and God were recently plagiarized by an Archbishop; the literary critic who enthusiastically announced the death of literature in the 1980s and who subsequently published work entitled *The English Novel* and *How to Read a Poem*. Yet through this seemingly diffuse range of positions runs a constant thread, concerning how criticism can be pushed into new social and intellectual engagements, and the responsibility of the critic towards fulfilling a political function within society.

It is towards tracing a route through Eagleton's career that this present study is conducted, in an attempt to analyse and understand the span of the remarkable career, as well as to seek out the continuities and breaks that have marked Eagleton's own critical trajectory. Consequently, while dealing with the major and prominent examples of Eagleton's work in critical theory, such as *Criticism and Ideology* (1976), *The Ideology of the Aesthetic* (1990), and *Sweet Violence* (2003), I have also sought to address some of the lesser-known areas of his work. One of the areas that this book hopes to detail and clarify is Eagleton's involvement in radical Catholic politics in the 1960s, and the range of publications that he made in this field. This is an area of Eagleton's output of which the details are almost unknown among his wider cultural-theory readership, but provides an important element to understand the formation of his critical perspectives, and as a precursor to the recent 'metaphysical turn' that his writing has taken. I have also dedicated considerable space to analysis of Eagleton's literary output, such as his unpublished play, *Brecht and Company* (1979), his novel, *Saints and Scholars* (1987), and his major published plays, *Saint Oscar* (1989) and *The White, the Gold and the Gangrene* (1993), with the purpose of understanding them as literary works in their own right, as well as works that intersect with and illuminate key areas of Eagleton's broader cultural-theoretical concerns. In such a way, I hope that this study manages to cover the breadth of Eagleton's career, while doing justice to the style and variety of his critical engagements, and by doing so also reflect upon a wider series of debates that have occurred within the fields of literary and cultural theory over the past several decades.

Background

Eagleton published a widely praised memoir, *The Gatekeeper*, in 2001. It was a work which combined a range of witty anecdotes concerning characters Eagleton had encountered in his career, as well as musings on politics, cultural theory, and religion, while at the same time offering a knowing scarcity of direct facts about his life (indeed, at one point Eagleton slyly remarks in an aside about the art of writing 'anti-autobiography', so as to 'outwit the prurience and immodesty of the genre by frustrating your own desire for self-display and the reader's desire to enter your inner life'). Before moving onwards in this study, I will therefore first offer a brief biographical sketch, to fill out some of these data missing from the memoir, and to establish a framework for subsequent chapters.[3]

Terence Francis Eagleton was born in 1943 to a working-class family, of Irish decent, in Salford in North-West England, an industrial city that suffered from major economic decline during the second half of the twentieth century. Eagleton was educated at the Catholic De La Salle College, before gaining admission to read English at Trinity College, Cambridge, the largest and grandest of the University of Cambridge's constituent colleges, in 1961. Eagleton, while writing at some length about his experiences as an undergraduate at Cambridge, paints a largely negative view of how his career was shaped by this experience, going so far as to state that 'My education was a waste of time' (*G* 136). Nonetheless, Cambridge English, with its emphasis on study in tragedy and practical criticism, remained a formative influence upon Eagleton's critical preoccupations across his career. In terms of general influence, Eagleton's time as an undergraduate at Cambridge coincided with the peak of the institutional sway of the great 'practical critic', and founder of the influential journal *Scrutiny*, F. R. Leavis (with Leavis having been appointed to the English Faculty Board in 1954 and finally to a University Readership in 1959, and being before his break with Cambridge in 1964). While Eagleton never was, in any substantial way, a 'Leavisite' critic, much of his work nonetheless bears the indelible influence of Leavis and engages, either explicitly or implicitly, with the *Scrutiny* group's critical paradigm, ranging from his polemical attacks in works such as *Criticism and Ideology* (1976) and *Literary Theory* (1983), to the more recent preface to the collection of his essays *Figures of Dissent*, where he explained the 'combative tone' in his writing as possibly being an 'heirloom of the Cambridge English school' in which he was trained. As Eagleton went on to explain, 'I studied English at Cambridge in the last days of F. R. Leavis, so trenchancy seems to come naturally to me' (*FD* ix), and this will be a thread of influence which will be examined in many of the subsequent chapters of this work.

If Leavis formed one of the general influences over Cambridge English at this time, there were also other, more personal, interactions shaping Eagleton's intellectual perspectives. *The Gatekeeper* describes at some length Eagleton's recollections of his college teacher, a 'Dr Leo Greenway', whom Eagleton not only derided as having had 'no more ideas in his head than a hamster' (*G* 128), but also described him as his major and formative exposure to the liberal and patrician mindset – the 'first truly civilized man I had ever encountered' (*G* 127). The 'Greenway' of *The Gatekeeper* was a thinly disguised caricature of Theodore Redpath, Trinity College's first fellow in English, and a figure whose life was indeed as varied as Eagleton's depiction. Redpath, besides his academic career as editor of Shakespeare and Donne, and sometime student of Wittgenstein, had also, through his life, variously served as an intelligence officer, been called to the bar as a barrister, and set up a business as a wine-merchant; and maintained a reputation as a rigid upholder of antiquated college traditions (such as refusing to shake a student's hand unless it was vacation) – representing, in many ways, the archetypical version of the donnish, politically conservative critic that Eagleton's project would come to contest. The experience of studying under Redpath shaped Eagleton's perspective to the extent that much of Eagleton's later writing appears to continue a latent dialogue with the views he encountered in Redpath's office. Perhaps the most indicative instance of this can be found in the fact that almost forty years later, in explaining his motivation for writing his study of tragedy, *Sweet Violence*, Eagleton described it in terms of settling a debate started with Redpath – as he stated in an interview, 'He used to wipe the floor with me then . . . but now I think I've got him.'[4]

A third, and probably the most pervasive, influence from Cambridge came in the figure of Raymond Williams, the socialist critic and leading figure in the British New Left who, through studies such as *Culture and Society* (1958) and *The Long Revolution* (1961), was at this time one of the most prominent and important voices in British cultural criticism. As an undergraduate, Eagleton was described as being 'utterly bound up with Raymond',[5] and Eagleton has told of how he would 'go round the same Williams lectures time and time again'.[6] The concerns that Eagleton here encountered as an undergraduate would shape the critical direction of his later career, whether in works that explicitly draw upon Williams's paradigm or in developments that react against it, and they will become among the most constant engagements examined throughout this study.

Eagleton graduated from his undergraduate years with a First in English, before moving to Jesus College, Cambridge, as a junior research fellow and doctoral student, where he was supervised by Raymond Williams. Here Eagleton took responsibility for the teaching of the college's undergraduates while working on his dissertation on the Victorian poet and writer Edward Carpenter. It was at this time also that Eagleton became heavily involved with movements within the Catholic Left, coming under the influence of radical Dominican theologians such as Laurence Bright and Herbert McCabe, and becoming a founding editor of the radical journal *Slant*, designed as a provocation and intervention into debates surrounding the direction of Catholicism in the 1960s. This period would see the first sequence of Eagleton's publications, with theological works such as *The New Left Church* (1966) and literary-critical studies such as *Shakespeare and Society* (1967), establishing his prolific rate of publication from the earliest stages of his career.

In 1969, after it became evident that he was unlikely to obtain a lectureship in the English Faculty at Cambridge, Eagleton moved, as a tutorial fellow, to Wadham College, Oxford, a college which had a reputation as being among the most progressive of those constituent in the University of Oxford, and which provided Eagleton with an academic base for a number of decades. Although politically and intellectually at odds with many of the prevalent practices of the English Faculty in the wider university, Eagleton developed a reputation as a popular and influential teacher, with his undergraduate lectures frequently full to capacity, and with his establishment of a weekly seminar providing a focal point for others interested in emerging currents of critical theory. Throughout this period, he also remained actively engaged in socialist political organizations, particularly with the Trotskyist 'Workers' Socialist League', led by Alan Thornett, a prominent trade-unionist based in the Cowley car works near Oxford.

The 1970s would see intense debates in the Anglo-American academy concerning emerging modes of critical theory, spurred by the translation of predominantly French structuralist and post-structuralist thought. This would be particularly felt among members of the political New Left, grouped around the influential journal *New Left Review*, as interest and controversy surrounded the newly available work of the French philosopher Louis Althusser and his theories of a 'structuralist Marxism', which challenged the forms of socialist humanism previously predominant in British New Left thought. Eagleton would be among one of the new wave of figures influenced by such forms of emergent thought, with the publication of the Althusser-inspired *Criticism and Ideology* in 1976 establishing his international prominence as one of the leading figures in the field of Marxist critical theory. This reputation was consolidated by further work in the early 1980s such as *Walter Benjamin* (1981), before *Literary Theory: An Introduction* (1983) launched Eagleton to the forefront of the wider movement challenging the long dominance of what he would term as liberal-humanist critical modes.

Eagleton would occupy a series of positions at Oxford through his thirty-odd-year association with the institution. He moved to Linacre College as lecturer in critical theory in 1989, before being appointed to the senior position of Thomas Warton Professor of English in 1992 – after having been turned down previously for a personal chair in the faculty. At this time, he was also considering an offer made by a university in the USA. The appointment to the professorship quickly attracted attention as being more than a simple academic promotion: it was, rather, suggested in the national press that this was the first time a Marxist had held one of Oxford's professorial chairs, resulting in a remarkably hostile response from commentators in mainstream newspapers. One writer claimed that 'The man who spent years carving radical slogans into the woodwork of England's high table is now to be found seated at it, the napkin of conformity tucked firmly into his waistband, the goblet of gentility lustrous and brimming. After the Marxist meals come the bourgeois banquets, after the long knives come the fish knives';[7] while perhaps the most savage assessment came in the pages of the *Guardian*, where readers were titillated with details of Eagleton's class-traitor furniture (which readers were informed included 'a large and comfy sofa, part of a bourgeois three-piece suite'), quotes from safely anonymous 'former students' and 'Oxford dons', and the suggestion that no billet could be 'comfier' that the Professorship, which only involved '36 hours of teaching a year, and supervising a few postgraduates, for a salary of £31,000'.[8] This reaction, while savage, would in fact serve to consolidate Eagleton's public position as one of the most prominent of British Leftist intellectuals, particularly in the wake of Raymond Williams's death in 1988. This period would see Eagleton emerge as one of the most forceful critics of postmodernism, embodied in works such as *The Illusions of Postmodernism* (1996), as well as being a period in which he diversified critical modes, with an increased range of output now occurring in non-specialized periodicals such as the *London Review of Books*, or in the form of dramatic works such as those published in *Saint Oscar and Other Plays* (1997), capturing a space as a 'public intellectual' in wider cultural debates. It would also see Eagleton increasingly concerned with Irish history and culture, as he released a trilogy of works on these issues, launched by *Heathcliff and the Great Hunger* (1995).

The final break with Oxbridge came in 2001, with a move to the University of Manchester as the John Edward Taylor Professor of English Literature, with Eagleton now dividing time between living in England and Ireland. In his most recent critical direction, his writing has undertaken what he has termed a 'metaphysical' turn, re-engaging with the themes that occupied his earliest works in the 1960s, in order to reconnect with topics such as tragedy, as undertaken in *Sweet Violence* (2003), as well as to goad the Left into new forms of critical engagement beyond the standard cultural theory topics of 'class, race and gender', a position most directly developed in *After Theory* (2003).

That then, in its barest outlines, has been the shape of Eagleton's career. I will thus now proceed back to the point where it all began, to Eagleton the Christian radical of the 1960s.

1

Eagleton and the Catholic Left

In March 1967, *Time*, the United States news magazine, published a brief article concerning a radical British political movement, whose ideas were now beginning to gain some degree of circulation in the United States of America. Noting that while most 'radical movements have [either] been founded in the name of Karl Marx, [or] others in the name of Christ', the *Time* correspondent nominated the English 'New Left Catholics' as one of the 'rare exceptions' which claimed direct alliance to both. The founders of this movement were described as 'a coterie of Cambridge-educated intellectuals who advocate a social revolution that is both Communist and Christian', and the article went on to describe the movement's politics in slightly puzzled terms: 'Not content to condemn capitalism as a moral evil, they also denounce the British Labor Party as the tired-blood expression of a bourgeois working class. In their view, the church is equally obsolescent in structure and needs to be seriously reconstructed if it is to share in organizing the revolution.' Various leaders of this movement were listed by the magazine: Neil Middleton, director of the publishing company Sheed and Ward; Brian Wicker, a lecturer in English and columnist for the *Guardian*; and a twenty-four-year-old named Terence Eagleton, who was described as being 'an editor of the New Left periodical *Slant*, [and] a fellow of Jesus College, Cambridge'.[1]

While Eagleton's name is now most commonly associated with the fields of literary theory and Marxist literary criticism, it is easy to overlook the fact that his first major area of publication and prominent intellectual activity was in the field of Catholic theology. Yet it is in this field where he was highly active during the 1960s, as one of the founding editors of the radical Catholic journal *Slant*, a publication that would serve as a rallying point for a group of like-minded radical Christians, seeking to develop both a challenge to the structures and beliefs of the Catholic Church, as well as to stage a distinctly Christian engagement with the wider movement of the New Left.

This chapter will trace Eagleton's involvement with the Catholic New Left in the 1960s, paying specific attention to his involvement with *Slant*, and his two significant book-length publications in the field, *The New Left Church* and *The Body as Language*. It is not my intention to provide a detailed theological critique of Eagleton's position at this time so much as to attempt to contextualize and examine Eagleton's position within the *Slant* movement and the Catholic Left in this period, and through this highlight such factors as the influence that the Dominican Herbert McCabe had upon Eagleton's writing – an influence that has come to the forefront of Eagleton's work in recent years.

The Context of the British Christian Left: The New Left and the Second Vatican Council

Eagleton's involvement in the Catholic Left, and the founding of the journal *Slant*, occurred at a unique political junction in the 1960s, when both secular left-wing organizations and the Catholic Church were undergoing renewal and reorganization. To understand his position and work that emerged at this time, it is thus necessary to examine the wider context of these movements, specifically that of the emergence of the New Left in Britain as an influential political movement, and the debates within the Catholic Church in the wake of the Vatican II progressive reforms.

During the period of Eagleton's involvement with the Catholic Left, the Catholic Church itself was undergoing significant reform, in the wake of the Second Vatican Council (or Vatican II), held in Rome from 1962–5: an issue that would serve as the major conjecture from which *Slant* emerged. Vatican II had undertaken a wide-ranging reconsideration of aspects of the Catholic faith, such as its relationship to other branches of Christianity and religions, the reconsideration of the role of the liturgy in favour of a more inclusive celebration, and the right of personal liberty in religious beliefs, providing significant impetus for modernizers and progressives in the Church. In *The Gatekeeper* Eagleton described the 'surge of spiritual renewal' that had swept across the Church in the wake of Vatican II, 'Bishops were mocked and heckled ... Priests who had kissed one another in private for decades began to do it in broad daylight', and 'aloof, ascetic monks suddenly reinvented themselves as raucous thigh-slapping Trotskyites' (*G* 21). While this is obviously a parody, to some degree, of the over-enthusiasm generated by the changes made by Vatican II, it still conveys some sense of the possibilities that infused Catholic progressives at this time – an enthusiasm of which *Slant* itself was a manifestation.

Eagleton and the *Slant* group were not simply concerned with the adaptation of the reforms, but instead used this momentum of initial change to push the Church into a more radical position: as Eagleton expressed in the preface to *Directions: Pointers for the Post-Conciliar Church* (a collection of essays that he edited, with contributions from many in the *Slant* group), the area of investigation and action that the Catholic Left in Britain needed to undertake was to examine 'the structure of parish and priesthood, problems of education and catechetics, issues of peace and communications, social morality and social reconstruction' in light of the reality of what had been achieved, and to highlight the 'real achievement ... to the frontiers where the council stopped short or the areas where its demands have been quietly and politely steamrollered in the interests of "harmony"'.[2]

If these were the internal debates occurring within Catholicism at this time, it was the emergence of the New Left that was forcing a fundamental rethink in the conception, theory, and action of left-wing politics in Britain, and thus proving the major political impetus for Christian radicals to draw upon, and an influence that was crucial to the formative direction of Eagleton's career. The British New Left had evolved as a political movement in the wake of 1956, when the Soviet leader Khrushchev's 'Secret Speech' (which both detailed much of the brutality of Stalin and denounced his legacy), and the Soviet invasion of Hungary, had prompted many members of the Communist Party of Great Britain to quit the party, and instead seek alternative forms of socialist political organization. Evidence of the intellectual activity that such political shifts generated can be seen in the variety of new publications and organization that were founded, in an attempt to outline new theories and modes of political engagement. Particularly significant among these was

The New Left Review founded in 1960,[3] the journal that would initially be the focal point of many of the major socialist-humanist New Left figures (such as Raymond Williams, E. P. Thompson, and Stuart Hall), and which would later be taken over by Perry Anderson and become increasingly concerned with engaging with new modes of Marxist theory available in Europe (to which Eagleton would be a noted contributor). One of the highpoints of New Left activity occurred with the release of the *New Left May Day Manifesto* in 1967, which both signalled the New Left's disillusionment with the direction of Labour under the leadership of Harold Wilson, and argued for the new modes of political activity necessary to revitalize the democratic socialist movement in Britain. The manifesto set out their claims:

> We intend to take part, as allies, in all the social conflicts, of every kind, which then follow. We will see each conflict as an opportunity for explaining the character of the system which is cheating us, and so as a way of helping to change consciousness: to follow the needs and the feelings through until they reach the point of demands which the system can neither satisfy nor contain.[4]

It was the New Left that provided much of the wider political context for the *Slant* group, with *Slant* attempting both to draw on the work of the New Left for their own analysis of their distinct Catholic political situation, and to bridge the gap between discourses on the Left and those in the Church, with the work of Williams and Thompson highly influential over the *Slant* journal's own analyses of culture and institutions. Indeed, from the outset there was direct crossover between members of the New Left and those in the Catholic Left and *Slant* group, with Raymond Williams (himself an agnostic) writing the introductory note to the first issue of *Slant*, which is interesting both in showing Williams's cautious but still receptive position regarding the *Slant* project, as well as his wider possibilities of the religious Left contributing to the wider New Left culture of the time:

> [T]hose of us who have grown within a Christian intellectual tradition, and who have come to reject religious belief, look anxiously yet deliberately for values of a comparable or greater depth by which we can live and act. We look also, with interest and concern, to what Christian thinkers are themselves able to believe, in a common world . . . we find – I have found many times – that the contemporary Christian inquiry into the central political issues has

positive qualities in its seriousness and energy, from which, if we cannot learn, we can take heart and fellow-feeling.[5]

If this was the broad historical junction in which Eagleton's involvement in *Slant* began, it is also important to note the direct theological and political inspiration that came from Herbert McCabe and Laurence Bright, both Dominicans and the leading members of the December Group. In 1965 McCabe had been sent to help establish (and later edit) the theological journal *New Blackfriars* (to which Eagleton would later be a frequent contributor). During his editorship McCabe established a reputation as a radical thinker within the Catholic Church, which was perhaps most famously highlighted after being suspended from both the editorship and (briefly) from the priesthood in 1967, after publicly stating the opinion that the Church was 'quite plainly corrupt', but that progressive members of the Church should stay within the institution and work for change, rather than abandoning it in political and theological disillusionment.[6]

Besides his editorial work, McCabe published a number of significant studies in his lifetime, such as *The New Creation* in 1964 and *Law, Love and Language* in 1968, in which he combined the influence of Thomas Aquinas with Wittgenstein and Marx in arguing a passionate case concerning the radical potentiality in both the practices of Catholicism and the figure of Christ; and these are two studies that, as will be seen later, profoundly influenced the writing of Eagleton. In *The New Creation* McCabe offered a wide study that ranged from examinations of the symbolism of sacramental systems to considerations of human sexuality and the nature of hell. Underpinning McCabe's investigations was his conception of the fractured nature of humanity, and the fact that humans are denied the ability to enter into a full relationship with one another, or achieve a society based on understanding and community: 'We are born with a constitutional inability to live together in love; we achieve a precarious unity only with great difficulty and for a short time; there is a flaw in the very flesh we have inherited which makes for division between us.' It is in the resurrection of Christ that McCabe sees the fulfilment of this long denied community, for the 'teaching of the Bible is that the goal of mankind, real unity in love amongst men, can only be reached by dying to our injured human nature . . . and rising again to a new physical human community in the risen Christ', with the sacraments of the Church 'as the ways in which men are able to break down the barriers between them and form a real community'.[7] In *Law, Love and Language* McCabe offered a more overtly politicized case (for example, raising the issues of the killing of children in Saigon to link the import of his debate on the question of the unfolding Vietnam War), as he sought to argue the grounds from which a radical Christian ethics could be based. Arguing against notions of ethics simply based on the categories of love or natural law, McCabe outlined a Wittgenstein-inspired case in which human ethics are seen to stem from 'communication, with the fact that human animals make use of conventional signs and symbols' and 'that men communicate not merely in a human language but in the language of God'.[8] In this view ethics is a struggle to achieve more significant modes of human community: 'Men belong to each other (and thereby exist) in trivial ways and in less trivial ways . . . we can say that ethics is the quest for less and less trivial modes of human relatedness.' In this way 'ethics points towards, without being able to define or comprehend, an ultimate medium of human communication which is beyond humanity and which we call divinity'.[9] It is this need to strive towards full human communication, towards 'divinity', that McCabe sees as commanding the Christian not just to undertake a 'personal' revolution, but actively to join the political struggles in a wider society. The conclusion of McCabe's study articulates the need for the Christian to view the coming of Christ not as an excuse for disengaging with the world, but rather as a motivation for the engagement, as a necessary precondition for creating the true kingdom of heaven:

> The Christian . . . is not concerned to extend the areas of an autonomy which in the end means irresponsibility, but to transform media of domination into media of communication, media of self-assertion into media of self-expression. He is aware that this will never be finally achieved without a transfiguration of man, a radical revolution that reaches down to the depths of our bodily life and which therefore means death and resurrection. He is not, however, solely concerned with this ultimate revolution. His business is the continuing transformation of the world that leads up to this final parousia.[10]

In McCabe's theology, Christianity and socialism are not seamlessly reconciled, but rather strategically and temporarily aligned: 'the Christians' relation to the revolution can never be a simple one, he needs to be constantly critical of the political revolution lest it should become a substitute for the final transformation of the world'.[11] In light of these works, McCabe established a prominent reputation as a controversial thinker in the Catholic tradition, and one who was prepared to push debates and reasoning forward into territories from which other Catholic theologians and intellectuals shied away.

A further direct Dominican influence over the group came from the figure of Laurence Bright. Bright was similarly active in debates on the Catholic Left at the time, a frequent speaker at symposiums and editor of collections such as *Christians and World Freedom* that sought to outline the Christian's duty 'to work actively for peace, for social justice, for the end of class inequality and race hatred, through the institutions which the secular community to which we belong has set up'.[12] As Eagleton detailed in some length in *The Gatekeeper*, Bright was a formative influence on the young Eagleton, being the man who 'finally liberated' him from his 'stiff-necked papist-correctness', and showed him that it was possible to remain both a Christian and a radical.

Bright was one of the major factors behind the founding of *Slant*, contributing both as editor and writer to the project, and it was from this particularly charged political conjecture that the impetus behind the *Slant* group was derived. As described by Adrian Cunningham, *Slant* had originally been conceived by a grouping of young Christian radicals as a direct political intervention into the situation of the Catholic community at the University of Cambridge, and specifically as a counter to the conservative chaplaincy of Alfred Newman Gilbey, the chaplain to Catholic undergraduates at the University of Cambridge. Gilbey, who had been appointed as chaplain in 1932, had refused to adapt to offering a mixed chaplaincy at Cambridge after women were admitted as full members of the university in 1948, preferring instead to maintain a segregated system which kept women from attending the main Sunday Mass. However, at the instigation of Bright, the *Slant* group expanded its aim towards establishing a professionally designed journal with a circulation of one thousand copies and widespread distribution, rather than a local organ of limited circulation aimed at a directly local political conjecture. *Slant* was launched in 1964 by an editorial group that mainly consisted of Cambridge students, with the first edition carrying contributions from, among others, Adrian Cunningham (now professor of religious studies at the University of Lancaster), Brian Wicker (now Chair of the Council on Christian Approaches to Defence and Disarmament), and Eagleton himself, with Anthony Downing as editor and Eagleton in charge of advertising. In the most immediate terms, *Slant* was a success: Gilbey was forced into an early retirement in 1965, allowing reforms to the Cambridge University Catholic chaplaincy to take place. But in wider terms, *Slant* emerged as a prominent movement in progressive British Catholicism of the 1960s, seeking to intervene in debates both within the Catholic Church itself, as well as in generating progressive Christian perspectives on wider debates and issues in society. Each issue saw editorials setting out provocations and statements of *Slant* positions, from '*Slant* on Abortion' to '*Slant* on Class War'; and would carry articles ranging from those on specific religious topics of theology, liturgy, and the contemporary organization of the Catholic Church; to wider investigations concerning world politics, such as on the situation of Israel and Palestine in the Middle East, and the results of protest in London concerning the ongoing Vietnam War. Equally, *Slant* was not limited to articles on current political events, but also detailed wider developments in progressive arts and culture, carrying (for example) an early review article on the ideas of Michel Foucault,[13] and works discussing the political implications of the aesthetics of Bertolt Brecht.[14]

Eagleton and *Slant*

This sets out the broad context from which *Slant* emerged, and I will now move to the specific case of Eagleton's involvement within this project. Aside from his work as one of the founding editors (and, later in its existence, editor-in-chief) of the journal, Eagleton's own contributions to *Slant* took a number of forms, ranging from poetry and book reviews, to essays and polemics. Many of his pieces published in *Slant* were intended as direct political interventions or statements of position, aiming to explain both why radicals should seek to stay in the Church, and how the Church can be revisioned in a socialist form. Eagleton's first article in *Slant*, 'Labour in the Vineyard', for example, offers an attempt to negotiate the question of what being 'political' means in the Catholic Church, decrying the fractured perception between 'religious' and 'political' concerns. Eagleton points to the hypocrisy of the situation where 'the parish priest can thus denounce capitalism in the morning and attend the local Catenian dinner [a Catholic businesses association] in the evening for the simple reason that he accepts . . . politics and religion, although occasionally impinging on each other's territory in the form of social encyclical acceptable to General Franco, are ultimately different kinds of reality', and instead reiterates the recognition that being a Christian demands contributing 'what Christian energies we still possess towards destroying what at the moment passes for "community" and constructing in its place a society where Christ can live in fact rather than word'.[15] Later articles would address areas ranging from demands for the abolition of the geographical parish and separate Catholic educational systems on the ground that it encouraged a political separatism; through to examinations of how Catholics should engage with the mass media of society.[16]

A significant proportion of Eagleton's project in his *Slant* publications was to theorize the possibilities and common ground between socialist and Christian thought, and show how the Christian faith, rather than being antithetical to radical political action, provided crucial ethical backing to a materialist political movement. In other articles, however, we can see the emergence of Eagleton as cultural theorist, as he begins to turn the McCabian-inspired critical discourse into an analysis of the structures of Catholic faith, and from here derive models with which to understand the operations of contemporary society. One of the most interesting examples of this early incarnation of Eagleton as cultural theorist can be found in the article 'Politics and Benediction', an article that attempts a critical analysis of the Catholic ceremony of the Benediction of the Blessed Sacrament. This article was later described by Eagleton as a work that was a 'kind of experiment, an attempt to discover how far one crucially important contemporary language – that of developed Marxism and phenomenology – could meaningfully be used about liturgy',[17] and it serves as a nexus of theoretical influences drawn into a form of cultural critique. The contention offered by Eagleton through the article is that, while this ceremony of Benediction did not in itself impart any particularly important religious moment, the structure of relationships embodied in the process seemed to offer a way of reflecting on 'the nature of political society, particularly about the nature of capitalism'. In Eagleton's analysis, the Mass, the ceremony in which the bread is consecrated as the body of Christ before being received and consumed by members of the congregation, is held to represent an immediate Christian community. This is not due to the eucharist functioning as some form of supernatural event, but rather, due to its position in a wider structure of communal activity, it serving as the focal point for a particular signifying system: 'Like a word in a language, the bread has no meaning outside an articulate context, and the context, the language, which gives the eucharistic bread its intelligibility – and thus its *being* – is the human, intersubjective activity which constitutes a mass.'[18] The relations within the Mass provide a mode of understanding the dialectical nature of human activity, where 'gestures, actions, objects, relations, are constituted as meaningful not as substances in themselves but in their intelligible relation to a whole world of meaning, a human historical action'.[19]

In contrast to this, Eagleton examines the Benediction of the Blessed Sacrament, the ceremony in which the bread, rather than being consumed by the congregation, is instead set in a monstrance (or display vessel) upon the altar during the service, before being used as an object with which the priest blesses the passive congregation. Eagleton, deploying concepts derived from the work of the young Marx, depicts this as involving the reification of relationships (or shift into abstraction), where the 'bread becomes dislocated from the practical, communal activity within which alone it has intelligibility, and is reified into an isolated commodity – a *thing* set over against the group with an alien and determining life of its own'.[20] Eagleton sees the point of this analysis as not being a simple theological critique, but rather that through analysis of these particular microcosmic structures of human relationship, an analogy can be developed for the wider pattern of relationships that humans undertake in society; specifically in contrasting an immediate community to an alienated one:

> Because of this alienation of its communal existence to a system of commodities and their autonomous relations, capitalist society is atomized in a similar way to a congregation at benediction: it is individual relationship to the all-determining economic system, which is paramount, and human interrelationship becomes therefore secondary and negative . . . What is important in benediction is simply that there should be a human group there to be blessed; in a mass, active relationship between individuals valued as concrete individuals is itself the ground of community.[21]

This article is both significant in showing the development of a theoretical language to put to use in cultural critique, as well as embroiling Eagleton in what is perhaps his first of many disputes in print over his use of 'theory' and 'jargon'. In the following issue of *Slant*, the Dominican Edmund Hill challenged Eagleton on a number of theological points concerning his method of criticism and depictions of the ceremonies, but one of his most manifest irritations was Eagleton's use of 'jargon', which 'obscures issues in at least two ways; by encouraging the use of clever jargon in the interests of one-upmanship – and *Slant* is full of jargon, exciting new jargon, perhaps, but still a language which is opaque to the uninitiated . . . and does not encourage its users to examine their own ideas critically'.[22] Eagleton's response was unequivocal: '*Slant* works on a kind of frontier, mediating different disciplines to each other, and to do this adequately – to press understanding and analysis to its limit – sometimes involves using language and concepts unfamiliar to many Catholics . . . For those to whom the attempt to work with these immensely difficult concepts is anyway irrelevant the impression is bound to be arrogance and assertiveness; attention will then be drawn to the style of speaking and away from the ideas, which are ignored as "jargon".'[23]

The New Left Church

Many of the issues and concerns that occupied the pages of the earlier editions of *Slant* were revisited and further examined by Eagleton in *The New Left Church*, Eagleton's first book-length publication. A work concerned with 'the church, literature and politics', whose aim was 'to persuade Christians that being in the church involves commitment to imaginative culture and the political left' (*NLC* vii), *The New Left Church* deploys an eclectic range of influences, ranging from the Christian theology of Thomas Aquinas through to the agnostic existentialism of Jean-Paul Sartre. Several threads of argument run through the work as a whole, but the overall method is one of fusing a form of socialist-humanist cultural criticism with a radical Christian perspective, engaging with areas such as the literary analysis of F. R. Leavis, and the political-cultural argument of New Left intellectuals such as Raymond Williams and Richard Hoggart, in an attempt to open and articulate a dialogue within Christian perspectives. In the preface to the work, Eagleton cites approvingly a 1962 lecture by Leavis, in which Leavis sets out an impassioned case for how humans must develop a 'basic living deference' towards the 'unknown and immeasurable' possibilities of a human future, and Eagleton sees the Christian perspective as one linked to the Leavisite case:

> If the Christian responds to the Spirit in a great novel he is respond-
> ing to what is centrally human in it: to say after the resurrection, that
> the poet is divine is to say he is in touch with what is most real in
> human life. To identify what is real, which actions make for life, is to

be politically committed: here the 'deepest vital instinct' is mea-
sured against an actual society, actual structures and relationships.
(*NLC* ix–x)

It is this task, of reflecting on how literature can inform us as to
what is most 'real' in human values and society, and how this links
with Christian conceptions, that forms the basis of the essays in the
work. For example, one of the crucial disjunctions that Eagleton
places at the heart of contemporary society is between the 'idea of
the common life' and 'the idea of intensity'. For Eagleton, the issue
of intensity (or following a belief system without comprise) is one
that occurs in numerous instances of modern tragic literature. Willy
Loman, from Arthur Miller's *Death of a Salesman*, symbolizes for
Eagleton the existence of an 'intense' man trapped in an alienated
capitalist society: he refuses to compromise in his belief that society
will recognize and reward him, and in the end destroys himself in
the self-inflicted car-crash at the conclusion of the play, rather than
compromising or giving in to the voices of family and friends who
suggest that he retire or modify his faith in the dream of success.
The question raised by much modern tragedy thus points to a
'general dilemma' where 'Intensity takes men outside the community' (*NLC* 10), with the urgent question being 'how is intensity to
be fed creatively into a society, how are we to stop it tearing through
the fabric of the common life?' (*NLC* 5). The answer, Eagleton suggests, would come when we fuse the intense expression of the now-
alienated individual into a full part of a new society, 'where the
means for entering into the most intense experience the society had
to offer were the normal means of life and production, and the
common culture which grew from this economic community' (*NLC*
14). Similarly, the intensity and 'gratuitous energy' of Christianity,
which demands vulnerability and always turning the other cheek
of its adherents, provides the spontaneous force for a political pro-
gramme, in which meekness will be transformed into a strength in
the cause of unilateral nuclear disarmament (*NLC* 27), and the wilful
and total embrace of vulnerability into a powerful challenge to a
capitalist society that must always coolly calculate definite values
and exact profits (*NLC* 29).

If modern tragedy thus allows us to glimpse the issues of intensity, and how the individual and society are thrown into mutual
antagonism through the alienation created by capitalist society,
Eagleton proposes that the alienated society can equally be
traced through history of modern poetry, in a way that has 'clear

connections' to the young Marx's discussion of the relation of the worker to the object under capitalist modes of production (*NLC* 55). Marx described the process in which the 'alienation of the worker in his product means not only that his labour becomes an object, an external existence, but that it exists outside him, independently, as something alien to him, and that it becomes a power of its own confronting him', and Eagleton traces a similar process occurring in the history of English poetry.[24] Offering a detailed reading of Wordsworth's *The Solitary Reaper*, for example, reveals the 'insidious' dangers of Romanticism. Eagleton tells us that it is 'a dangerous and possibly immoral kind of poetry' in the same way 'as capitalism is a dangerous and immoral way of life', in that both of them betray a 'characteristic stance towards reality' that 'is essentially imperialist': Romanticism is a form of poetry 'which sets out to convert objective reality *totally* into subjective emblems – which allows objective reality significance only insofar as it provides the expression of a personal vision' (*NLC* 40-1). Eliot's *The Waste Land* is equally criticized on the grounds of an intellect alienated from society: 'it is a personal version which seems to grow, not from genuine responsiveness to how things are, but from a pre-existent consciousness which then arranges reality in corresponding patterns' (*NLC* 45). The nature poetry of Jon Silkin from his *Nature and Man*, and specifically his poem 'Violet', is offered by Eagleton as the exemplar of a way out of this alienated situation, not just for poetry, but for human perceptions of the political, 'he is trying to find a point of balance between the two, so that what comes through powerfully is both a sense of the violet as a unique, self-developing life with its own impulses and growth, and a sense of the relation of this movement and growth to what we know about ourselves' (*NLC* 68).

Having thus diagnosed the forms of alienation in society which are manifested through the modes of literature, Eagleton turns to the question of how to solve this alienation, and how to develop 'community as the way of life in which all men can be simultaneously free subjects, present to each other without mutual exploitation'. The solution that Eagleton sees is to re-examine the ideas of Christian community through the seemingly irreconcilable existentialist perspective:

> Christ, to use Sartre's expression, is a 'here-everywhere', the constitutive unity of the group in fully present and interiorized within each component . . . Each member of the group encounters Christ as the

centre of the subjectivity of the other, and as the centre of their own
subjectivity, so that there is no more possibility of one man objectifying and exploiting another than there is of a man objectifying and
exploiting himself. (*NLC* 166–7)

Thus Eagleton proposes the idea of Christ as a way out of Sartrian
angst about the responsibilities of freedom – the oft-quoted conflicting situation where 'Man condemned to be free carries the whole
world' – with Christ the figure who presents the ultimate symbol
of freedom for humans.

At the time of publication, *The New Left Church* received some
cautious but warm reviews, with one critic writing that 'Whether
these programs will succeed or not one cannot tell, but students of
society who wish to observe a social movement *in medias res* should
sit up and take notice.'[25] But it is now tempting to look back on the
earnest humanism of *The New Left Church* as something from part
of the prehistory of Eagleton's writing; and indeed there is much
material in the work that will undoubtedly generate a wry smile
from a knowing, later reader. For example, we can read the critic
who would, in *Criticism and Ideology*, introduce many of Althusser's
anti-humanist concepts of ideology to an Anglo-American readership, here offering us such platitudes as 'What the church, the arts
and politics have in common is that they all offer basic descriptions
of what it is to be human' (*NLC* viii); or the rebel who would be
become a worldwide name in the 1980s on his polemical announcements in *Literary Theory: An Introduction* concerning 'the death of
literature' informing us that 'Literature teaches us how to live or it
does nothing' (*NLC* 127).

But beyond these obvious and somewhat superficial points of
difference between the early and later Eagleton, *The New Left Church*
displays many issues and problems of theory that Eagleton's later
writing was in some sense an attempt to resolve. The attempt to
articulate the need for Christians to understand their links with the
political world is passionate and challenging, but the methods of
expressing these links expose an irreconcilable theoretical weakness:
the Church, politics, and literature all offer 'the same description'
of societal ideas of 'what it is to be human', and the practical criticism of a narrow selection of literature seemingly given the wide-
ranging ability to diagnose all manner of social and political ill.
Equally, the heterogeneous theoretical reference points are ambitious, and lead at many points to insight, not least in extending
a radical Christianity into dialogue with other critical currents such

as those of F. R. Leavis and Sartre – but in extending the dialogue in this way, in many places it seems to be stretched to breaking point. Can the concepts of a staunch agnostic and existentialist such as Sartre really be so easily assimilated into a Christian perspective, or does the linking of the two seemingly contradictory positions too easily glide over fundamental differences? Indeed, this simple model of the interaction between modes of discourse in society would increasingly become one subject to scrutiny by Eagleton, with much of his writing of the 1970s being dedicated to developing theories of ideology that could account for a more complicated mediation between these levels, which leaves the methods of *The New Left Church* looking distinctly threadbare in comparison.

But, having registered these reservations, *The New Left Church* is an interesting work to re-examine for a number of reasons. For one, Eagleton attempts a unique mode of cultural and literary criticism: for all the limitations of the eclectic blend of Williams, Leavis, and Christ, the attempt to fuse new understandings of areas such as modern tragedy and poetry from a committed and radical Christian perspective challenges conventional barriers separating these modes of discussion. It also shows the intellectual range of formative influences that are not explicit in much of Eagleton's later work but directly evident here, especially the strong emphasis on the humanist writings of the young Marx, and the existentialism of Sartre. Perhaps most suggestively, and on a wider level, even from this earliest stage we are seeing the emergence of the concerns that will echo through Eagleton's work throughout his career: how can literature be understood not as an object itself, but instead as a mode of access into a wider society; and how can the literary critic seek to comment not just on literature, but on the society from which the literature emerges?

Over the following years, Eagleton would feature, as both editor and contributor, in a number of other book projects emerging from the Catholic Left. One of the most interesting would also appear in 1966; the collaborative work *The Slant Manifesto*, edited by Adrian Cunningham, Eagleton, Wicker, Martin Redfern, and Bright, which set forth, in a range of provocative essays, the challenges the *Slant* group issued to the Catholic Church. Eagleton would co-author with Cunningham the opening part, 'Christians against Capitalism'. Eagleton's and Cunningham's work set out a confident and lucid statement of position explaining the rationale for the *Slant* movement, and a challenge for Christians to recognize that 'Christ's teaching is political teaching, concerned with how men are to live together, not with man in isolation', and that 'Christians can never be conservatives or liberals or even right-wing socialists; they must fight capitalism as evil; they must align themselves, perhaps, with all those traditional enemies of the Church, left-wing socialists and atheistic Marxists.'[26] The vision of a socialist society that they outline is one that opposes both the reformism of the Labour Party and the hardened position of bureaucratic Stalinism, and one that instead allows 'the greatest degree of participation by everyone in social processes', achieved by the opening 'political decisions to the vote of a whole society', in order to realize 'a genuinely Christian society – one which acted by the ethic of co-operative equality, of shared and active responsibility'.[27] In 1968 Eagleton would edit *Directions*, which, as noted above, offered collections of essays intended as interventions in the post-Vatican II circumstances of British Catholicism, assessing the extent of changes achieved and advocating the further social, political, and liturgical reforms necessary for the Church to continue its progressive direction. Also in 1968 he would edit and introduce, with Brian Wicker, *From Culture to Revolution*, the collection of essays stemming from a 1967 *Slant* Symposium, to which he also contributed the essay 'The Idea of a Common Culture'. This chapter, a piece largely under the shadow of Raymond Williams's work on the 'Culture and Society' tradition, traces notions of culture from Romanticism through the 'dilemma of liberalism', and the subsequent positions of T. S. Eliot, F. R. Leavis, and Raymond Williams regarding culture, and the implications of this for the construction of a common socialist culture (and, as will be seen in a later chapter, provides much of the background for his later *The Idea of Culture*).[28]

The Body as Language

Eagleton's final major publication in Catholic theology at this time was *The Body as Language* (1970), which is his most developed and coherent contribution to this field, analysing many of the themes that had tentatively appeared in *The New Left Church*, through a more coherently and developed theoretical framework. It was a work that Eagleton described as attempting 'to reveal both the relations and divergences between Christianity and Marxism' (*BL* ix), and one that rethinks the Christian concepts of the fall and redemption through the concepts of language theory and Marxism. It is a study that again shows the strong influence of McCabe, and specially McCabe's discussions from *Law, Love and Language* concerning the fact that human community is, uniquely, both a 'biological unity' and a 'linguistic unity': communities stemming from our physical characteristics as well as shared ability to communicate.[29]

Taking as his starting point Wittgenstein's statement from the *Philosophical Investigations* that, as a dog is not a linguistic animal, it cannot be a hypocrite but neither can it be sincere, Eagleton locates the uniqueness of the 'fallen' human condition in the fact that the entrance to the linguistic world has opened humans to both the creative and destructive potentials of language: 'Man, unlike the other animals, is not passively trapped within the determining limits of his "species-life": language, by distancing and objectifying man's animal nature, allows him to enter into transformative relationship with it'(*BL* 3). The 'fall' into language thus opens up the twin horizons of human existence, at once allowing humanity the possibility of creativity and expressiveness that a dog cannot achieve (the 'sincerity' of which Wittgenstein spoke), but, in turn, unleashes the potentiality for 'human destructiveness' (*BL* 3), with language opening up 'the continual possibility of *reification*: the chance that the codes into which reality is ordered, with a consequent dawning of intelligibility and loss of practical immediacy, may become autonomous, manipulating rather than mediating the world' (*BL* 20). Language, in other words, always carries with it the destruction of the immediate community of humanity, for 'to have language is to be capable of forming projects which extend beyond an immediate present, to wrestle a personal perspective from the world and order reality within it towards the goal of a personal intention' (*BL* 51), with this split in seeing other human bodies as commodities that can be exploited for private gain resulting in the spiritual and political fall: 'When man . . . uses others as objects for his private self-advancement . . . he commits what the Christian calls sin and the Socialist calls capitalism' (*BL* 52).

The issue, then, that Eagleton pursues through *The Body as Language* is how the fallen human linguistic animal can escape reification, this transformation of perception in which other human bodies are seen as separate things. Again, the liturgy provides an example of an already existing non-reified community, and specifically a symbolic activity that escapes from the deferred signification of other semiotic systems, one in which 'the symbols themselves cease to exist in their usual modes and become the reality they mediate . . . that disjunction of sign and reality which I have argued to be

endemic in human history is abolished' (*BL* 29). The political challenge is thus to extend this new community of bodies prefigured in
the liturgical community into the general condition of society, and
again it is the figure of Christ who provides this solution:

> The only way in which this condition could be successfully trans-
> formed would be for man's universal modes of communication and
> relationship to achieve all the sure, close, solid controllability pos-
> sible to his directly physical action: for the human race to be able
> to live together, in its linguistically created global networks, at the
> same level of unbreakable achievement which two men can estab-
> lish in sawing down a tree. By their faith in Christ, the eternal word
> made animal, Christians subscribe to a belief that this absurd vision
> is the future reality of man: that the opaqueness of our present
> bodies will be transfigured into pure transparency by the power of
> God. (*BL* 55)

It is in building this interconnectedness that Eagleton sees the
radical demands and potentials of Christianity: not in building an
isolated enclave against the fallen outside world, but instead 'in
sharing in the construction of human community', striving to
'creat[e] a common culture' (*BL* 60). In other words, the construction
of a socialist society in which the bodily reification, the perception
of other humans as separate objects, can be overcome. The figure of
the *anawim*, the oppressed and exploited, thus becomes central to
the mission of the Christian revolution, as symbols of those currently excluded from this full social integration, with Jesus himself
the ultimate form of *anawim*, at once the dangerous challenge and
outcast from the social order, but also the truth, 'a manifestation of
ultimate, authentic reality in a false society' (*BL* 73-4). Christ
demands of us a Trotskyite 'permanent revolution' (*BL* 68) to in-
corporate these dispossessed into the full life of a society: the challenge is to 'transform human society to the point where the truth of
Christ can be lived out in the detailed praxis of social life: to embrace the consecrated power of the *anawim* so that society can be
born again' (*BL* 74). The function of the Catholic Church within this
project to create an integrated human community is, Eagleton
suggests, similar to the function of the vanguard party within
Marxist-Leninist political revolutions, with the revolutionary priest
entering into a dialectical relationship between the masses and the
future society, both leading and representing the congregation.

The Body as Language displays the increasing interest Eagleton
had developed in critical theory, drawing on emerging currents

of linguistic, structuralist, and phenomenological theory through critical engagements with the concerns of Wittgenstein, Barthes, Merleau-Ponty, and McLuhan. As will be seen in the following chapter, this move was not just occurring in his theological writing, but was also present in his more directly literary-critical writing, as he engaged with emerging issues from the continental Marxist tradition. However, perhaps the most interesting situation is the position of Marxism within Eagleton's theoretical framework, and its firm subordination to the figure of Christ. Marx is frequently referred to, and indeed the humanist-Marxism based primarily on the young Marx's *Economic and Philosophical Manuscripts* emerges as one of Eagleton's primary theoretical reference points. Yet, while fully acknowledging contradictions in capitalist society as not just symptoms of a dislocation in a deeper human nature but the direct result of unjust class relations, Eagleton also challenges Marxism with 'a case to answer', due to its inability to resolve the alienation stemming from humanity's position as a 'fallen' linguistic animal. Marxism may offer the ability to prevent alienation caused by a capitalist economic order, such as the exploitation of one human by another for personal profit, for example. But it does not possess the ability to resolve the alienation of an 'interpersonal crisis', such as the collapse of a marriage, or other forms of human suffering not stemming directly from an economic contradiction. The case then is that Marxism and a radical theology are not just comparable techniques trying to get to the same point, or different theoretical frames for saying the same thing. Rather, radical Christianity offers a necessary supplement to Marxist conceptions of revolution, for while a socialist revolution may heal a world-historical crisis, it is only a spiritual revolution which will fully heal a fractured humanity. In this view, it is the figure of Jesus who symbolizes the ultimate possibility for the reconciliation of these positions:

> The Jesus who confronted and conquered tragedy in the world-historical action of the cross was also the Jesus who wept over the death of an historically insignificant friend: it is only in the kingdom of heaven, where 'death shall be no more, neither shall there be mourning nor crying nor pain', that the redemptive power of that first tragic action will penetrate the darkness of the second with its own victory. (*BL* 113)

The Body as Language represented the high point of Eagleton's articulations of the possibility of a radical Christianity. Eagleton had taken on the mantle of editor of *Slant* in 1969, and his first editorial enthusiastically praised the developments which *Slant* had been part of:

> During the few years of *Slant's* existence there has been an accelerating growth of critical theory in the politics of both church and state: a growth which in some areas constitutes, and in others is on the way to constituting, a more or less complete counter-culture. Whatever the significant obstacles to revolution are now, they are likely to be less and less the absence of a coherently articulated critique of the status quo.[30]

Despite this optimism concerning the growth of a counter-culture to dominant modes of capitalism, and the contribution towards the removal of the theoretical obstacles to socialist revolution, the *Slant* project, and Eagleton's substantive involvement in the Catholic Left, would soon come to a conclusion. After having run for 30 issues, *Slant* concluded publication in February 1970 due to a combination of factors, such as Sheed and Ward withdrawing their financial support, and the general feeling among the group, as described by Adrian Cunningham, that *Slant* had pushed its political project as far as possible. Eagleton himself would continue to publish a number of essays in *New Blackfriars* during the 1970s, ranging from pieces concerning faith and revolution, to essays on figures such as William Hazlitt, Freud, and W. H. Auden.[31] But, as will be explored in the following chapter, Eagleton's intellectual concerns would increasingly shift their focus away from questions of socialist theology and into the secular areas of Marxist theory, as new areas of radical theory began to emerge from Europe; and Eagleton's essays would increasingly appear in journals such as *New Left Review*, rather than those of Catholic philosophy. By the 1980s the influence of the Catholic Left would seem to have been wholly erased from Eagleton's theory and writing, and his relationship to this movement drifted into obscurity, occasionally conjured up by later critics puzzled at how the young Catholic they remember from this 1960s grouping evolved into a Marxist intellectual eschewing modes of idealistic criticism.[32] Indeed, Eagleton himself has wryly commented on the obscurity that the *Slant* movement now languishes in, remarking in his memoir that 'Nowadays people write the odd doctoral thesis on the Catholic Left, which I suppose is one up from oblivion' (G 28).

While this chapter has offered a necessarily brief overview of the diverse areas of Eagleton's contribution to the Catholic Left activity in the 1960s, a number of central concerns and themes emerges, and it becomes apparent that the reconsideration of Eagleton's involvement with the Catholic Left has importance for a number of reasons. On the level of intellectual and political history, the *Slant* group represents a particularly vibrant moment in both the career of Eagleton and the history of the British New Left, where Christ and Marx were tentatively but nonetheless genuinely enlisted as allies in the same political cause. While the exuberance regarding the revolutionary potentiality of reforming the Catholic Church may, in retrospect, seem overly optimistic in both its belief in the compatibility of Marxism and Christianity, and in its belief in the structures of Catholic institutions being open to socialist change, it nonetheless shows a progressive religious culture in stark contrast to the current climate of religious fundamentalism, whether of the Islamic-extremist or the Christian evangelical variety. It also shows the development of Eagleton's own theoretical and political position, from an early Christian-humanist, and the specific role that theological debate played in the development of both his critical background and theoretical perspectives.

More specifically, it suggests the extent to which the work of Herbert McCabe has provided a crucial, and under-acknowledged, influence over Eagleton's writing. Raymond Williams is normally held as being the decisive influence upon the career of Eagleton, and indeed I will go on in subsequent chapters to see the interactions with Williams's ideas as being the crucial driving force behind much of Eagleton's literary criticism and theoretical development. Yet I also want to suggest that it is probable that the influence of McCabe has been important and pervasive to an almost equal extent. This is a view that, over the past decade, Eagleton has increasingly stressed. For example, in 1996 Eagleton would claim, in an article celebrating McCabe's seventieth birthday, that 'Dismally few people, when you come to weigh it up, really change your life, even those who are traditionally supposed to. My supervisor at Cambridge changed my life about as much as Vera Lynn did. But without my long friendship with Herbert McCabe I wouldn't be at all what I am. So you can blame it all on him.'[33] Similarly, Eagleton would dedicate *Sweet Violence* to McCabe, and state that the influence of McCabe on *After Theory* was 'so pervasive . . . that it is impossible to localize' (*AT* ix). Eagleton's 'theological turn' (as discussed below) thus offers an obvious point of re-engagement with McCabe, but it is also suggestive, however, that McCabe's influence extends beyond Eagleton's manifest articulations of religious and ethical concerns, and into the latent current of Eagleton's very critical style across much of his career. Even in Eagleton's most widely known work of the 1980s when he would, on the surface, appear at his furthest away from the theological writing from prior decades, the presence of McCabe seems to hover, not in the sense that McCabe's theology is directly being invoked, but in that Eagleton's rhetorical and argumentative strategies seem in many ways to echo those of McCabe. McCabe's essays, with their disarmingly straightforward style used to convey a radical argument, offer a stylistic precursor to much of Eagleton's mode of writing; and particularly, McCabe's ability to convey complex points of argument through the mode of sudden rhetorical links with a stark, lower, reality prefigures what would become one of Eagleton's most characteristic argumentative traits. At one point, for example, McCabe punctuated his argument about love and ethics with a statement concerning the killing of children ('Now a man who says that killing babies is always wrong may not, after all, be a legalist seeking to stifle man's creative inspiration under a load of rules and regulations [but instead] may be simply trying to explain what love means to him – whatever it comes to mean, it can't mean this'):[34] a rhetorical strategy that directly prefigures what Willy Maley would later coin as an 'Eagletonism'. Maley offered a detailed description of what he considered Eagleton's distinctive rhetorical trait, describing it as 'a flexible polemical device which takes the form of a rhetorical flourish designed to debunk an image of high culture, through a gesture in the direction of some banal, bizarre, or brute "reality" '. Maley states that 'The Eagletonism is a type of oxymoron, but rather than a seeming contradiction, we get a juxtaposition of politesse and politics. Eagletonisms are bathetic, deflationary measures taken against the exorbitant claims of metropolitan high culture.'[35] Maley went on in this article to offer a critique of the Eagletonian strategy, complete with a list of the 'top thirty' examples of Eagletonisms in action; yet it appears that the Eagletonism is less a distinct invention, and more an interesting mutation of an older 'McCabeism'.

Finally, the concerns of Eagleton's early publications in the field of radical Christian theology are increasingly finding new voice in Eagleton's contemporary work. As Eagleton stated in 2005, in the introduction to *Holy Terror*, his work seemed to have taken a 'metaphysical or theological turn (or full circle) . . . in recent years', bringing him directly back to the issues and concerns first argued in the 1960s (*HT* vii). *Sweet Violence*, for example, shows Eagleton directly re-addressing the issues of tragedy, sacrifice, and the *anawim*, to the point that many of the arguments in the later work are drawn directly from his writing of the 1960s. *After Theory* would see him pointing to the limits of secular critical theory, and instead attempting to reinvigorate a discourse by returning to issues such as morality, death, and 'non-being'; and *The Meaning of Life*, in offering visions of how humans achieve their ultimate value through participation within a commonly constructed culture, is in many ways a reformatting of the arguments presented by Eagleton in *The New Left Church*. Eagleton's involvement with the Catholic Left in the 1960s is thus not a curious part of his background, but the direct foundation for many of the mutations his later work would undergo.

2

From Williams to Althusser:
Eagleton's Early Literary Criticism

At an age when many academics are still working on their PhDs or embarking on their first steps in academic careers, Eagleton was already a prolific author, having published, in addition to his works on Catholic theology, his first book of literary criticism, *Shakespeare and Society*, in 1967 while working on his doctorate. This was followed over the next decade by a further series of books – *Exiles and Émigrés* (1970), *Myths of Power* (1975), *Marxism and Literary Criticism* (1976), and *Criticism and Ideology* (1976). This chapter outlines the main thematic and theoretical concerns raised by these works, placing them in the context of wider theoretical developments occurring in Western Marxism. Engaging in significant debates with the critical theories of Williams, Lukács, Goldmann, Althusser, and Macherey among others, Eagleton moved in this period from a pre-Marxist humanism towards a scientific Marxist criticism in an attempt to develop new forms of political literary criticism. Consequently, the works discussed in this chapter are significant as more than just interesting examples of Eagleton's critical development, but also mark out many of the crucial theoretical shifts in the development of twentieth-century Marxist critical theory.

Early influences

The person with most influence over Eagleton's early literary criticism was Raymond Williams, an issue touched upon in the last chapter but one that I will now seek to draw out in more detail.

Williams, one of the most important British socialist intellectuals of the twentieth century, is commonly described as the founder of the critical movement of cultural materialism, and as one of the co-founders of British cultural studies, although his work is more complicated than these convenient tags imply.[1] Williams was influenced as an undergraduate by both the Marxist literary criticism practised by members of the Communist party (of which he was briefly a member), and also the work of the great Cambridge critic F. R. Leavis, but quickly grew frustrated with the limitations inherent in both approaches. For Williams, the orthodox Marxist criticism of the 1930s and 1940s was too prescribed and therefore unable to account for the complexity of working-class culture, while Leavis's disdain for modern culture and his yearning for the organic, pre-industrial society struck Williams as ignoring the real benefits that the Industrial Revolution had brought to the lives of working people.[2] Instead, Williams embarked on a long investigation, in seminal works such as *Culture and Society* and *The Country and the City*, aimed at providing a socialist-humanist understanding of modern culture and evaluating the changes in key cultural concepts and institutions. Williams retrospectively defined his position as that of cultural materialism: 'a theory of the specificities of material cultural and literary production within historical materialism'.[3] Williams began lecturing at Cambridge in the same year that Eagleton became an undergraduate, and Eagleton has described hearing Williams lecture as an 'extraordinary personal liberation'.[4] Williams would go on to become Eagleton's dissertation supervisor, and Williams's desire to have a second Fellow, to take responsibility for teaching undergraduate English at his college, led to Eagleton being appointed to a fellowship at Jesus College, Cambridge, at the remarkably young age of 21, highlighting the strong influence Williams had in the formative stages of Eagleton's career.

This influence, as has been discussed in the previous chapter, was certainly present in aspects of Eagleton's *Slant* writing, but it is brought clearly to the fore in Eagleton's first book of literary criticism, *Shakespeare and Society*, written while Eagleton was working on his doctorate. Dedicated to Raymond Williams, Eagleton states that *Shakespeare and Society* was 'an extension of [Williams's] own explorations' (*SS* 6), offering a 'consideration of individual and society' in the plays of Shakespeare, with the stated purpose of providing not only 'an extension of our understanding of Shakespeare' but also, more ambitiously, of our more general

'understanding of person and society' (*SS* 10). The relationship
between an individual and society was for Williams a crucial area
of investigation throughout his career, with his 1961 *The Long
Revolution* devoting a chapter to consideration of this issue, believed
by Williams to be 'at the centre of the conflicts of our times'.[5] Very
briefly, Williams argued that the beginning of the capitalist
economy created an antagonism between the two concepts, so that
we 'see the terms of relationship separating out, until "individual"
on the one hand, "society", "community", and "state" on the other,
could be conceived as abstractions and absolutes'.[6] For Williams,
the only resolution to the conflict between the individual and
society could occur with the fulfilment of the 'long revolution' of
cultural, democratic, and economic change, which would provide
the conditions for a truly democratic socialist society: 'If man is
essentially a learning, creating and communicating being, the only
social organization adequate to his nature is a participating democracy, in which all of us, as unique individuals, learn, communicate
and control.'[7]

Eagleton, investigating this problem outlined by Williams, reads
the plays of Shakespeare as works that themselves interrogate this
conflict between individual and society. *Hamlet*, for example, is
read as the 'tragedy of the authentic man in false society' in which
'men have to stifle themselves in the interests of the State' (*SS* 65),
and where characters such as Claudius represent a society 'which
weighs and measures, balancing consequences according to a fixed
and rational scale of values' (*SS* 64); while *Macbeth* depicts the situation in which the individual rejects society in the pursuit of personal
ambition, with Macbeth himself undergoing a fall from 'a place
within the community to the pure negativity of evil, the area of
nameless deeds' (*SS* 134). On the other hand, in *The Tempest* people
are depicted as living 'authentically', and Eagleton argues that the
'theme of *The Tempest* is that men are not wholly active, shapers of
their individual lives, nor wholly passive, parts of a larger design in
which they are merely manipulated objects; human life is in some
way an interpenetration of the two' (*SS* 156). Prospero, in particular, is invoked as an example of the 'authentic' individual existing
in society, and as someone who 'achieves for the others in the play
his own fusion of spontaneity and aware responsibility: he orches-
trates the individual, clashing and combining wills into a harmony
within which they can find fulfilment and identity in terms of an
awareness of others' (*SS* 163), allowing 'new, creative life' to grow
(*SS* 169).

In his closing chapter Eagleton extends his political argument by offering an innovative comparison of Shakespeare's plays with the 'crisis' experienced in nineteenth-century culture in the wake of the Industrial Revolution, in particular with regard to the arguments about the nature of socialism. Eagleton's doctoral dissertation, *Nature and Spirit: A Study of Edward Carpenter in his Intellectual Context*, focused on the English poet and political writer Edward Carpenter (1844–1929) and his relationship to progressive political organizations and intellectual circles, and thus Eagleton's concluding chapter to *Shakespeare and Society* presents many of the main political arguments stemming from his doctoral research.[8]

Examining the writing of Arnold, Carlyle, and Carpenter among others, Eagleton traces how these thinkers have attempted to reconcile the life of the individual with the conditions of society after the Industrial Revolution, where 'spontaneous living is crippled by industrial capitalism' (*SS* 205). While agreeing with this concept, that in the face of capitalism the existence of the spontaneous individual is threatened, Eagleton also accepts that simply developing this spontaneous life in a 'merely personal' way and 'in opposition to society itself' is essentially a negative retreat (*SS* 205). This is a central flaw identified by Eagleton in aspects of the nineteenth-century socialist tradition, and in particular he argues against the individualist socialism espoused by Oscar Wilde in his essay *The Soul of Man Under Socialism*, stating that 'Wilde makes no attempt to heal the gap between social and individual, spontaneous and socially responsible: he tries to solve the problem by accepting and ratifying the gap, turning the breakdown itself into a kind of strength' (*SS* 202). Instead, Eagleton argues for a socialist society that achieves the 'fusion of spontaneous life and social responsibility' (*SS* 205). The ambivalent conclusion that Eagleton proposes, then, is that 'We can learn a good deal from the way Shakespeare faces his own problems, but the ultimate answer, inevitably, must be our own' (*SS* 206).

While the overarching political aim of *Shakespeare and Society* is derived from Williams, there are a number of other influences that can be detected. Eagleton's constant reference to the idea of how the 'authentic' individual can exist in a false society again suggests the influence of the existentialist philosophy of Jean-Paul Sartre, although the use of such terms is never subjected to an explicit critical examination.[9] The influence of F. R. Leavis and the *Scrutiny* critics is also detectable, specifically in the frequent use of Leavisite shibboleths such as 'spontaneous life',[10] and more generally in the critical method used in the readings of Shakespeare's plays, offering close 'practical' criticism of the texts at hand combined with a distinctive moral argument. Indeed, Eagleton offers a slightly self-conscious apology for his adoption of such a vocabulary: 'I have used a vocabulary in discussing Shakespeare which may seem self-consciously modern: "authentic", "spontaneous", "reciprocal" probably recur too often as critical terms, but this kind of language seems to me the way we can get closest to Shakespeare's ideas and feelings' (*SS* 9–10). But it is the attempt to grasp these nebulous 'ideas and feelings' that leads to the problems inherent in Eagleton's approach. In the concluding chapter, Eagleton attempts to advance a political argument concerning the necessary shape of a socialist society, but his Williams-inspired political aim sits uneasily with the existentialist vocabulary and Leavisite practical criticism; and it is hard to avoid the feeling that, although the arguments presented in the closing chapter are original, their links to the earlier discussion of Shakespeare are tenuous. *Shakespeare and Society* is an interesting study for its attempt to use the plays of Shakespeare as a basis for wider social criticism (a point recognized by early reviewers),[11] but it also demonstrates the lack of a necessary critical language for Eagleton to bridge successfully the divide between literary texts and social experience.

Further investigation of the relationship between the individual and society occurs in Eagleton's second book, *Exiles and Émigrés*, this time with regard to the state of twentieth-century British society as reflected in the literary work of Joseph Conrad, Evelyn Waugh, George Orwell, Graham Greene, T. S Eliot, W. H. Auden, and D. H. Lawrence. While still primarily a work of practical criticism, offering close readings of specific literary texts, it displays a number of significant changes from *Shakespeare and Society*, with Eagleton addressing a number of critical concerns surrounding the politics of the canon of English literature. In *The Great Tradition* (1948), F. R. Leavis had offered a controversial and influential working of the canon of the English novel, arguing that only Jane Austen, George Eliot, Henry James, Joseph Conrad, and D. H. Lawrence reach the status of great literature in their 'awareness of the possibilities of life'.[12] In the same year that *Exiles and Émigrés* appeared, Raymond Williams published *The English Novel from Dickens to Lawrence*, offering an implicit challenge to Leavis's idealistic critical assumptions, by emphasizing the political and economic circumstances that shaped the context of the works in 'the great tradition'.[13] *Exiles and Émigrés* can therefore be read as a work engaging in this specific canonical debate, siding with Williams in offering a politically aware criticism of movements in the English literary canon. Perhaps more significantly, *Exiles and Émigrés* also shows an engagement with a central aesthetic debate in the Western Marxist tradition, albeit in a tentative way. Although not explicitly cited in *Exiles and Émigrés*, the writing of the Hungarian Marxist critic Georg Lukács nonetheless forms an important theoretical backdrop to Eagleton's arguments. In influential works such as *The Meaning of Contemporary Realism*, Lukács had examined the difference between the realist and the modernist novel, and argued that, while the great realist literature presents 'total' visions of humans as 'social animals' with their individual existence bound up in their social and historical environment, modernist writers such as Kafka, in their depictions of human existence as fragmentary and solitary, surrender to a sense of impotence and acceptance of the status quo of capitalism. Lukács, to counter this, advocated the rise of the aesthetic of 'socialist realism', as 'socialist perspective, correctly understood, and applied, should enable the writer to depict life more comprehensively than any preceding perspective'.[14]

Eagleton draws a similar distinction in the history of the English novel, arguing that nineteenth-century realist novelists such as Dickens and George Eliot are able to depict society as a 'totality': they are 'able to fuse the profoundest inwardness with the specific life of their own times with a capacity to generalize that life into the form of a complete vision' (*EE* 10), and this ability, Eagleton argues, is virtually non-existent in the writings of twentieth-century novelists (*EE* 11). Unlike Lukács, however, Eagleton does not see the centre of this problem lying with the aesthetics of realism or modernism as such, but rather the problem is traced to the dominance of two strands of the English novel in the early twentieth century: the 'upper-class' and 'lower-middle-class' novel, with the resulting contradictions inherent in this ethos limiting the ability of the author to achieve the totality and transcendence possible in the greatest of nineteenth-century literature. Evelyn Waugh, the main representative of the upper-class novelists examined by Eagleton, is held to embody the flaws of this type of novelist, with Waugh's 'vivid kaleidoscope' of satire betraying the fact that his novels are unable to portray any profound social reality as, while 'all is possible to this privileged social class and to the literary form which mirrors it, nothing is especially valuable' (*EE* 69). In contrast, Orwell's novels are represented as embodying the ethos of the lower-middle class (even though, as Eagleton admits, Orwell's own social position was more upper than middle class), offering a 'naturalist' concern with the gritty detail of daily middle-class life, insecurely situated between the working and ruling class. Therefore, while Waugh's novels offer a privileged and detached vision far removed from social reality, the lower-middle class novels of Orwell and others are held to display the opposite problem, being too closely linked to a particular insecure petty-bourgeois social reality, and therefore limited in their ability to offer a wider social vision. Despite the apparent disparity between the two styles of novel, Eagleton argues that both are linked by their failure to achieve a complete vision of society: 'Both genres are acutely aware of the impoverishment of their own typical experience; but neither is in the end capable of rising above their fragmentary living to grasp a more "total" and "objective" version of its society' (*EE* 69).

The result of this split is that the 'outstanding' literature which has been produced in twentieth-century Britain 'has been, on the whole, the product of the exile and the alien' (*EE* 10), with Eagleton holding up Conrad, James, T. S Eliot, Pound, Yeats, and Joyce as the most significant authors of the period (with the inclusion of these modernist novelists and poets indicating Eagleton's difference from Lukács). Whereas English writers, caught in their one-sided cultural attachment, were unable to 'totalize' in their novels, these exiles and émigrés had 'immediate access to alternative cultures and traditions ... broader frameworks against which, in a highly creative tension, the erosion of contemporary order could be situated and partially understood' (*EE* 15), such as in the use of mythology in the work of Yeats and Eliot (see *EE* chapter 5, 138–78). The one exception to this rule, Eagleton notes, is the Englishman D. H. Lawrence, but Lawrence's proletariat class-position effectively positions him as outsider, allowing him to 'generalize, from this basis, a critique of England which seemed at times as alien as the judgement of a foreigner, yet as intimately acquainted with its real issues as a native' (*EE* 17), with Eagleton holding Lawrence's *The Rainbow* up as the novel able to offer a 'total' vision and 'able to grasp the interior connections between particular relationships and the shape of a common history' (*EE* 203).

Exiles and Émigrés is a more developed work than *Shakespeare and Society*, largely due to its more focused argument on a distinct literary and political problematic. But also noticeable is that Eagleton shies away from drawing on an explicit theoretical framework or Marxist vocabulary, instead still content to offer close readings concerned with the relative merits of individual works. Therefore, despite the introduction of social class as a critical concept, and the seemingly controversial discussion concerning the social basis for shifts in twentieth-century literature, the emphasis is still strongly on the formation of a canon which, while it may upgrade or down-grade individual works, looks suspiciously similar to the great tradition of Leavis, in ranking works on their ability to offer the fullest vision of 'positive life' (as Eagleton remarks approvingly of Lawrence, *EE* 216). Again, the problem with critical language encountered in *Shakespeare and Society* manifests itself. Eagleton is attempting to offer a socialist critique of twentieth-century British society in what is essentially a liberal-humanist critical language. Therefore, while the individual readings of texts are insightful and intelligently provocative, it is evident that Eagleton is still searching for a critical language capable of synthesizing both theory and practice.

It is in *Myths of Power* that Eagleton first draws on an unequivo-cally Marxist vocabulary, and as a result this work represents an important marker in Eagleton's career. Offering readings of the novels of the Brontë sisters, Eagleton strongly signals the shift in his theoretical orientation. The subtitle itself – *A Marxist Study of the Brontës* – is a provocative one, confidently declaring its Marxist credentials when Marxist literary criticism had, as yet, little cur-rency in the Anglo-American academy.[15] In the introduction Eagle-ton polemically asserts Marxism as the only complete theory, and boldly outlines his manifesto for the aims of a Marxist literary criti-cism: 'Marxist criticism must refuse to occupy its modest niche within that formidable array of critical methods . . . which reflects the tolerant pluralism of a liberal democracy', and rather 'must claim to shift the terrain of . . . debate', instead of resting 'content as one component within it' (*MP* 2).[16]

Eagleton's growing interest in Marxism was influenced by his new awareness of theoretical works by Continental European Marx-ists, then comparatively little known in Britain, that offered a more sophisticated historical-materialist account of culture than previous orthodox Communist party literary criticism had allowed. *Myths of Power* displays the beginning of an engagement with the theories of the French Marxists Louis Althusser and Pierre Macherey (which will be discussed in more detail in the following section on *Criticism and Ideology*), but it is the work of the Romanian Marxist Lucien Goldmann that provides the primary theoretical concepts for Eagleton's study, in particular the concept of 'categorical structures'. Goldmann, a proponent of a 'genetic structural sociology of culture', approached the study of literature from the perspective that a rigorous political literary criticism should resemble more an objective science than a subjective art, and advocated that the literary critic should adopt an attitude 'similar to that of the physicist or the chemist who is recording the results of an experiment'.[17] Goldmann argued against the idea of a single genius author as the full creator of a literary text, as 'the experience of a single individual is much too brief' to create a coherent mental or categorical structure displayed in a literary work. Instead, he argues that categorical structures 'can only be the result of the conjoint activity of a large number of individuals who find themselves in a similar situation'.[18] It is the role of the literary sociologist, he asserts, to search out these structures in individual literary works, and relate them to the wider social structures that explain the genesis of these categorical structures.

In *Myths of Power*, Eagleton adapts Goldmann's theory in order to examine the 'recurrent "categorical structure" of roles, values and relations' in the novels of the Brontës (*MP* 4). Unlike Goldmann, Eagleton is less concerned with linking the Brontës with a larger structure (as Goldmann linked Pascal's and Racine's structures to the wider social class of the *noblesse de robe*),[19] than with working within a predominantly practical critical model, as opposed to Goldmann's scientific sociology. Instead, Eagleton uncovers political structures at play in different levels of the novels of the Brontës, using these as the basis for a comparison of the ideology in the sisters' work, and through this formulating a basis for a more objective aesthetic judgement concerning the superiority of Emily's *Wuthering Heights* over Charlotte's novels.

Chapter 5 of *Myths of Power*, 'The Structure of Charlotte Brontë's Fiction' represents probably the most significant example of Eagleton's strategy in action. In previous chapters, Eagleton undertakes readings of Charlotte's novels, tracing out recurring categorical structures of characters and relationships in the works. This leads Eagleton to the position of being able to formulate what he sees as the key categorical structures common to all of Charlotte's novels. In Eagleton's reading, the 'fundamental structure of Charlotte's novels is a triadic one: it is determined by a complex play of power-relations between a protagonist, a "Romantic-Radical" and an autocratic conservative', such as the relationship between Jane, Rochester and St John Rivers in *Jane Eyre* (*MP* 74). This 'vertical' triadic structure of character types coincides with a 'horizontal' triadic structure of periodization, with each novel being 'more or less trichotomized into a preliminary phase of domestic settlement, a break to isolation and independence, and a final integration' (*MP* 94). The specific ideological significance of these vertical and horizontal triadic structures is that each phase of the horizontal periodic structure corresponds, to 'some extent', with the vertical character structure: 'the preliminary settlement corresponds to the function of conservative authority, the transitional period of independence belongs to the protagonist, and the concluding integration is with the "Romantic-Radical" figure' (*MP* 94). It is therefore possible to use the consideration of the interaction between these dual triadic levels as a basis for both political and aesthetic analysis, with Eagleton ranking *Jane Eyre* as being the 'aesthetically superior' novel, due to its more complicated 'second phase', in which St John Rivers is portrayed as a more complex 'authoritarian' character than corresponding second phase characters in the other novels of Charlotte (see *MP* 95–96).

Eagleton also identifies a 'primary structural relationship' *between* characters in the novels, which he argues is 'between two characters who are *both* blends of conformism and rebelliousness, but where one stands in deferential relation to the dominative other. This is the case with Jane and Rochester, Crimsworth and Hunsden, Caroline and Shirley, Lucy and Paul' (*MP* 74–5). Eagleton describes this fundamental structure as a tension between 'Romance' and 'Realism', and proposes that this structure embodies the ideological reproduction of what Eagleton had earlier argued was the conflict between the 'landed and industrial sectors of the contemporary ruling class' (*MP* 4):

> The structure of Charlotte's fiction, then, must achieve an appropriate balance between nostalgic reaction and forward-looking enterprise – or, conversely, between Romantic panache and realist prudence. In searching out that point of balance, the novels, as I have argued, are attuned to a real history: their ideological interplay has its source in a pattern of conflicts and alignments between contemporary social classes. (*MP* 76)

An understanding of the structures operating in Charlotte's fiction forms the basis for comparison with Emily's *Wuthering Heights*, and for an exploration of the reason why, aesthetically, Emily's novel is thought to be more successful than her sister's work. Eagleton describes Charlotte's novels as 'mythical', in the sense that they 'weld together antagonistic forces, forging from them a pragmatic, precarious coherence of interests' (*MP* 97) which, while attempting to 'reconcile' the gap between Romance and Realism, still sometimes shows 'severe structural disjunctions between the two' (*MP* 100) due to the ideological contradictions inherent in such a move. In contrast, *Wuthering Heights* is more successful as a work, as it refuses such a false reconciliation. In Eagleton's view, it 'achieves its coherence of vision from an exhausting confrontation of contending forces' (*MP* 98), and 'fastens thematically on a near-absolute antagonism between these modes but achieves, structurally and stylistically, an astonishing unity between them' (*MP* 100). In short, Charlotte is unable to achieve a complete artistic unity in her work because she seeks to falsely reconcile conflicting ideologies, while Emily, with her more authentic grasp of social reality, is able to transcend the problems of reconciliation faced by Charlotte and portray the conflict in a more complete form.

This is only a brief explication of what is a detailed argument presented by Eagleton, but shows both the main lines of thought advanced in the work, as well as the practical and theoretical differences between *Myths of Power* and Eagleton's earlier books. While I have argued that this presented an important theoretical advance, it is also necessary to explore some of the limits inherent in Eagleton's approach. Firstly, as is evident above, Eagleton depicts the concept of 'unity' as the primary criterion for judging the aesthetic value of a literary work. However, this itself implies a particular aesthetic ideology that equates unity with artistic success, stemming, in Eagleton's case, from the influence of Lukács's aesthetics of realism. Eagleton later acknowledges the presence of this implicit Lukácsian aesthetic in *Myths of Power*, and recognizes that it would be entirely possible to read Charlotte's apparent failure to achieve a complete unity in her work not as an aesthetic flaw, but instead as an attempt to expose the limits of the genre and offer 'a radical challenge to orthodox realism rather than a thoughtless deviation from it' (*MP:* 1988 xvi). Secondly, while Goldmann's concept of category structures provides an important critical tool for Eagleton, allowing him to surmount many of the problems found in *Shakespeare and Society* and *Exiles and Émigrés* (specifically in providing a theoretical method for moving between the levels of history, authorial ideology and text in his critical discussion), it is also evident that the adaptation of Goldmann's methodology introduces a new set of problems to be addressed. A frequent post-structural critique of structuralist thought is that, despite the claim made by structuralists of an objective scientific method, no structure obtains a total objectivity, for they must still rely on a centre that limits the 'play' of a structure.[20] A similar problem evident in Eagleton's method is that his readings, despite the confident talk of uncovering seemingly objective structures throughout the novels of the Brontës, do not obtain the level of objectivity to which they purport. As certain slips in Eagleton's vocabulary indicate, the categorical structures that he uncovers are by no means clear-cut: Charlotte's novels display a '*roughly* triadic structure' that can be seen '*more or less*' as operating on both a horizontal and vertical level; they are structured around an opposition between what he has '*crudely* termed "Romance" and "Realism"' (*MP* 94, 100, emphasis mine), to give only a couple of possible examples. The use of such imprecise, hedging qualifiers suggests the prospect that Eagleton is not so much explicating definite objective structures in the text that are waiting to be uncovered, but instead interpreting rather more ambiguous, shifting concepts that could be read in disparate ways, potentially undermining Eagleton's attempts to pin down an overarching structure. This leads to the third point: that Eagleton, following Goldmann, assumes a relatively unproblematic mediation of categorical structures between society, author, and text. The novels are said to 'express' the mental structures of the author, which gives little consideration to the fact that the ideological and material factors that contribute to the production of a literary text complicate the structural interaction proposed by Eagleton. This is a problem, as will be seen below, that becomes a central concern for Eagleton, and leads to one of the significant theoretical differences between *Myths of Power* and *Criticism and Ideology*.

Eagleton, in his preface to the second edition of *Myths of Power* (1988), notes the potential for such criticism of his book, and also cites his failure to move decisively beyond the 'practical criticism' model of textual analysis, and his silence on issues such as gender and race, as omissions from which the work suffers (*MP*: 1988 xi–xix). Indeed, these are important areas overlooked in this book, but it is also necessary to note that, whatever the weaknesses of *Myths of Power* may be, the book has played a significant role in Eagleton's theoretical development. An early anonymous review of *Myths of Power* in *The Times* could not disguise the reviewer's irritation with the content and method of the book, writing it off with the statement: 'Heavy going in style and content for 138 pages, with something to irritate everyone who loves the novels.'[21] This, however, presumably was the point. *Myths of Power* is not a work written to promote an uncritical 'love' for the Brontës or to depict them as genius sisters, serenely untouched by history or politics. Instead Eagleton provides a challenging and rigorous reading attuned to both the political and aesthetic levels of the novels, extending new areas of Marxist critical theory into the field of Anglophone literary studies.

Towards a Marxist science of the text: *Criticism and Ideology*

We have seen in the above sections the critical and theoretical shifts present in Eagleton's earliest publications, beginning with the early influence of Williams, Leavis and 'practical criticism', and moving towards a more explicit engagement with Marxism and the theories of ideology. This critical journey culminates in *Criticism and Ideology* (1976), which stands out as the most consciously theoretical work in Eagleton's corpus. Unlike Eagleton's earlier literary critical books, all of which were based on the study of distinct literary-critical problematics, concerning specific genres, periods, or authors, *Criticism and Ideology* presents itself as a break with such a method, offering a new 'scientific' theory of criticism. In the following section, I will outline the main areas of the argument presented by Eagleton in each of these chapters, and consider the main issues that subsequent critics have debated concerning Eagleton's work. Due to the complexity of Eagleton's work, I will make no pretence of offering an exhaustive explication of every element of the study, but rather highlight certain elements which seem to me to encapsulate the key issues arising from the work.

   The opening chapter of *Criticism and Ideology* presents an attempt by Eagleton to account for the main currents of English literary criticism, focusing on the political shifts in the British academy, and concerned primarily with a critique of Raymond Williams. For Eagleton, such a task is necessary to account for the apparent failure of the British to develop their own theories of Marxist criticism – a sense of failure that Eagleton makes plain in the preface (*CI* 7) – and also to establish his own point of intervention in the debate. The three main currents Eagleton identifies in the history of British literary criticism are the 'Leavisite' criticism of F. R. Leavis and the school of criticism that formed around the journal *Scrutiny*, the early Marxist criticism of the English Marxist Christopher Caudwell, and the 'Left-Leavisite' criticism of Raymond Williams that represents a partial combination of the first two currents. Eagleton praises the *Scrutiny* movement, characterized as the product of the entry of the petty bourgeois into the ancient universities, for its challenge to the amateur literary critical approach of the early professors who established the discipline of English, and argues that 'No more militant, courageous and consistent project is to be found in the history of English criticism' than the project instigated by Leavis. Nonetheless, Eagleton remains scathing of their 'pathetically obsolescent and idealist' reaction to the modern world and lauding of the non-existent organic past, as well as their vastly inflated claims made for the civilizing value of the study of literature (see *CI* 13–16).[22]

In light of the contradictions of the Leavisite tradition, the lack of an English materialist criticism to offer an effective counter is particularly significant. Eagleton characterizes the British Marxist literary tradition as a 'fragmentary, notably uneven body of materialist criticism', most of which 'is now of merely historical interest'. The main figure Eagleton cites is Caudwell, the 'major English Marxist critic . . . *helas*'. But for Eagleton, there is 'little, except negatively, to be learnt from' Caudwell, due to Caudwell's apparent isolation from Continental debates in Marxist aesthetics, and his 'vulgar' Marxist understanding of the relationship between literature and the dominant political ideology (*CI* 21).

It is this lack of a viable Marxist tradition in the work of Caudwell that Eagleton sees as the basis for the theoretical problems in the work of Raymond Williams. Central to Eagleton's criticism of Williams is the fact that Williams was forced to adapt other, ill-suited critical methods to his own purposes of providing a socialist cultural criticism. Eagleton provides a detailed reading of Williams's oeuvre, which I will not recount here, save to point out the central theoretical contradiction for which Eagleton rebukes Williams's work. Eagleton characterizes Williams as a 'Left-Leavisite', and sees that Williams has been forced to adapt 'what is still in many ways a Leavisian perspective to a "socialist humanism" radically hostile to *Scrutiny's* political case' (*CI* 24–5). Eagleton's criticisms of Williams were controversial, and it is hard to escape the sense of parricide as Eagleton attacks Williams's work in what is quite often a savage manner. Nonetheless, it remains an important reconsideration of areas that are problematic in Williams's writing, necessary for British Marxist critics to confront if the movement was to reach beyond Williams's shadow.

Having thus distanced himself from his English critical precur-
sors, Eagleton moves on to propose a radical rupture with previous
forms of criticism in the Anglo-American academy, arguing that
'criticism must break with its ideological pre-history, situating itself
outside the space of the text on the alternative terrain of scientific
knowledge' (*CI* 43). In order to grasp what Eagleton was attempting, it is necessary to consider briefly the wider debate in Marxist
literary criticism, specifically concerning the issue of 'base' and
'superstructure'. Marx, in a famous passage from the preface to *The
Critique of Political Philosophy*, outlines the fundamental distinction
that would form the basis for all subsequent Marxist cultural
thought:

> In the social production of their life, men enter into definite relations
> that are indispensable and independent of their will, relations of
> production which correspond to a definite stage of development
> of their material productive forces. The sum total of these relations
> of production constitutes the economic structure of society, the real
> foundation, on which rises a legal and political superstructure and
> to which correspond definite forms of social consciousness. The
> mode of production of material life conditions the social, political
> and intellectual life process in general. It is not the consciousness of
> men that determines their being, but, on the contrary, their social
> being that determines their consciousness.[23]

Literature, therefore, is a product of the superstructure of society,
which is 'conditioned' by the economic base. The problems arise
when one tries to establish how close the link between base and
superstructure actually is. In the economically determinist or
'vulgar' Marxist style of Marxist literary criticism that was dominant in the earlier twentieth century, a simple cause-and-effect
model was often adopted. In such a scheme, a Marxist critic would,
for example, seek to explain Shakespeare's plays as expressing the
conflict between the absolute feudal monarch and the rise of the
bourgeois class, or see Byron's poetry as representative of the dying
ideology of the aristocratic class. Alick West, a notable British
Marxist critic of the 1930s, baldly stated in one of his articles on
poetry that 'The ruling ideas being the ideas of the ruling class, the
poet during the rise and prime of capitalism necessarily thinks and
feels in terms of capitalist ideology', a statement that is too broad
to account for the diverse range of poets and opinions in this era
if they all reflect the same 'capitalist ideology'.[24] Such a style of criticism has been rightfully condemned as being too reductive, but this

leaves the problem of how to enact a form of Marxist criticism that would not only allow a rigorous historical materialist reading of the text, but also account for the specific aesthetic and authorial aspects of the text that a mechanical base/superstructure model fails to account for. Eagleton's criticism of Caudwell and Williams in the opening chapter confronts exactly this problem in the history of English Marxist criticism: Caudwell for being too reductive, and Williams for substituting a Romantic humanism in place of Marxist criticism, resulting in an evasion of a necessary historical materialist problem.

As has been seen in the discussion of *Myths of Powers*, Eagleton found a partial solution to this problem in Goldmann's concept of 'categorical structures', but Eagleton increasingly saw this, as well, as too simplistic a concept to account for the complexity of ideology. To overcome this issue, Eagleton turned to the theories of the French Marxist philosopher Louis Althusser, and Althusser's student, Pierre Macherey. Althusser, commonly termed a 'structuralist Marxist', was involved in important reinterpretation of key texts by Marx, emphasizing both the 'scientific' nature of Marx's thought, and reconsidering certain Marxist concepts in light of Freud's and Lacan's psychoanalytical work. As Althusser explains in the preface to the English edition of his collection of essays, *For Marx*, he sought to ' "draw a line of demarcation" between the true theoretical bases of the Marxist science of history and Marxist philosophy on the one hand, and, on the other, the pre-Marxist idealist notions on which depend contemporary interpretations of Marxism as a "philosophy of man" or a "Humanism".'[25] His seminal essay, 'Ideology and Ideological State Apparatuses', drew on Antonio Gramsci's concept of hegemony, and Freud's and Lacan's theories of the unconcious, to analyse the relationship between ideology and the historical 'real', proposing that ideology does not reflect the real world as such, but instead 'represents' the 'imaginary relationship of individuals' to the real world.[26] Althusser's understanding of ideology, as will be seen below, forms an important backdrop to Eagleton's discussion, as Eagleton refines these general concepts with regard to the relationship between history, ideology, and the literary work itself.

Althusser did not write in any detail on specific literary theory topics, save from one short letter in which he stated that he did not 'rank real art among the ideologies'. Instead art, while not presenting scientific knowledge, nonetheless shows something 'which *alludes* to reality'.[27] It was Althusser's student, Pierre Macherey, who clarified Althusser's general argument into a specific consideration of literature in the seminal work *A Theory of Literary Production*. Traditional criticism, Macherey claimed, has a 'tendency to slide into the natural fallacy of empiricism, to treat the work (the object of the enterprise of criticism) as factually given, spontaneously isolated for inspection. The work thus exists only to be received, described, and assimilated through the procedures of criticism'.[28] Macherey also criticizes what he terms the 'normative fallacy': the tendency for the critic to assume the position of judge, pointing out that 'the work should be other than it is'. Macherey proposed a new purpose for literary criticism, advocating that it should no longer merely concern itself with the act of literary consumption, but rather would ask the 'new critical question': 'What are the laws of literary production?':

> Can there be a criticism which would not be commentary, which would be a scientific analysis adding an authentic knowledge to the speech of the work without, meanwhile, denying its presence? Instead of an *art of reading* could there be a *positive criticism* which would speak of the conditions for making a book?[29]

What interested Macherey was not so much what the text under consideration purports to signify, but rather what is in the 'unconscious' of the text, or what the gaps and omissions in a text reveal about the ideological circumstances of its production. As he states:

> We should question the work as to what it does not and cannot say, in those silences for which it has been made. The concealed order of the work is thus less significant than its real determinate disorder (its disarray). The order which it professes is merely an imagined order, projected onto disorder, the fictive resolution of ideological conflicts, a resolution so precarious that it is obvious in the very letter of the text where incoherence and incompleteness burst forth.[30]

Althusser's ideas were beginning to circulate in English publications by the late 1960s, with the *New Left Review* publishing a number of his articles in translation, and by the 1970s Althusser's ideas were being subject to intense debate among theoreticians, as one of the most challenging new critical formations being adapted by members of the New Left,[31] and particularly drew controversy over the Althussarian claims to a scientific Marxist methodology, attracting attacks from many of those in the socialist-humanist tradition of the 'older' New Left.[32] *Criticism and Ideology* thus represents a sophisticated mediation of a major area of Marxist theoretical development to a broader critical theory audience, and also an important engagement in debate with the theories of Althusser and Macherey in its own right.

Following Macherey's proposal to establish the 'laws for the production of the text', Eagleton presents a comprehensive categorical theory of the various levels of ideological and productive influences that contribute to producing a text. These interlocking levels are:

(i)   General Mode of Production (GMP)
(ii)   Literary Mode of Production (LMP)
(iii)   General Ideology (GI)
(iv)   Authorial Ideology (AuI)
(v)   Aesthetic Ideology (AI)
(vi)   Text

The general mode of production refers to the 'unity of certain forces and social relations of material production': in classic Marxist terms, both the economic system (slavery, feudalism, capitalism) and the relations between classes that are unique to these means of production (the bourgeois exploitation of the proletariat under capitalism, for example). Within each general mode of production there will be a distinct literary mode of production, which refers to the 'unity of certain forces and social relations of literary production in a particular social formation' (*CI* 45). This is often a complicated interaction as, 'In any literate society there will normally exist a number of distinct modes of literary production' for, as Eagleton highlights, 'if it is possible in Western societies to produce fiction for the capitalist market, it is also possible to distribute one's handwritten poetry on the streets' (*CI* 45), and it is also possible that a single LMP (such as the little magazine) may contain features from a variety of other LMPs.

The separation of ideology into the three distinct categories of general, authorial, and aesthetic offers the opportunity to distinguish between complex layers of ideological influence upon a text. The general ideology is the dominant ideological formation produced by the general mode of production: a 'relatively coherent set of "discourses" of values, representation and beliefs' that perpetuates the dominant social relations (*CI* 54). The authorial ideology refers to an author's specific biographical insertion into the general ideology, 'a mode of insertion overdetermined by a series of distinct factors' such as 'social class, sex, nationality, religion, geographical region and so on' (*CI* 58). The aesthetic ideology denotes a specific region of the general ideology, of which the literary aesthetic is a particular subset, made up of levels such as 'theories of literature, critical practices, literary traditions', and so forth (*CI* 60).

It is important to note that these levels are not proposed as autonomous categories, but rather as categories in constant dialectical interaction with each other. The literary mode of production, for example, is provided by the general mode of production, but in turn, the literary mode of production may contribute to the general mode of production itself, such as with the rise of the printing press and the growth of literature as a commodity production. Similarly, a complicated interaction occurs between the aesthetic ideology, general ideology, and literary mode of production, for: 'A GMP produces a GI which contributes to reproducing it; it also produces a (dominant) LMP which in general reproduces and is reproduced by the GMP, but which also reproduces and is reproduced by the GI' (*CI* 60). It is by analysing the complicated interaction between these different ideological and productive factors that the basis of this scientific literary criticism is formed, and this in turn sets the framework for the later analysis undertaken in *Criticism and Ideology*.

Eagleton's categories offer an important advance in Marxist criticism, refining the precarious base/superstructure model into more flexible categories which, while still offering a materialist theoretical basis for understanding a literary work, also allow a more sophisticated interrogation of the multiple layers of ideological, aesthetic, and economic factors that shape the production of a text. However, the very notion of attempting to install literary criticism as a 'science' instigates a new range of theoretical issues. Howard Felperin criticized Eagleton for engaging in what is essentially a theoretical sleight-of-hand with his claims towards 'science', stating that:

> This impulse to create a scientific critical discourse – a system of fixed signifiers, adequate to denote the signified object of explanation without slippage – leads Eagleton not only to the specific adoption of a pseudo-mathematical terminology and an elaborate set of laws and formulas that supposedly 'govern' literary production, but to the more general stylistic trick of deploying a concrete vocabulary for the highly abstract concepts and processes he wants to describe.[33]

It is fair to say that Eagleton does get carried away with constructing seemingly scientific formulas for describing the interaction
between the constituent levels of his theory of literature.[34] But
to write Eagleton's discussion off as a 'stylistic trick' ignores the
difficult but significant task that Eagleton was trying to carry out.
It is certainly true that Eagleton was trying to bring 'highly abstract
concepts and processes' into a critical discussion, but it is exactly
for this reason that the theoretical framework of this chapter is of
value.

Having thus outlined the complicated interaction of structures
that contribute to the production of a literary text, Eagleton turns
to an examination of the relationship between the text, ideology,
and history. This is a discussion that generally seeks to use Althusser's understanding of ideology and clarify Althusser's enigmatic
claim that a literary text is not knowledge or ideology, but instead
something 'which *alludes* to reality'. The mechanical formulations
of vulgar Marxist literary criticism had seen a relatively uncompli-
cated relationship between a literary text and ideology, with the
former simply reflecting the latter, and it is this conception that
Eagleton seeks to replace with a more sophisticated model. As
Eagleton distinguishes: 'The literary text is not the "expression" of
ideology, nor is ideology the "expression" of social class. The text,
rather, is a certain *production* of ideology . . .' The analogy Eagleton
uses is the relationship between a dramatic text and a dramatic
production of that text, for such a production is not said directly to
'express' the text on which it is based, but rather offer a production
that is a 'unique and irreducible entity' (*CI* 64). As such, the literary
text does not have a 'direct, spontaneous relation' to history, for
while language 'certainly denotes objects . . . it does not do so in
some simple relationship, as though word and object stood adja-
cent, as two poles awaiting the electric current of interconnection'
(*CI* 70). Unlike Georg Lukács, Eagleton does not propose ideology
in the sense of a 'false consciousness' that can be escaped to grasp
the historical 'real', but rather sees it, following Althusser, as 'an
inherently complex formation which, by inserting individuals into
history in a variety of ways, allows of multiple kinds and degrees
of access to that history' (*CI* 69). History, therefore does certainly
enter the text, 'but it enters precisely *as ideology*' (*CI* 72).

While he argues that literature may access history in this way,
Eagleton also maintains the distinction between literary and histo-
riographical discourse, with the latter being distinguished as having
'history itself' as its object, while the former appears to have 'no

determinate object' (*CI* 72). It is exactly this apparent distance from 'history itself' that provides the specific value of literature:

> Literary and historiographical texts are thus 'ideological' in quite distinct senses. The literary text does not *take* history as its object, even when (as with 'historical' fiction) it believes itself to do so; but it does, nevertheless, *have* history as its object in the last instance, in ways apparent not to the text itself but to criticism. It is this *distantation* of history, this absence of any particular historical 'real', which confers on literature its air of freedom; unlike the historiographical work, it seems to be liberated from the need to conform its meanings to the exigencies of the actual. (*CI* 74)

This point is well applied to the case of Jane Austen. Austen's fiction, Eagleton argues, is not to be dismissed as the work of ideological delusion due to its clearly ideological and reactionary social vision, for 'on the contrary, it also offers us a version of contemporary history which is considerably more revealing than much historiography', as Austen's forms 'are the product of certain ideological codes which, in permitting us access to certain values, forces and relations, yield us a sort of historical knowledge' (*CI* 70–1). This leads Eagleton ultimately to make the bold claim that it is literature that offers 'the most revealing mode of experiential access to ideology that we possess', allowing us to observe in 'a peculiarly complex, coherent, intensive and immediate fashion the workings of ideology in the textures of lived experience of class-societies'. It is therefore the function of the materialist critic 'to refuse the spontaneous presence of the work' and, as Macherey proposed, interrogate the unconscious gaps present in the work and to 'make its real determinants appear' (*CI* 101).

From here Eagleton moves on to demonstrating this criticism in action, specifically through an examination of the same 'Culture and Society' tradition that he first addressed in *Shakespeare and Society*, and traces the decline of the 'organic' literary form in the English literary tradition, characterized as the form of writing that sought to portray society as existing in spontaneous unity. D. H. Lawrence, for example, is characterized as the twentieth-century inheritor of the Romantic humanist 'Culture and Society tradition' and his work is read as a dramatization of the 'contradiction within the Romantic humanist tradition itself, between its corporate and individualist components' (*CI* 158). Therefore, whereas Lawrence was praised in *Exiles and Émigrés* for the 'total' vision presented in *The Rainbow*, it is now the 'fissuring of the organic form' present in

Women in Love that is held as the significant aspect of Lawrence's work (*CI* 160). The discussion of the 'Culture and Society' tradition offers an important practical investigation of a literary problem using the theoretical methods outlined, but it is far from a problem-free example. Firstly, the very return to the 'Culture and Society' tradition in this section raises the problem of canonical politics, as to whether he is replicating the very Leavisite canon that earlier sections had subject to critical attack. It is possible to defend Eagleton here by arguing that he essentially puts the problems of canonical politics and aesthetic temporarily in brackets, and instead demonstrates how the theory outlined in chapters 2 and 3 can be put into use to offer counter readings of the received canon. But nonetheless Eagleton, despite the polemical attempts to signal a definitive break with the prehistory, continues to work implicitly within the same basic canonical assumptions as Leavis and Williams; assumptions that will be seen later to present a significant blind spot in Eagleton's work. Secondly, what is also notably absent is the move beyond this generalized ideological critique into specific acts of literary criticism, save for the occasional terse statement regarding an example of a contradiction found in a novel. It is true that Eagleton was attempting to break with the 'practical criticism' tradition, but the attempt leaves Eagleton's critical method (in form if not in content), looking remarkably similar to that of Christopher Caudwell, albeit in a more sophisticated and nuanced way. Significantly, Eagleton chose to omit an essay – 'Form, Ideology and *The Secret Agent'* – offering a specific reading of Conrad's *The Secret Agent*, which was later published in *Against the Grain*. In this Eagleton offers what is perhaps the strongest development working out of his Althusserian-inspired critical method, teasing out the contradictory levels of signification at work in the novel, in areas concerning the complexity of the 'Conradian ideology' and how this plays out in the complex interaction of literary forms of the text. This essay, one could argue, provides the necessary move from theory to practice, and its omission leaves a gap in *Criticism and Ideology* that is not satisfactorily resolved.

The final chapter of *Criticism and Ideology* addresses perhaps the most difficult question of all: the question of a materialist aesthetics of literature. In the previous chapters, as has been seen, Eagleton worked within the framework of an accepted canon of 'valued' literary texts. He now attempts to account for the value of these texts in material terms. Significantly, he does not advocate the position of dismissing out of hand the notion of the established canon, arguing that 'nothing is gained by that form of literary ultra-leftism which dismisses received evaluations merely because they are the product of bourgeois criticism'. He is also explicit in his disdain for the supposedly 'anti-elitist' drive behind much of the (then embryonic) movement of cultural studies, asserting that 'It would seem absurd for Marxist criticism to be silent on the qualitative distinction between, say, Pushkin and Coventry Patmore' (*CI* 162). But equally, Eagleton is scathing towards the concept of 'Literature' in the sense of a particular canon of works only truly appreciated by a limited caste of 'cultured' individuals, arguing that in these circumstances 'Criticism becomes a mutually supportive dialogue between two highly valorized subjects: the valuable text and the valuable reader' (*CI* 164). This leaves Eagleton with the difficult task of negotiating the middle ground and providing a materialist explanation for the basis of literary value.

This issue has been one of the most problematic areas in Marxist aesthetics, first broached by Marx's own notoriously unsatisfactory pronouncements on the continued value of ancient Greek art stemming from its 'child nature'.[35] Lenin and Trotsky both attempted to extend this debate in their writing on literature, and this is Eagleton's point of entrance into the topic. Eagleton argues that, while Trotsky may have intelligently tried to defend aesthetics from the problems of historical reductionism and the artistically bankrupt *proletkult*, he significantly contradicts himself when trying to understand whether Dante was a great writer, as Trotsky was unable to decide whether this was because of, or despite, Dante's own historical circumstances (*CI* 172–3). Lenin, however, was unable even to confront this issue, as he was 'simply incapable of enjoying art which he found theoretically unsympathetic' (*CI* 173). This had led both writers, despite their differences, to arrive at a similarly evasive position with regard to the cause of aesthetic value: they fall back on the Romantic concept of individual greatness, and fail to provide a properly materialist critical account (*CI* 174).

Eagleton, following Brecht, sees the most basic criteria necessary for literary works to have aesthetic value as being their ability to 'make us think' or allow us to 'get something out of them'. This fact, then, establishes the necessary areas of investigation for a materialist criticism, concerning 'the ideological matrix of our reading and the ideological matrix of their production' (*CI* 169). The specific example that Eagleton returns to is Dante's *Divine Comedy*, in an attempt to expand on Trotsky's work. In Eagleton's view:

It is not that Dante's work is valuable because it 'speaks of' an important historical era, or 'expresses the consciousness' of that epoch. Its
value is an effect of the process whereby the complex ideological
conjecture in which it inheres so produces (internally distantiates)
itself in a play of textual significations as to render its depths and
intricacies vividly perceptible. (*CI* 177–8)

The reason we can find continued value in Dante many centuries
later is because we are part of the same long history of class struggle: the *Divine Comedy* 'belongs to the general history of class-
society *by virtue* of occupying a particular moment in medieval
Italy' (*CI* 178).

Eagleton also recognizes that transhistorical literature such as
Dante's (which, in Engels's view, stands at the point of the world
historical shift from feudalism to capitalism) is not the only valuable
form of literature, and that indeed much valuable literature 'comes
into being not *despite* its historical limitations . . . but *by virtue of*
them' (*CI* 179). This is the reason given by Eagleton for the value of
the 'Culture and Society' writers. Eagleton notes that all these
'agreed "major" authors' were 'significantly displaced from the
hegemonic bourgeois ideology' (*CI* 180), allowing them to throw
'the "fault-lines" of that formation into partial relief' (*CI* 181), specifically *because of* their particular historical and ideological limita-
tion developed in reaction to contemporary society. But Eagleton
here appears to assume that the ability to depict the fault-lines of
ideology is in itself enough to create a major work, an assumption
that has drawn strong criticism. In Tony Bennett's opinion, the
theories concerning literary value presented in *Criticism and Ideology*
'must be judged a failure', for 'there is simply no way in which a
given text can be said to be valued *because* of the circumstances of
its production'.[36] While I would not be so quick as to dismiss it as
a failure, Bennett indeed identifies a crucial gap in Eagleton's argument. Eagleton also argues 'that all texts signify, but not all texts are
significant' (*CI* 185), but his clarification of this claim is only
partial. Eagleton is evasive when it comes to distinguishing between
'Literature' (in the canonical sense) and literature (in the sense of
all imaginative writing), a fact that presents a serious problem in
his formulation. He holds up the example of a love story in a
teenage magazine as an obvious example of inferior literature, as
whatever the transformative textual production undertaken, the
ideological matrix in which it is formed renders it unlikely to
produce a significant work. In a sense, this is an easy and obvious

example, but does not bring us any closer to a solution. Eagleton cites the play of textual signification in *The Divine Comedy* as revealing the complex ideological circumstances in which it was formed, proving this as a valuable text. But this evades the question of what is specific to *Dante's* 'play of textual signification' to make it valuable or 'significant', as opposed to other writing emerging from the same ideological and productive circumstance. Eagleton seems to accept Dante's 'value' as given, which is a curiously unscientific lapse for someone proposing a scientific interrogation of literary aesthetics. He faces similar problems when discussing the value of the works examined in chapter 4. He cites the 'power' of the 'aesthetic signification' of the 'Culture and Society' tradition as stemming from its ideological position, which, again, takes for granted that the 'aesthetic signification' of this tradition *is* indeed powerful (*CI* 181). Essentially, Eagleton is in a bind. He wants to reject the idealistic notion of 'literature' and replace it with an objective scientific understanding of literary value. Yet he simply assumes that the texts that he discusses *are* aesthetically valuable, and explains this as arising from the productive circumstances of the texts – a neatly sealed circle. It would be entirely possible for Eagleton to attempt to justify his choice of significant texts, but this would mean resorting to the subjective method of 'practical criticism' and comparatively analysing examples of 'significant' and 'non-significant' literary texts – the very critical method from which he has just sought to distance himself. Therefore, Eagleton's refusal actually to provide analysis of why a specific 'play of textual signification' is more aesthetically significant than another means that his assertions, while suggestive, are never satisfactorily resolved.

Aftermath

Criticism and Ideology met with enthusiastic initial reviews, praising it as a significant contribution to the field of Marxist aesthetics, with Francis Mulhern, in an early and substantial critique, citing it as 'the first major study in Marxist literary theory to be written in England in forty years'.[37] Yet, despite this initial excitement, the critical impact of the work was negligible. While *Criticism and Ideology* is still sometimes cited as an important work of Marxist literary theory, it never generated a corresponding 'Eagletonian' movement in literary criticism, something which the initial response might have suggested would happen. Eagleton himself, in his later publication, makes very little direct reference to the theoretical framework laid out in *Criticism and Ideology*, and instead (as will be detailed in later chapters) developed a less explicitly theoretical, more journalistic, critical style, markedly different from the dense, scientific style of *Criticism and Ideology*. Looking back at *Criticism and Ideology* from the vantage point of the preface to his next major publication, *Walter Benjamin* in 1981, Eagleton remarked that the earlier work was 'less overtly political in timbre and more conventionally academic in style and form', which subsequent shifts in Marxist cultural theory sidelined:

> What seemed important when I wrote my earlier book, at a time when 'Marxist criticism' had little anchorage in Britain, was to examine its pre-history and to systematize the categories essential for a 'science of the text'. I would still defend the principle of that project, but it is perhaps no longer the focal concern of Marxist cultural studies. Partly under the pressure of global capitalist crisis, partly under the influence of new themes and forces within socialism, the centre of such studies is shifting from narrowly textual or conceptual analysis to problems of cultural production and the political uses of artefacts. (*WB* xii)

There are a number of factors that influenced this shift in critical theory. Partially, this was due to the increasing problems evident with Althusserian structuralist Marxism. As Eagleton admitted retrospectively, 'The benefit of each of Althusser's major theoretical concepts was that it sought to correct what could often be convincingly exposed as flawed or false conceptions in other traditions of Marxist thought; but, in almost every case, the alternative formulations offered turned out to be gravely and sometimes equally at fault', with Althusser's theories of ideology and anti-humanism threatening to 'marginalize both subjects and class struggle' (*AG* 2, 3). But wider shifts in critical theory also decisively influenced the subsequent reception of Eagleton's work. 1976 saw the publication of the English translation of Jacques Derrida's *Of Grammatology*, and the following year also saw the appearance of the English translations of Michel Foucault's seminal work, *Discipline and Punish*, as well as a selection of Jacques Lacan's *Écrits*.[38] *Criticism and Ideology*, situated as it was on the cusp of the shift in the Anglo-American academy from structuralism to post-structuralism, with its high-structuralist formulations, was thus easily theoretically sidelined from the debates that were about to engulf the literary academy.

Conclusion

What I want to propose briefly in concluding this chapter, however, is how *Criticism and Ideology* still offers a significant counter to problems frequently found in contemporary post-structuralist criticism. In recent decades one of the major movements in literary criticism has been the so-called 'New Historicism', associated with the work of Stephen Greenblatt, the author of *Renaissance Self-Fashioning* and *Shakespearean Negotiations*. Drawing on the work of Foucault, Greenblatt's method is characterized by its refusal to allow 'literature' a privileged place in critical discussion and instead sees the literary text as only one mode of a wider network of discourse. Such a technique often makes for lively and ingenious writing but also, in its seamless melding of various forms of discourse, excludes the study of literature as a distinct signifying process. One of the most frequent criticisms levelled against New Historicist critics is that, in seeing a literary text as only one document in a wider ideological matrix, they ignore the complicated interaction between history, ideology, and literature: in the words of one critic, New Historicism chooses 'merely to observe or describe juxtaposable events, practices, and texts, but never to explain the causal connections between those practices and texts'.[39] *Criticism and Ideology*, as has been argued in this chapter, is a work vulnerable to criticism on a number of fronts: its claim to 'science', its continued assumptions concerning a stable canon of 'Literature', and its partial demonstrations of how the theorical framework could function in practice. Yet this vulnerability does not render the difficult issues that it was attempting to explore any less valid or important. *Criticism and Ideology*, in offering one of the most sophisticated Marxist considerations of the relationship of the production of the literary text to the wider idelogical and historical circumstances, continues to offer a contribution to a debate that New Historicism has, by and large, evaded.

3

The Critic as Azdak: Eagleton in the 1980s

In 1982, Eagleton published an article in the journal *Diacritics*, which offered an assessment of the work of the American Marxist critic and theorist Fredric Jameson. Eagleton was firm in his admiration for the innovation and political impulse behind Jameson's writing, saluting Jameson's achievements as a political critic, and citing him as an example of 'one of the few American critics for whom "radicalism" extends beyond the terrors of tropology . . . to embrace the fate of the political struggles in Poland or El Salvador'. Nonetheless, Eagleton was motivated to rebuke Jameson on the grounds of his style, seeing his intricately wrought prose and intimidating intellectual range as raising significant questions regarding the political effectiveness of his mode of discourse. He claimed that:

> The most uncharitable way of putting the point would be to say that his work resembles nothing quite so much as some great Californian supermarket of the mind, in which the latest flashily dressed commodities (Hjelmslev, Barthes, Deleuze, Foucault) sit stacked upon the shelves alongside some more tried and trusty household names (Hegel, Schilling, Croce, Freud), awaiting the moment when they will all be casually scooped into the Marxist basket . . . such appropriation too often leaves the texts in question relatively untransformed, intact in their 'relative autonomy,' so that the strenuously *mastering* Jameson appears too eirenic, easy-going and all-encompassing for his own political good.

In Eagleton's view, Jameson's radical politics was limited by its inability to articulate its concerns through similarly revolutionary modes of expression, instead relying on a mandarin-like critical sublimation that avoided direct confrontation. Eagleton went on to localize the problem as one residing in the *style* of engagement undertaken in Jameson's criticism: 'The fact that [Jameson] is in no sense a polemical or satirical writer – essential modes, to my mind, for a political revolutionary – may be taken to confirm this impression.'[1]

This essay is symptomatic, I would hold, not just of Eagleton's engagement with the work of Jameson at this time, but also of Eagleton's emerging concerns with the nature and mechanisms of radical cultural criticism, and the shift in strategic priorities that such a reconsideration entailed. If Eagleton's writing through the 1970s was marked by its attempts to move away from the perceived theoretical weakness of the socialist-humanism of Raymond Williams, towards adapting emerging forms of theory in the construction of a comprehensive and scientific Marxist criticism, the 1980s would see Eagleton undertake a major reconsideration of both the goals and methods of a socialist cultural criticism. During this period, his critical output markedly shifted away from the narrowly textual attempts to derive a 'total' theory of cultural or textual production, and instead into more diffuse and pluralistic forms and concerns, seeking to engineer a politicized criticism that drew on the emerging insights and concerns of post-structuralism, psychoanalysis, and feminism without compromising on the political function. Similarly, this shift in theoretical priorities manifested itself in the level of Eagleton's practical style, as he increasingly investigated and used the 'essential modes' of polemic and satire as critical tools in his own work, resulting in a series of publications functioning as self-conscious interventions into the politics, scope, and methodology of contemporary criticism.

This chapter will trace these concerns as they emerged through Eagleton's work in the decade. I will start by examining his unpublished play, *Brecht and Company* (1979), in which Eagleton created a provocative and engaging portrait of the dramatist Bertolt Brecht. This work debuted at the Edinburgh Festival of 1979, where it was praised by one reviewer as 'an impressive analysis of Brecht in Brechtian styles',[2] but it is a work that has subsequently slipped into obscurity, with the occasional ironic references later made by Eagleton concerning its existence.[3] It is a work that occupies an important place in understanding Eagleton's shift in critical orientation, standing silently, as it does, between two major periods of his critical output, and this growing interest in Brecht's life, theory, and practice reflects and influences Eagleton's own critical preoccupations. This chapter then turns to the trilogy of 'critical-historical' works, *Walter Benjamin, or Towards a Revolutionary Criticism* (1981), *Literary Theory: An Introduction* (1983), and *The Function of Criticism* (1984), to analyse how these theorize the new emphasis on a radical critical pluralism, as well as how they show Eagleton's increasing experimentation with forms of critical style. This chapter concludes by briefly considering the two works from this decade – *The Rape of Clarissa* (1982) and *William Shakespeare* (1986) – which offer the major direct examples of this form of radical critical pluralism in action, and how they bring into practical focus the theoretical issues generated by Eagleton's writing in this period.

Brecht and Company: making Brecht strange

In the preface to *Walter Benjamin*, Eagleton cites one of the decisive factors behind the theoretical shift from the high Althusserian *Criticism and Ideology* as being the experience of writing *Brecht and Company*, 'which both in its writing and in the final product raised questions of the relations between socialist cultural theory and cultural practice, the relevance of both to revolutionary politics, the techniques of intellectual production and the political uses of theatre and comedy' (WB xii). What, therefore, were the questions raised by the writing and subsequent production of this play, that provoked such a profound shift in Eagleton's career? Bertolt Brecht, as one of the greatest socialist artists and aestheticians of the twentieth century, represents an obvious and crucial marker for subsequent Marxist critical theorists, but Eagleton's turn to Brecht as a source of literary inspiration is not an attempt at hagiography, so much as being, through this biographical investigation, a work designed to both enact and question Brecht's own drama and theory. In his life, Brecht produced a corpus of work marked by its attempt to push socialist theatre into new forms of expression capable of engaging with the complexities of developing capitalist society, ranging from his earlier anarchic plays such as *Mahagonny* and the *Threepenny Opera*, to his experimental political Lehrstüke, and his mature historical epics such as *Galileo* and *Mother Courage*. Similarly, Brecht's innovation was not confined to practical dramatic works or theatrical techniques, but was constantly refined and debated on a theoretical level. This was most famously shown in his often-cited debates with Lukács over the position of realism and

modernism as modes of socialist art,[4] as well as the corpus of theoretical works that culminated in the *Short Organum for the Theatre*
and *The Messingkauf Dialogues*, which developed his famous concepts of 'Epic Theatre' and 'Alienation Effects'. Brecht sought a form
of theatre that would resists the urge of creating simple modes of
dramatic illusion in which members of the audience were passive
spectators, and instead desired to foreground the play as a site of
debate and artificial construction, in which the audience would be
challenged to adopt an active role in critically assessing the material
presented to them.[5] As he famously quipped in relation to the challenges presented to the socialist artists by the demands of modernity, 'petroleum resists the five act form', and his career can be seen
as a series of experiments and developments in order to find new
modes of expression to audiences suitable for conveying the complex
political climate of an advanced capitalist society.

At the same time, Brecht's own biographical details raise a series
of important questions concerning the relation of Brecht's personal
life to his political position. A man who would profess a revolutionary Marxism but would not actually become a member of the Communist party; who would travel the entire length of the USSR to
evade the Nazis before choosing to end up in the bosom of American capitalism in Hollywood; who was a famously abrasive personality, and accused by subsequent critics of severe plagiarism from
the work of his various mistresses; and who would throw his lot in
with East Germany and become one of the East German's cultural
stars, while maintaining an ambivalent relationship with the Party
hierarchy, especially after writing a letter expressing 'solidarity'
with the Party First Secretary Walter Ulbricht in the wake of the
violent suppression of the 1953 Worker Uprising in Berlin: Brecht's
career posed a series of questions which have generated a range
of subsequent debate over the sincerity and effectiveness of Brecht's
own political commitment.[6]

These ambivalences are the focus of *Brecht and Company*, as
Eagleton turns Brecht's theory and practice back on Brecht himself.
Eagleton constructs a work that moves back and forth across Brecht's
career in an epic style, offering a series of episodic scenes taken from
various stages of Brecht's career, while frequently interrupting its
own narrative with asides from the cast, projections on screens
behind the stage, and sudden breaks into Shakespearian verse, in
witty and apt deployments of Brechtian-style alienation effects.
Through this, Eagleton interrogates the figure of Brecht himself,
offering coherent snapshots of Brecht at various stages of his career;

and also sets Brecht's life and political claims against the wider backdrop of Nazism, in a juxtaposition that sets a stark contrast between the claims of Brecht's aesthetic, and the actual political demands made on socialist intellectuals in light of the rise of fascism.

This is a tension that Eagleton skilfully binds into the opening of the play, where the famous Brecht–Weill song 'Mack The Knife' from *The Threepenny Opera* is rewritten as 'Bert the Knife', satirically casting Brecht's own story in the modes of his dramatic works. To provide a few stanzas:

> Oil your holster, Hermann Goering
> Get your shades on, say you're dead
> For Bert's pen stabs swift and sharp, friend
> Kills without a trace of red

> Hear his old typewriter rattle
> Mowing fascists to the ground
> Clutch your crotch there, Third Reich baby
> 'Cos old Bertie's back in town.

The manifest level of this song would indicate a valorization of Brecht's role in resisting the Nazis through his literary creations, but irony quickly seeps through. The instability of the word 'red' implies a double negativity: at once suggesting the death that Brecht wreaks on the Nazis is purely a textual one that leaves their physical body intact (and thus able to carry out their political project), and that Brecht's lack of red symbolizes the distance between his textual interventions and actual socialist revolution. The rattle of a machine-gun transposed to Brecht's typewriter creates a similar incongruity, between the idea of writing as literary creation and writing as a weapon in a struggle. A series of questions is thus starkly raised by Eagleton: in what ways and to what extent can cultural production serve as an effective political tool, in the face of an acute struggle and the rise of Hitler?

The issue that Eagleton circles around is the role of irony as a critical tool, and the power of satire to function as a political intervention, and this is a debate that Eagleton again and again implicates Brecht's work within. In an exchange with his actors that occurs in one of the early scenes of the play, set against the backdrop of the political upheaval of the Weimar Republic, Brecht explains the choices that he makes for his theatrical methods, and argues with them about the demands faced by theatre in light of

political reality. The actors joke with Brecht about his political pretensions, as a man who would 'rather show the bourgeois your arse
than your fist', but in response what Brecht stresses to his actors is
the subversion that he finds inherent in the comic mode, where
'anything can become anything else':

> ACTOR   Six million out of work and he talks about comedy.
> BRECHT   Look: six million out of work today, maybe sixteen million
> tomorrow. Hitler a housepainter yesterday, Chancellor tomorrow.
> And the day after? Maybe Hitler down a sewer and Soviets in Berlin.
> Everything can be stood on its head . . . If you can't smash it you can
> wear it out, with wit and cunning.

As Brecht tells his debater, there is political value in the seedy and
irreverent: his hero is not the tiger, but instead the rat, a creature
who 'is slimed with the sewers but he survives, forages here and
there. And he can kill too. He isn't a mouse.'
    The play jumps from this scene forward into 1947, as Brecht faces
the House Committee on Un-American Activities (HUAC) in New
York, deploying exactly this wit and cunning in the face of the questions of those who sought to use his political allegiance to entrap
him. The historical Brecht had originally stated that he would not
give testimony to the congress (in solidarity with nineteen other
Hollywood workers who had been summoned), but answered the
questions put to him in the end, slyly evading incriminating himself
through a series of bluffs, half-truths and claims of mistranslation.
What Eagleton portrays is Brecht not just avoiding the questions
put to him, but Brecht mimicking the very values and discourses of
those conducting the inquisition, tying them up in their own logic
and ideology so as to present no target to attack. In defending his
own work against the committee's charges of Communist sympa-
thies, Brecht instead describes his corpus of theatrical work in the
image of wholesome Christian values – the very value system that
the committee believe they are upholding. *St Joan of the Stockyard* is
about the 'Salvation Army'; the *Seven Deadly Sins* 'my most religious
piece', *Man is Man* a work intended as being 'against homosexual-
ity' and *Mother Courage and her Children* 'essentially a defence of the
family': all statements that, while perhaps tenuously true and thus
plausible descriptions with which to placate the ideological distrust
of the committee, are nonetheless canny evasions, glossing over the
fact that these seemingly banal topics hide works espousing a revolutionary politics. As such, Brecht survives the hostile interrogation

with flair, baffling the committee, allowing him to leave the USA, with the equivocation and mock-innocence in front of the committee buying him the necessary freedom to continue his work unhindered.

But from here Eagleton jumps back to a Germany in the early 1930s, in a stylized scene entitled 'What is Fascism?', showing the debate between six political types – a worker, a social democrat, a Communist, a Nazi, a member of the petty bourgeois, and a capitalist – as they debate who will side with whom to resist the Nazi's rise to power. The worker stands unsure, while the social democrat and Communist abuse each other with slogans, all ignoring the petty bourgeoisie, capitalist and fascist aligning with each other. The popular front occurs too late, and the sectarian political equivocation has prevented the opportunity to halt fascism at its most vulnerable stage. In light of this personified historical clash, Brecht's previous performance is not erased or degraded, but instead is held open for questioning: how far can the rat go when a direct stand is needed?

Eagleton offers a similar juxtaposition between images of the subservience of women under the Third Reich, and Brecht's own relationships with the various lovers and mistresses that he maintained throughout his life. Moving from a mock-Shakespearian scene depicting the rise of Hitler, the play points to the forgotten 'shy, hunted race, whom the Nazis crushed with a ferocity remarkable even for them' – the women of the Third Reich, valued only in terms of serving as the 'biological vessel of the master race', and barred from employment or education. After a rendition of the 'Song of the Sexist', the focus of the play moves back to that of the young Brecht composing poetry for *Baal*, refusing responsibility for his partner's pregnancy, instructing her to have an abortion, and walking out to continue his career in Berlin – where he casually talks, in turn, about philandering between various mistresses while working on his plays. Again, the point of this is not a simple condemnation of Brecht's sexual politics, or direct equation between his treatment of women and the institutionalized oppression under the Nazi regime. It instead raises the issue of how far a socialist can talk about exploitation in the factory without assessing the exploitation occurring in their own home, and how far Brecht's great drama was achieved through the silent work of the mistresses with which he surrounded himself.

This pattern of dialectical assessment reaches its culmination at the conclusion of the play, as Brecht undergoes a final interrogation.

The inquisitors are now no longer HUAC members accusing him of harbouring socialist sympathizers, but instead a series of inter-loquers who accuse Brecht of betraying or compromising his social-ist political beliefs, due to his compromised position as cultural star of a Stalinist state. The final speech given by Brecht, then, directly echoes Galileo's final speech in *Life of Galileo*, in which Galileo explains the nature of his compromise with the state, that at once allowed his work to continue and the manuscript of the *Discorsi* to be written, but that also severed the position of the scientist from the society for whom knowledge could be a liberating force. Brecht, too, is left handing over the manuscript of his plays, and explaining his balance between the politics of his compromise and survival:

> Well, maybe I have compromised. But I've survived – I haven't gone soft, or mad, or metaphysical. I came to the theatre when it was a centre for spiritual dope trafficking. And I took that apparatus and tore it apart, stripped off the magic and let in the light [. . .] I wrote simply and concretely, so that the workers could understand it. My theatre was a theatre for the exhausted who needed to learn, not for the sleepy who wanted to dream [. . .] I never believed that art itself could change society; but I was, after all, an artist, and I had to do what I could. Every gesture, every positioning of an arc-lamp, was a struggle against mystery, and so against oppression [. . .] we did what we could, making all things serviceable, using such scraps as history permitted us.

The final words of the play are thus Brecht reciting the conclusion of his famous poem, 'To Posterity', which at once combines a mourning for the corruption of the political ideal – where 'Anger, even at injustice / Makes the voice hoarse' – while maintaining a prophetic optimism for the order that will some day fulfil their stalled aspirations:

> But you, when the time comes at last,
> And man is a helper to man
> Think of us
> With forbearance.

This is only a brief description and reading of the play, but a number of major thematic issues can be traced out, concerning Eagleton's treatment of Brecht, and how this, in turn, illuminated new con-cerns that would come to the forefront of Eagleton's writing in the subsequent decade. In *Brecht and Company*, Eagleton does not allow an easily polarized view of Brecht as either heroic theatre visionary, or hypocrite seduced by a Stalinist regime. Instead the focus is predominantly on the question of *effect*: what a socialist intellectual can hope to achieve in a given political climate, what methods and fields of criticism they must engage with, what compromises can be endured in order to find an outlet for their work, and what forms of cultural work can be adopted for this purpose. The contrast between these questions and Eagleton's previous Althusserian mode are immediately apparent. No longer is the business of Marxist criticism most urgently concerned with the development of a dispassionate, scientific methodology, to theorize 'the laws of literary production' (as Pierre Macherey claimed for his project). It is instead to work out ways of taking this fight to the ground level of opinion and debate – as Brecht famously said, 'the proof of the pudding is in the eating'.

Developing a revolutionary criticism

The questions of *Brecht and Company* are thus ones that directly feed into *Walter Benjamin*. It is a work structured around a seemingly diffuse series of essays, with Eagleton's interests ranging across debates within the Western Marxist tradition, with the overarching aim of enquiring as to what the strategic priorities of a socialist criticism should entail. It is a work Eagleton described as reflecting 'the pressure of global capitalist crisis, [and] the influence of new themes and forces within socialism', which demanded that the focus of such interventions move 'from narrowly textual or conceptual analysis to problems of cultural production and the political use of artefacts' (WB xii). *Walter Benjamin* thus situates itself as an intervention on several levels: as the subtitle *Or, Towards a Revolutionary Criticism* suggests, the work of Benjamin is not so much the entire focus of his concern, but rather the starting point from which to engage a wider consideration with the role and function of a socialist critic.

On the first level is the question of the figure of Walter Benjamin himself, and the politics inherent in Eagleton's return to Benjamin. Benjamin, friend of Brecht and associated with the Frankfurt School of critical theorists centred around Theodor Adorno, was among the most strikingly original cultural critics, with his writing representing a unique nexus of thought in the Marxist tradition, offering heterogeneous combinations of cultural criticism, historical materialism, and Judaic messianic thought. His essay 'Work of Art in the Age of Mechanical Reproduction' would become a seminal text in the development of modern cultural criticism, and specifically his 'Theses on the Philosophy of History' would serves as one of the key points of influence upon Eagleton's work. In this work, Benjamin offered a series of cryptic musings on how a historical materialist should seek to engage with history as a political tool, contending that:

> A historical materialist cannot do without the notion of a present which is not a transition, but in which time stands still and has come to a stop. For this notion defines the present in which he himself is writing history. Historicism gives the 'eternal' image of the past; historical materialism supplies a unique experience with the past. The historical materialist leaves it to others to be drained by the whore called 'Once upon a time' in historicism's bordello. He remains in control of his powers, man enough to blast open the continuum of history.[7]

In Benjamin's view, a socialist cultural critic must 'brush history against the grain' in order to retrieve from it those aspects of the tradition that can be turned to progressive uses – a concept that provides the driving force behind the interventions that Eagleton undertakes in *Walter Benjamin*, and a statement that Eagleton would, in turn, seize as the title for his own 1986 collection of essays and come back to in many of his creative works, indicative of the wider, hovering, influence that Benjamin had across Eagleton's subsequent work.

While Benjamin had committed suicide at a border-crossing in 1940, fearful of falling into the hands of the Gestapo, it was only many years after his death that Benjamin's work was emerging in an accessible form, with a significant span of his work only published in English translation during the 1970s. Given that Benjamin himself always had an ambiguous relationship to Marxism, never joining the Communist Party (just as Brecht did not), and with his intellectual interests resisting easy categorization, the question of his political legacy was thus one to be actively contested: whether he was a man for whom socialism was only one interest out of a range of many, or instead a committed thinker for whom separating radical politics from his work would be a fundamental misreading. To offer just one example, Susan Sontag's introduction in 1979 to the collection of Benjamin's writing, *One Way Street*, offers a

detailed description of Benjamin's concerns, but one that empha-
sized Benjamin as the melancholic eccentric, for whom communism
was just one of the many 'positions' he kept open.[8] Thus Eagleton's
turn to Benjamin at this critical moment was the first of a number
of significant attempts to assess the importance of Benjamin's work,
and definitively re-inscribe him as an intellectual working within
the socialist tradition.[9]

If this was perhaps the most obvious political reason for
Eagleton's interest, it is equally evident that Benjamin was of more
importance than that of simply being a historical figure to be added
to the pantheon of great Marxist intellectuals, but rather as a living
resource, whose body of work prefigured developments occurring
in the later twentieth-century criticism, such as the 'various forms
of psychoanalysis, linguistic theory, deconstruction, avant-gardism,
and Marxism', and thus allowing a point of intervention into contemporary debates. As Eagleton described in an interview published in 1982:

> To go back to Benjamin and look at how he interrelates these motifs,
> and uses these various themes, is to see in a quite different kind of
> light the need to do this in an era of political crisis. One is not looking
> back to Benjamin for any kind of neat theoretical synthesis, but to see
> how those different theoretical positions shape up, interrelate, con-
> flict, within the context of Benjamin's concern for revolutionary
> politics.[10]

Therefore, Eagleton's work in *Walter Benjamin* is not an attempt at
systematic explication so much as a seizing of the possibilities in
Benjamin's text and forging a new critical practice out of his suggestive monads: as Eagleton described, in a way that Benjamin
would no doubt approve, 'it is more than ever necessary to blast
Benjamin's work out of its historical continuum, so that it may fertil-
ize the present' (*WB* 179). For example, Benjamin's *The Origin of
German Tragic Drama*, with its study of the baroque art of the six-
teenth and seventeenth centuries and specifically the *Trauerspiel*
works (lit. 'tragedy'), provides Eagleton with a launching point of
intervention into the debates of Leavis and Eliot concerning English
literature of the seventeenth century and the 'living voice' of poets
such as Donne compared to those such as Milton; while his notions
of 'aura' are pressed into a dialogue with Freud and Lacan in a
meditation on the nature of art and the commodity (see *WB* chapter
2). Eagleton's concern is not so much with a sustained application

of Benjaminian 'theory' to a scenario as it is to offer a series of
meditations, a series of deft interventions into various symptomatic
debates within both Western Marxism and wider literary-critical
fields, the fluidity which stands in marked contrast to the previous
methodology, structure and style of *Criticism and Ideology*.

If Benjamin himself proved a tool with which to rub contemporary debates against the grain, the other major trajectory encom-
passed in *Walter Benjamin* was Eagleton's emerging consciousness
of, and engagement with, the critical theories of post-structuralism,
and particularly the ideas of Jacques Derrida as they were assimilated into the Anglo-American literary-critical practice thorough
the 1970s and 1980s, under what quickly became known as the
deconstructive critical movement. A crucial marker of this influence
was the so-called 'Yale School' of critics, consisting of major figures
such as Paul de Man, Geoffrey Hartman, J. Hillis Miller, and Harold
Bloom, who published a collection of essays in 1979, *Deconstruction
and Criticism*, that provocatively set forth examples of deconstructive criticism in action, pursing a literary-critical method less concerned with synthesizing a 'univocal' textual reading (as was the
predominant aim of New Critical practice), and instead one that
privileged notions of indeterminacy and textual aporia, influenced
by Derrida's concerns with language as an inherently unstable
system.[11]

Eagleton's engagement with deconstruction in *Walter Benjamin* is
two-fold, and is worth considering in some detail, as Eagleton
would come to function as one of the most prominent Leftist critics
of Derrida and deconstruction over the subsequent decades (repeating, for example, similar criticisms in both *Literary Theory* and *The
Function of Criticism*). Eagleton is by no means universally hostile to
the possibilities offered by Derrida for the purpose of establishing
a 'revolutionary criticism', constantly assessing what can be use-
fully drawn from this post-structural discourse. For example, in
many of the critical debates that Eagleton examines in *Walter Benjamin*, he draws suggestively on Derrida's ideas, such as his reconsideration of Milton's position in the literary canon in light of
Derrida's discussion of 'speech' and 'writing' (*WB* 13), or his proposal of Swift as a proto-deconstructionist (*WB* 19). But in the majority of his engagement, Eagleton's analysis is focused on drawing
out the political contradiction that lurks at the basis of the deconstruction, characterizing it as both 'reformist' and 'ultra-leftist' (*WB*
134), turning the deconstructive methodology on to deconstruction
itself, mimicking its methods while at the same time mocking its

pretensions in a powerful deployment of a satirical mode of criticism. In operating as a form of textual subversion, deconstruction is described by Eagleton as a disillusioned political move at the level of theory: 'a sort of patient, probing reformism of text, which is not, so to speak, to be confronted over the barricades but cunningly waylaid in the corridors . . .'. But at the same time, Eagleton argues, there is an ultra-leftist urge in deconstruction, of '*madness and violence*' and a 'scandalous urge to think the unthinkable', that 'poses itself on the very brink of meaning and dances there, pounding away at the crumbling cliff-edge beneath its feet and prepared to fall with it into the sea of unlimited semiosis or schizophrenia' (*WB* 134, emphasis in original). In one sense, Eagleton proposes, these contradictions are a result of the 'death drive at the level of theory' that 'turns masochistically upon itself' (*WB* 136), with Derrida's position being ultimately unassailable as 'there is nothing to . . . outmanoeuvre; he is simply the dwarf who will entangle the giant in his own ungainly strength and bring him toppling to the earth' (*WB* 136–7). But in another sense, Eagleton argues, lurking beneath deconstruction there is, in fact, little more than a new reworking of bourgeois liberalism. In a critical formulation that would be repeated in many of Eagleton's subsequent critiques of Derrida, Eagleton accuses deconstruction of adapting a form of purely textual radicalism: 'it is doubtless pleasant to find one's spontaneous bourgeois-liberal responses shorn of their embarrassing eclecticism and tricked out as the most explosive stuff around' (*WB* 138). Thus, while Eagleton remains open to the possibility of deconstruction acting as a radical textual force, in the end, it is argued that Derrida's 'petty bourgeois' concerns with doubt and indeterminacy render deconstruction a method that will ultimately not be reconcilable with Marxist *praxis* (*WB* 142).[12]

In the face of this, Eagleton sees that there is a tradition, within Western Marxism itself, that has already anticipated many of the concerns that seemed to have been generated by the new-found notions of deconstruction, providing not only a counter to what Eagleton sees as the joyful but ultimately destructive anarchy of Derridian deconstruction, but also a theoretical framework with which to fuse together the contemporary impulse of post-structuralism and the demands of a radical politics. If Benjamin's hybrid writing offers Eagleton a wide cache of work to be raided, it is again through an engagement with Brecht that Eagleton finds the crucial material to push forms of radical criticism forward into new territories. In the scope of the debates within *Walter Benjamin*, Brecht offers several strategic resources for Eagleton. For one, he offered a unique development within Marxist thought, and the importation of his work fills a particularly acute absence in the English-language tradition of progressive modernist aesthetics. As Eagleton noted, while Raymond Williams and E. P. Thompson could be described in the 'rough sense as the English equivalent of Lukács ... there is no English Brecht' (*WB* 96), and the harnessing of the Brechtian method for Anglo-American forms of socialist criticism provides a crucial new opportunity in cultural debates. In Eagleton's account, Brecht's championing of modernism was a radical advance, not by offering alienation, irony, and fragmentation as an aesthetic opposed to realism, but rather one that portrayed political and social reality in a far more profound and comprehensive way than the pretensions of a false unity offered by realism. As his method is characterized: 'Brecht's practice is not to dispel the miasma of "false consciousness" so that we may "fix" the object as it really is; it is to persuade us into living a new discursive and practical relation to the real', or a rationality based on 'scepticism, experiment, refusal and subversion' (*WB* 85).

But beyond offering the grounds for engagement with the politics and aesthetics of realism and modernism, Eagleton finds within Brecht's *style* a fundamentally different ideology from the mainstream of Western Marxism. While the work of Western Marxists has been dominated by a strain of pessimism, particularly those associated with the Frankfurt school, Brecht offered a unique break: 'Of Bloch, Lukács, Brecht, Benjamin and Adorno, only Brecht is comic ... Brecht stands ideologically apart from that "Western Marxist" melancholy which in its various ways broods over the other four, and infiltrates the very sinew of their prose styles' (*WB* 159). Brecht, in this understanding, stands forth as a proto-post-structuralist, who had already anticipated the subversive possibilities of deconstruction, but bound them to the service of a Marxist aesthetic. Brecht shows how the comic can be deployed in a radical criticism, in an argument directly carried over from *Brecht and Company*, with the willingness to laugh, mock, upend, and look again holding revolutionary potential: '[Brecht's] comedy lies in its insight that any place is reversible, any signified may become a signifier, and discourse may be without warning rapped over the knuckles by some meta-discourse which may then suffer such rapping in its turn' (*WB* 160).

The figure of Azdak, the lowly clerk who stumbles into the position of Judge in Brecht's *Caucasian Chalk Circle*, thus for Eagleton comes to symbolize the politically subversive deconstructive critic, who apes the customs and logic of ruling-class law and justice only to subvert it from within. In the action of Brecht's play, Azdak cheerfully grasps the contradiction of his position: as he happily tells the courtroom in which he solicits bribes, 'Judgement must always be passed with complete solemnity – because it is such rot.' Azdak sits in the judge's seat and mouths the rhetoric of the law at the same time as wilfully subverting it, using the institution that had previously been one to enforce unjust class relations as one to instead redistribute wealth to those who need it most, who 'To feed the starving people . . . broke the laws like bread.' It is in the methods of Azdak that Eagleton sees a new model for a radical criticism, which would harness the subversive possibilities of moving within an existing discursive system only to be working against it from within, a form of deconstruction put towards definite political ends:

> Living provisionally yet self-protectively, having a quick eye to the main chance, bowing humbly to the mighty only the more effectively to butt them in the stomach, entangling the enemy in his own rhetoric: all these may be qualities of the clown, but they are qualities of the revolutionary too, and Brechtian drama continually invites us to ponder their identity and difference. (*WB* 170–1)

Walter Benjamin thus represents, in both form and content, a decisive marking point in Eagleton's career. In its specific engagements, it sets up many of the arguments and debates that Eagleton would pursue across the subsequent decade, ranging from Benjamin's view of history, the function of rhetoric, the poverty of Yale-style deconstruction, or the critical possibilities of comedy. But in wider terms, it shows Eagleton's exploration of a new mode of criticism, with the style of criticism now an active concern – a fact borne out in the detail of Eagleton's single most important book, to which I will now turn.

An introduction and an exit:
Literary Theory: An Introduction

Literary Theory: An Introduction (1983) is in many ways the fulfilment of the issues pointed towards in *Walter Benjamin*, concerning how the literary critic could establish new modes of engagement. It is not only Eagleton's most widely read book; it is one of the most influential and popular books of literary criticism and theory ever published. In its pages, Eagleton offers deft chapters surveying the history of modern literary criticism, tracing areas such as the rise of English studies in the Victorian period, the developments of the liberal-humanist *Scrutiny* group and American New Critics, through the rise of phenomenology, structuralism, post-structuralism, and psychoanalysis. Combined with his pithy summations of the key figures and debates in literary theory is searching criticism of both the legacy of F. R. Leavis and the contemporary state of theory, with his central case being an attack on the idea of 'literature' itself as an institution of reaction and ideological conditioning.

What has made *Literary Theory* such an influential book? A number of factors can be suggested. In general terms, *Literary Theory* was published at a crucial historical junction in the development of academic literary criticism, when theory was moving out of the realms of specialized journals and graduate seminars, and offering fundamental challenges to the nature of undergraduate syllabuses and critical methodologies of English studies as a whole. As a result, questions that previously could be confined to scholarly quarrels at academic conferences were now increasingly present at the coalface of the academy, in the structuring of academic departments, and in the methods of teaching undergraduates. While many of the more progressive departments of English were enthusiastically adapting the insights and priorities that these new perspectives had raised, the arrival of theory created bitter divisions in many others. One particularly public example of this institutional debate in Britain occurred in 1981 at the University of Cambridge, and has subsequently become known as the 'MacCabe Affair'. In this peculiar debacle, the promising assistant lecturer Colin MacCabe was denied promotion to a full lectureship (and thus tenure) in the Cambridge English Faculty, despite the support of leading professors such as Frank Kermode and Raymond Williams. The opposition to MacCabe's appointment was lead by Christopher Ricks, and the objections centred on MacCabe's book *James Joyce and the Revolution of the Word*, and its supposed lack of critical rigour and distinction, due to his use of allegedly opaque 'structuralist' theory. As a result of the ensuing public debates, the Cambridge Faculty almost split in two, with Frank Kermode (himself no militant theorist, but someone who recognized the necessity of critical openness) resigning from his position in disgust. On a wider level, however, the debate over this case became symptomatic of broader concerns, and was quickly picked up by the national media, for whom the situation became representative of the split between 'traditional' literary studies on the one hand, and alien forms of 'Marxism' and 'Structuralism' on the other, which were seen as threatening the study of literature through the academy as a whole (although MacCabe was in no real sense either one of these, and indeed threatened legal action against those who had termed him a Marxist, which is perhaps indicative of the politicized nature of the ordeal). The situation was even more pronounced at Oxford (where Eagleton was teaching): as he bemoaned in a 1978 essay, English at Oxford had not even yet got around to having its Leavisite revolution, let alone taking on board the implications of recent theoretical developments.[13]

In light of this form of institutional inertia, and fierce rearguard action by traditionalists (which was by no means just limited to Oxbridge), the direct effectiveness and importance of *Literary Theory* becomes apparent. By providing a guide that was both intelligently polemical and directly accessible, it effectively undercut the opposition to theory as a necessary component of the academic syllabus, arming students with not just an interesting collection of new theories, but also with an awareness of how these theories challenged many of the orthodoxies of literary study. Indeed, as some reviews suggested, *Literary Theory* was as much read by well-established academics, desperately trying to come to terms with this new field of which they were increasingly required to show familiarity, as by students, showing the cross-hierarchical influence that this 'introduction' achieved.

Literary Theory is, of course, significant for more reasons than that it happened to be published at a particular junction in academic critical practice, and several specific factors stand forth as deserving closer scrutiny. The first major aspect is in the nature of the style of the work itself, and how Eagleton deploys the polemical and satirical forms, which he saw as crucial to developing a radical criticism and which had been manifested in *Walter Benjamin*, into a coherent work. To put it in the simplest terms, *Literary Theory* is a book that is radically challenging in its arguments, but engaging, accessible, and enjoyable to read. This is an important point to clarify, as a criticism that has often been levelled against Eagleton is that the enjoyment and accessibility of his work is somehow a weakness, or entails a necessary lack of seriousness. For example, in an early review, one critic sniffed that *Literary Theory* was 'a spotter's guide to the various contemporary schools of criticism, providing easy ways to memorize their distinguishing features', achieved by amassing 'each group's prejudices about the absurdities of its rivals'.[14] It is a mistake, however, to confuse the idea of something being popular with that of being simplistic. As Eagleton would argue in a subsequent publication, 'one of the most vital tasks of the socialist intellectual' is the 'resolute popularization of complex ideas, conducted within a shared medium which forbids patronage and condescension' (*FC* 113), and on this criteria *Literary Theory* manifestly succeeds.

The major tool which Eagleton deploys, to this end, in the pages of *Literary Theory* is that of the comic. As was seen in the previous discussion on *Brecht and Company* and *Walter Benjamin*, Eagleton theorized that the comic alienation techniques of Brecht offered a vital tool to the Marxist critic, evading the strain of negativity and melancholy that had permeated Western Marxist thought, seizing the radical and subversive potential available in comedy and irony to both present an image or concept, and force us to reconsider it in a new light, exploiting the comic incongruity generated as a source of energy put towards questioning and thought. The argument is born out in the detail of *Literary Theory*, with almost every page using such a method to bring some point of literary theory into a sudden, ironic, clarity. To give only a few of the most controversial examples, at one point the civilizing mission of F. R. Leavis and the *Scrutiny* group are juxtaposed with the Holocaust: 'When the Allied troops moved into the concentration camps some years after the founding of *Scrutiny*, to arrest commandants who had whiled away their leisure hours with a volume of Goethe, it appeared that someone had some explaining to do' (*LT* 35); while later the subversion of post-structuralism is derided as a textual cop-out from real political work: 'Unable to break the structures of state power, post-structuralism found [it] possible instead to subvert the structures of language. Nobody, at least, was likely to beat you over the head for doing so' (*LT* 142). Given the sheer audacity of such nuggets, it is hard not to be amused. That is not to say there is not a danger in such compact quips: in bringing two such starkly different cultural moments into a direct sequence, Eagleton risks over-inflating the importance of one side of the equation, while downplaying that of the other. Can *Scrutiny* and Nazism really be linked so easily together into this historical moment (or is the project of Derrida et al. really reducible to a fear of being hit with a truncheon), or does the undoubted attention commanded by the statement too glibly synthesize what are complex and separate historical phenomena into a single soundbite? Nonetheless, this technique serves as an effective provocation, at once linking events in literary theory with a wider historical span, while at the same time using humour as a means of deflating the opaque seriousness of modes of critical discourse, and showing it as something upendable, fallible, and open to critique.

The second major area is Eagleton's radical articulation of the links between the politics of the institutions of 'literature' and literary theory, and their relationship to the wider society. This is a thread that runs throughout the work, linking the early discussions of what 'literature' consists with Eagleton's analysis of the progression of critical movements, and this is brought to the fore in the polemical concluding chapter. The issues and questions that Eagleton outlines in the conclusion are directly confronting:

> As I write, it is estimated that the world contains over 60,000 nuclear warheads, many with a capacity a thousand times greater than the bomb which destroyed Hiroshima . . . Anyone who believed that literary theory was more important than such matters would no doubt be considered somewhat eccentric, but perhaps only a little less eccentric than those who consider that the two topics might be somehow related. (*LT* 194)

It is important to note that this gesture towards nuclear warfare was not simply a glib grab at a suitably apocalyptic scenario, but an attempt to link the question of literature into the most urgent and visible contemporary area of actual progressive political action. In 1983, the Coalition for Nuclear Disarmament organized a march of an estimated 200,000 people in London (at that time, the largest ever protest for the city), to protest against the instillation of a new range of American nuclear cruise missiles in Britain, matched with similar protests through the NATO countries of Europe. The question proposed by Eagleton is one of how to make direct connections to the most pressing contemporary political concerns: to question how the study of literature in the academy is linked to the overall ideological climate that perpetuates such belief systems, and how the theory and critical practice in schools and the academy can establish a direct relevance for those who seek to challenge such a political order.

Eagleton's answer, drawing implicitly on the ideas of Michel Foucault concerning the permeation of structures of power through society, is that notions of 'literature' and conventional literary theory have played a crucial role in these ideological formations in society. As Eagleton directly claims: 'My own view . . . is that literary theory has a most particular relevance to this political system: it has helped, wittingly or not, to sustain and reinforce its assumptions' (*LT* 196), and that 'Departments of literature in higher education, then, are part of the ideological apparatus of the modern capitalist state' (*LT* 200). This is a point of ambiguity in Eagleton's account: while literature undoubtedly forms a 'part' of this apparatus, it is by no means clear from Eagleton's account how crucial a part he attributes it, which offers the danger that the struggle over literature is being given a value out of proportion to its political import. Nonetheless, Eagleton argues that the skills and implications of literary criticism should not so much be abolished as taken towards their logical conclusion, subjecting the whole field of society's 'discursive practices' to its analysis rather than an artificially limited body of literature.

In light of this death-knell for literature, what does Eagleton propose as the methodology for this new field? In a significant move, he does not offer a counter-theory of Marxist literary criticism. While noting that there 'are indeed Marxist and feminist theories of literature, which in my opinion are more valuable than any of the theories discussed here', he also states 'any reader who has been expectantly waiting for a Marxist theory has obviously not been reading this book with due attention' (*LT* 204). This is a curious point in the work: the reference to the most 'valuable' aspects of literary theory only existing in the bibliography of *Literary Theory*, combined with the admonishing of the readers for their naive expectations that such theories may actually be addressed, would seem to glide too easily from the challenge of developing a positive theoretical case, into an essentially pragmatic and eclectic position of using whatever one can. But again what Eagleton offers is a championing of this Azdakian impulse, of not meeting opposing modes of criticism head-on, but instead assuming the robes of other discourse when strategically viable, as a vessel with which to carry a socialist criticism. The focus of criticism now is not on the generation of an acceptably orthodox political method, but rather in the actual *results*: 'Any method or theory which will contribute to the strategic goal of human emancipation, the production of "better people" through the socialist transformation of society, is acceptable. Structuralism, semiotics, psychoanalysis, deconstruction, reception theory and so on: all of these approaches, and others, have their valuable insights which may be put to use' (*LT* 211). In light of this strategic goal of human emancipation, Eagleton suggests that literary studies will be replaced with the broader field of 'rhetoric' – a term that, slyly, allows Eagleton to position himself as the upholder of the Western critical tradition against the modern upstart of liberal-humanist literary studies, and follows on from his consideration of rhetoric as a mode of political criticism first undertaken in *Walter Benjamin* (see *WB* 101–13). The result of this is a fundamental restructuring not simply of the methods of study, but the material which must form the basis of intellectual critique: the entire field of discourse becomes the subject of study and analysis, rather than the limitations of an ideological motivated canon of great works, which will instead be downgraded to a sub-branch in the wider pursuit of cultural studies:

> Within all of this varied activity, the study of what is currently termed 'literature' will have its place. But it should not be taken as an *a priori* assumption that what is currently termed 'literature' will always and everywhere be the most important focus of attention. Such dogmatism has no place in the field of cultural study. (*LT* 213)

Literary Theory is thus both a primer and a radical rallying cry, advocating a new way forward for the study of culture, beyond the limits of liberal-humanist canonical discourse, into a mode of politicized cultural studies that will shrug off the confines of literature in pursuit of bold new political goals. The significance of *Literary Theory*, then, was not simply in its ability to articulate an analysis and criticism of the various schools of thought that had contributed towards the growth of modern literary theory, but also in Eagleton's ability to construct a counter-narrative, as deeply passionate as anything offered by Leavis and the *Scrutiny* tradition. Whereas the *Scrutiny* project was deeply nostalgic, seeing literature as the bastion of values of the fading organic past against the vulgarity of modernity, Eagleton's narrative is one of promise for the future to come, with the students of culture serving as an intellectual vanguard for wider socialist politics. As he announces, 'this book is less an introduction than an obituary, and we have ended by burying the object we sought to unearth' (*LT* 204), with this sacrifice, however, carrying the promise of a rebirth: 'It is not out of the question that the death of literature may help the lion to awaken' (*LT* 217).

It is also significant to note that, while Eagleton issued the call for the move away from canonical literature into the field of rhetoric and cultural studies, it was not a call that he himself followed in his future work (save for one particular incarnation, which will be addressed in chapter 5). In subsequent published writing, Eagleton remained working within a framework of canonical literary studies that, while a dissenting figure within, nonetheless still kept the same recognizable names of the great tradition in circulation, with books on Samuel Richardson and William Shakespeare appearing a few years on either side of *Literary Theory* (as will be discussed later in this chapter). In a related but wider way, Eagleton's editorial work of this decade manifested a similar preoccupation: the 'Rereading Literature' series that he would edit for Blackwell (of which his *William Shakespeare* is a part), was dominated by studies of canonical authors, ranging from Chaucer, through Shakespeare and Pope, to W. H. Auden – works that were often exciting and innovative studies, offering new modes of theoretical and political readings, but nonetheless not a series of works that seemed to move in the exact direction that Eagleton was urging. Indeed, most recently Eagleton has fought against the decline of traditional literary genre studies. In *After Theory*, Eagleton criticized the results of the growth of cultural studies in the academy, while his most recent books have dwelt on topics such as the understanding of tragedy in Western art and the development of the English novel – not to mention his guide to reading poetry, in which he remarked upon the fact that 'hardly any of the students of literature I encountered these days practised what I myself had been trained to regard as literary criticism', and that 'literary criticism seems to be something of a dying art' (*HRP* 1).

The point of outlining these more recent positions adopted by Eagleton against the conclusions offered in *Literary Theory* is not intended as a trite condemnation, or to suggest that Eagleton, absurdly, should be bound in later work to adhere to positions that he outlined some quarter of a century earlier. But, again, it highlights an important theoretical ambivalence running as a counter-current in Eagleton's career, even at the points where it seems most polemically denied. As was explored in the previous chapter, *Criticism and Ideology* both attacked the political implications of the *Scrutiny* position and canon, but then conducted his own critical evaluations using a body of works little different to the great tradition it had attacked. *Literary Theory*, again, finds itself bound in a similar dynamic, explicating and attacking literature and 'literary theory', and going further in calling for the study of the field of rhetoric to replace that of literature, yet speaking of a paradigm shift in which Eagleton himself never chose to work.

Having pointed to these ambivalences that can be located in Eagleton's argument, it is equally important to note why *Literary Theory: An Introduction* remains an important and valuable work. On a general level, it presented a major contribution towards a democratization of a field of knowledge that has frequently been criticized on the grounds of its obscurity and cant, and on a specific level, presented a radical and challenging political thesis that both undercut claims concerning the 'apolitical' nature of literature and literary discourse, and demands consideration of how the study of literature is implicated in the wider structures of ideology and power in a society.

The critic and the public sphere:
The Function of Criticism

The call for a renewal of cultural criticism's link with a wider public role informs Eagleton's subsequent work, *The Function of Criticism*, a work that extends the lines of investigation undertaken in *Literary Theory*, as well as more directly addressing the question of the social function of the contemporary critic in its own right. The book is a short account of the profession of the critic in England, from its origins in the coffee-houses and periodicals of England through to the poverty of post-structuralism, with the overarching allegation being that 'criticism today lacks all substantive social function', being 'either part of the public relations branch of the literary industry, or a matter wholly internal to the academies' (*FC* 7), a situation in which the position of the critic 'has ended up, in effect, as a handful of individuals reviewing each other's books' (*FC* 107). Through this, Eagleton attempts to derive a renewed possibility for a contemporary politically and socially engaged critical practice, by harnessing the historically radical position of the original critical project: 'Modern European criticism was born of a struggle against the absolutist state', where a 'polite, informed public opinion pits itself against the arbitrary diktats of autocracy; within the translucent space of the public sphere it is supposedly no longer social power, privilege and tradition which confer upon individuals the title to speak and judge, but the degree to which they are constituted as discoursing subjects by sharing in a consensus of universal reason' (*FC* 9).

The predominant theoretical framework that Eagleton draws on to trace this development was the idea of the 'public sphere', a theory first developed by the German Jürgen Habermas, who had been a student of Adorno and a member of the Frankfurt School. In his widely influential study *The Structural Transformation of the Public Sphere* (1962) Habermas had outlined how the public sphere (a model of which was the coffee-houses of eighteenth-century London, where debates on topics of social and political importance could be undertaken, on equal footing, by the rising professionalized class of men) had played a crucial role in the development of bourgeois society, establishing opinion and reason as modes of political operation:

> The bourgeois public sphere may be conceived above all as the sphere of private people come together as a public; they soon claimed the public sphere regulated from above against the public authorities themselves, to engage them in a debate over the general rules governing relations in the basically privatized but publicly relevant sphere of commodity exchange and social labor. The medium of this political confrontation was peculiar and without historical precedent: people's public use of their reason.[15]

Eagleton's task in his book is to extend Habermas's category into an understanding of the genealogy of criticism in Britain, from the earliest emergence of the critical periodicals, through to its increased commodification and specialization as it became integrated into an industrialized economy. Eagleton points to the role criticism played in the consolidation of the political power for the rising bourgeois: '*The Tatler* and *Spectator* are catalysts in the creation of a new ruling bloc in English society, cultivating the mercantile class and uplifting the profligate aristocracy' (FC 11). With the expansion of the publishing industry in the mid eighteenth century Eagleton places one of the crucial dislocations in the position of the writer and critic in the public sphere, with the greatly expanding middle-class market disrupting the clubbable relationships of the early periodicals and resulting in an 'intensifying penetration of capital into literary production . . .' (FC 31), with 'the bounded space of the public sphere . . . aggressively invaded by visibly "private" commercial and economic interests, fracturing its confident consensualism' (FC 34), and the rise of working-class movement challenging the pretence at the universality claimed by the bourgeois discourse (FC 35–6). The subsequent history of criticism has seen attempts to recreate this public sphere in light of the increasing displacement of the critic from the society to which their critical discourse is aimed, with the Victorian man of letters no longer an equal in discourse with his peers, but rather an instructor trying to guide an audience through intellectual turmoil (*FC* 48), a dislodgement which finally ends in the specialization of knowledge in the form of the academic (*FC* 66). F. R. Leavis and *Scrutiny* represented a heroic but contradictory last stand in attempting to recreate the public sphere, while the subsequent theoretical debates which gripped the academy 'helped to provide a progressively discredited criticism with a new rationale' that allowed criticism to avoid questioning its own social roles.

Although a short work, *The Function of Criticism* outlines a number of significant areas, which both build upon the case presented in *Literary Theory* and circle the same problems concerning the future role Eagleton envisages for a politically engaged critic. For one, Eagleton undertakes an explicit revaluation of the significance of Raymond Williams, saluting him as the 'single most important critic of post-war Britain' (*FC* 108). This was not just a personal tribute, but also marks a shift in Eagleton's theoretical orientations: 'While other materialist thinkers, including myself, diverted into structuralist Marxism, Williams sustained his historicist humanism only to find such theoreticians returning under changed political conditions to examine that case less cavalierly, if not to endorse it uncritically' (*FC* 109). Yet even here Eagleton's assessment of Williams is marked by its reservation, not so much as to the commitment or theoretical position of Williams *per se*, but rather, linking with Eagleton's wider concerns in this period, the social position Williams established as a critic: 'The borders which Raymond Williams's work has finally been unable to cross . . . are the frontiers between the academic institution and political society, which the absence of a counter-public sphere throws into graphic relief' (*FC* 115). The urgent need, then, is to generate this 'counter-public sphere', with such a form of counter-public sphere, Eagleton holds, having existed in Weimar Germany when the working-class movement was 'equipped with its own theatres and choral societies, clubs and newspapers, recreation centres and social forums' (*FC* 112), and it is in some nascent state present in contemporary feminist discourse.

Having outlined a coherent narrative of the decline from the politically engaged role of criticism from the classic public sphere into the splintering of the twentieth century, what is to be done to reconnect the critical act with a social relevance? Literary criticism, in an argument that echoes that of *Literary Theory*, is curtly dismissed as pointless: 'It is hard to believe that, in a nuclear age, the publication of yet another study of Robert Herrick is justifiable' (*FC* 108). But, in light of the absence of any existing counter-public sphere – to such an extent that there is 'a simple, glaring lack of a popular socialist newspaper in Britain' (*FC* 113) – which could serve as forum for such a debate, a wider form of socialist cultural criticism is also peripheral, leaving an acute, practical gap in Eagleton's call for criticism to reconnect with its radical heritage. Thus, just when *The Function of Criticism* seems to be at the point of decisively theorizing a distinctly new form of critical engagement, the role for the critic that Eagleton returns to again is a curiously brief and tentative one, once more calling for a theoretical eclecticism as a way out of this impasse:

> Just as the eighteenth-century bourgeois critic found a role in the cultural politics of the public sphere, so the contemporary socialist or feminist critic must be defined by an engagement in the cultural politics of late capitalism . . . The role of the contemporary critic is to resist [mass-market public sphere] dominance by re-connecting the symbolic to the political, engaging through both discourse and practice with the process by which repressed needs, interests and desires may assume the cultural forms which could weld them into a collective political force. (*FC* 123)

This, Eagleton again argues, is simply the 'traditional' role of criticism, with the contemporary pursuits of 'semiotics, psychoanalysis, film studies, cultural theory, the representation of gender, popular writing, and of course the conventionally valued writings of the past' presenting a way of recapturing previous forms of radical critical modes (*FC* 123–4). Thus, a generously inclusive but vaguely defined form of cultural studies is again gestured towards as the future of academic criticism, as a means of analysing the 'symbolic processes' of political power – but this call for a shift in superstructural practice as a way of re-establishing a radical public sphere would seem also to be at odds with the historical account that Eagleton's own study had just traced out. As Richard Azcel argued in an article in *New Left Review*:

> At such a conjuncture, Eagleton's continual appeals to tradition are in danger of concealing more than they make strategically possible. The criticism which was 'born of a struggle against the absolutist state' in the seventeenth and eighteenth centuries was the ideological instrument of a confident and coherently revolutionary class on the

offensive, rather than a politically ambivalent practice defended within a liberal academy whose entire future is increasingly uncertain.[16]

The Function of Criticism thus pushes at the same issues as *Literary Theory*, forging an incisive analysis and intervention into the politics of contemporary criticism and the institutional position, but at the same time raising questions as to how far this criticism based on the pragmatic principles of resistance could pursue its aims. But the measure of the strategic possibility of this criticism is perhaps best addressed by examining how Eagleton deployed these ideas in his two major 'literary' studies offered in the decade, *The Rape of Clarissa* and *William Shakespeare*, to which I will now turn.

Deconstructive Marxism in action: *The Rape of Clarissa* and *William Shakespeare*

Given that as Eagleton's theoretical preoccupations during the early 1980s were concerned with developing new forms of strategically effective cultural criticism, the decision to write a monograph on Samuel Richardson would initially appear a strange one. Richardson's great eighteenth-century epistolary novel *Clarissa* (first published 1748), purportedly the longest novel in the English language, was also purported to have been one of the most unread, and thus an apparently unlikely site for a struggle to enact some form of Azdakian critical method. What, then, is the motivation behind the turn back to this novel at this particular junction in his career? Eagleton's contention is not that the work is simply an under-appreciated classic, for which sympathetic critical attention is needed so as to restore it to a wider readership. It is, rather, that these new modes of theoretical approach can interrogate the novel in fundamentally new ways, and make *Clarissa* 'speak' of a series of radical concerns particularly relevant at this contemporary historical junction. Eagleton takes up as his starting point the idea that formed the conclusion of *Walter Benjamin*, the necessity for criticism to '"blast open the continuum of history"', forging conjunctures between our own moment and a redeemed bit of the past, imbuing works with retroactive significance so that in them we may better read the signs of our own times' (RC vii), and by doing so unlock the unread masterpiece as a work that is 'scandalous' for modern criticism.

The tools that Eagleton thus deploys in this interrogation are a fusion of Marxist, post-structuralist, psychoanalytical, and feminist modes of criticism, not conceived of as separate practices, but rather as resources that interact, inform, and interrogate each other, to open planes of debate in the text. For example, the introduction to *The Rape of Clarissa* offers historical materialist analysis of Richardson's political and cultural contexts. Drawing on Gramsci's concept of the 'organic intellectual' (intellectuals who come organically from within a rising social class, rather than being the product of the dominant social order), Eagleton places Richardson as one of the 'most vitally significant' of such intellectuals who, by transforming both the English fiction and the world literary tradition, played 'a key role in the English class struggle' (*RC* 3). But, extending this Gramscian perspective into a post-structuralist mode, Eagleton sees the text as a site of active discursive struggle, not just reflecting or interpreting ideological debates, but rather active textual interventions: 'Richardson's novels are not mere images of conflicts fought out on another terrain, representations of a history which happens elsewhere; they are themselves a material part of those struggles, pitched standards around which battle is joined, instruments which help to constitute social interests rather than lenses which reflect them' (*RC* 4).

It is the process of writing that particularly fascinates Eagleton throughout his account in the *Rape of Clarissa*, as he articulates a series of concerns which draw suggestively from the work of Jacques Derrida. The process of writing was the subject of many of Derrida's philosophical investigations, ranging from the influential argument *Of Grammatology*, where Derrida explored the ideas of 'speech' and 'writing' as it had occurred through key texts in Western philosophy, to his most radical texts, such as *Glas*, which consciously played with the mode of an academic work, weaving his text around two separate columns which offered a simultaneous discussions of Hegel and Jean Genet, challenging the separation between 'author' and 'reader' in determining how such writing must be reconstructed and assimilated.[17] For Eagleton, Richardson's novels – or 'kits', as Eagleton refers to them (*RC* 20) – already illuminate a similar Derridian tendency, with the instability of writing and signification explicitly foregrounded in Richardson's work. For one, Richardson's own writing process draws attention to this instability of the final text, combining 'ceaseless revision' with works that encompass 'Prefaces, introductory letters, footnotes, appendices, indexes, postscripts, tables of contents' where the 'whole of this dangerously labile writing is merely one enormous spare part, permanently capable of being recycled into something else' (*RC* 21). Yet it is in the letter writing that constitutes the novel *Clarissa* itself that Eagleton finds the most radical element to draw out, and one that directly lends itself to feminist and deconstructive critique:

> For all the ardent immediacy of the letter, for all the traces of the body inscribed on it . . . the one contract unattainable in correspondence is the sexual union of bodies. This, which is what all the letters of *Clarissa* are ultimately *about*, must also be what is palpably absent from them. Richardson sees well enough that sexuality is mainly a matter of discourse: the sexual power struggle between Clarissa and Lovelace is a primarily rhetorical affair, a matter of strategic textual moves, the gaining of a momentary linguistic advantage, the reluctant concession of meaning. Yet this great flurry of signifying presence, the very soul of the real, merely foregrounds a material lack: letters can be no more than 'supplementary' sexual intercourse, eternally standing in for the real thing. (*RC* 44–5)

It is investigating this concern, reading the rhetorical struggles over sexual power and gender position against the physical rape and persecution of Clarissa at the hands of Lovelace, that impels Eagleton's treatment of the novel. Resisting modes of criticism that would cast Lovelace as a canny, Byronic hero, and portray a prudish Clarissa as complicit in her suffering, Eagleton instead holds Clarissa as a 'young woman of outstanding kindness, virtue and intelligence' (*RC* 63), a victim of Lovelace's 'Oedipal difficulties' (*RC* 62), whose true scandalous nature is her refusal to compromise in the face of an oppressive social system: 'What Clarissa's death signifies, in fact, is an absolute refusal of political society: sexual oppression, bourgeois patriarchy and libertine aristocracy together' (*RC* 76). The title *The Rape of Clarissa*, therefore, takes on a double meaning that illustrates Eagleton's concerns: the actual suffering of Clarissa at the hands of Lovelace, as narrated by Richardson in the novel, and the subsequent treatment of the novel in the hands of literary critics – 'the cavaliers, deconstructionists and debunking liberals' (*RC* 71) – who perpetuated the Lovelacian discourses of oppression in their assessments of the work. Overall, Eagleton's aim is not to claim Richardson himself as some sort of proto-feminist, but rather highlight that his text produced 'genuinely subversive effects' that 'far exceed its author's intentions' (*RC* ix), that can now be prised out and made to speak in our historical moment via such an interventionist reading.

The response to *The Rape of Clarissa* from subsequent critics proved mixed, but perhaps in a surprising way. For one, among Richardson scholars, Eagleton's work often received warm, if not outright, praise. For example, one reviewer, despite some reservations regarding Eagleton's being a 'strident gate-crasher into eighteenth-century studies', saluted it as a 'truly illuminating book', and interestingly also finding it 'oddly "conservative" . . . in its spirited defence . . . of Clarissa against "the cavaliers, deconstructionists and debunking liberals" '.[18] While *The Rape of Clarissa* was thus finding a degree of cautious accommodation from some (but by no means all) 'traditional' scholars of Richardson, it was from other critical theorists that some of the most trenchant criticism of Eagleton's methodology came, raising issues not so much with Eagleton's specific interpretation of Richardson's novel, but with Eagleton's position as a 'feminist' critic. The most significant of such attacks came from the critic and theorist Elaine Showalter, among the leading figures in contemporary feminist critical practice and author of works such as *Toward a Feminist Poetics* (1979), who in a 1983 essay launched an attack on the perceived politics of appropriation inherent in Eagleton's move. Showalter's critique focused on the accusations that Eagleton was not so much engaging in feminist criticism as annexing aspects of it for his own critical purpose, with the charge being that Eagleton had conducted a 'raid' on feminist critical methods. In Showalter's view, the choice of critical methodology cannot be simply a matter of pragmatically cherry-picking radical positions in order to arrive at a predetermined goal, for to do so is to risk 'borrow[ing] the language of feminist criticism without a willingness to explore the masculinist bias of their own reading system . . .' For Showalter, the central point of concern was not so much Eagleton's turn to feminist concerns, but rather his very confidence displayed in doing so: that he failed to show that there 'is something equivocal and personal in his own polemic, some anxiety of authorship that is related to his own cultural position'.[19]

Eagleton did respond to Showalter's criticism, but his own response was interestingly restrained.[20] Rather than meeting Showalter in an outright polemical exchange (a mode that Eagleton would not normally shy away from), Eagleton instead offered a personal anecdote, stemming from his experiences as a student socialist, and the perceptions that he had held concerning the contradiction in the class backgrounds of many of his fellow comrades. Eagleton outlines how the 'genuine' socialists, those from working-class backgrounds, came to scorn these supposed inter-lopers; yet in later life it was predominately these working-class socialists who had sold out their beliefs in the pursuit of their careers, while the students who had become socialist as a matter of intellectual conviction rather than class-background were the ones who had maintained their political faith – an obvious chiding of Showalter over her reluctance to credit the genuineness of Eagleton as a 'male' feminist.[21] In return, Eagleton's allegory drew a caustic counter from Showalter. In a brief response, Showalter refused to be drawn into debates about Eagleton's personal experiences, and indeed charged Eagleton's very method of argument as replicating a 'recent study of male–female interaction in conversation', which showed how 'men dominated, both by ignoring topics introduced by the women, and by developing topics that they had initiated themselves'. Showalter went on to accuse Eagleton of either not reading her article and instead falling back on a stock with which to rebut criticism from feminists, or to have been unwilling to engage with an argument or narrative generated by Showalter, and instead trying to force the discussion back into a narrative of his own creation.[22]

The point of recounting this debate is more than to highlight one particularly memorable intellectual scuffle in which Eagleton was embroiled, and is instead to focus on a theoretical crux con-cerning Eagleton's position at this time.[23] While Showalter's criti-cism focused on the specific case of adapting feminism, other critics would raise concurrent problems, questioning what was at stake in this refusal to theorize a basis for the discourse wielded in the name of a radical criticism. Just as Eagleton had asked of Brecht (in *Brecht and Company*) how far the discourse of subversion can go in the face of direct political need, *The Rape of Clarissa* raises the question of how far the yoking of differing strands of theory can go in the face of refusing to justify the terms of investigation. Despite the range of theoretical positions wielded by Eagleton in *The Rape of Clarissa*, the response he offered to Showalter showed Eagleton having to fall back on to the subjective grounds of anec-dotes and personal expressions of good faith in order to justify his critical acts – a vulnerability at an almost opposite pole to the previous problems of the Althusserian claims to scientific ideology critique.

If *The Rape of Clarissa* thus demonstrates the possibilities of fusing forms of post-structural, feminist, and psychoanalytical criticism, as well as some of the theoretical questions raised by such a move, *William Shakespeare* marks the highpoint of Eagleton's deconstructive turn. Described by Eagleton as a work that was 'in no direct sense an historical study of its topic', but rather 'an exercise in political semiotics, which tries to locate the relevant history in the very letter of the text' (*WS* ix), the focus is not so much on the discrete units of Shakespeare's plays, but instead upon the variety of discursive modes that manifest in the works: Language, Desire, Law, 'Nothing', Value, and Nature are all thematic headings under which Eagleton groups his critical readings. Thus, whereas almost twenty years earlier Eagleton's concern was with reading the plays of Shakespeare in terms of the unity of the vision that they sought to depict, his task was now to show such unity as unachievable.[24] The manifest depictions of unity in *The Tempest* are no longer grounds for praising the 'wedding [of] the merits of spontaneous, creative living with the value of a common, responsible way of life' (*SS* 170–1), but instead ideological mystification open to deconstruction:

> What it fails to draw attention to is the glaring contradiction on which its whole discourse effectively founders: the fact that this 'organic' restoration of a traditional social order founded upon Nature and the body rests not only on a flagrant mystification of Nature, gratuitous magical device and oppressive patriarchalism, but is actually set in the context of the very colonialism which signals the imminent victory of the exploitative, 'inorganic' mercantile bourgeoisie. (*WS* 96)

However, at the same time there is a profound irony at work in this study, that at once mouths the forms of deconstructive arguments, while drawing attention to the arbitrariness of these positions – an irony that would seem to present a more self-conscious edge to this work than that possessed by *The Rape of Clarissa*. This is established from the outset, when Eagleton anachronistically declares: 'Though conclusive evidence is hard to come by, it is difficult to read Shakespeare without feeling that he was almost certainly familiar with the writing of Hegel, Marx, Nietzsche, Freud, Wittgenstein and Derrida' (*WS* ix–x) – a mock historical naivety that at once highlights the range of theoretical influences drawn upon, yet downgrades their originality, with Shakespeare now being the precursor to the theorists in an inversion of the philosophical hierarchy. This playful anachronism extends into the reading of the plays themselves. His reading of *Macbeth*, for example, slyly upends conventional notions of the play in its assertion of its hierarchy of values:

To any unprejudiced reader – which would seem to exclude Shakespeare himself, his contemporary audiences and almost all literary critics – it is surely clear that positive value in *Macbeth* lies with the three witches. The witches are the heroines of the piece, however little the play itself recognizes the fact, and however much the critics may have set out to defame them. (*WS* 1–2)

This is more than a symptomatic reading, teasing out hidden contradictions, but rather a deliberate provocation, delighting in reversing the values normally attributed to the play, claiming the grounds of the 'unprejudiced reader' while forcing *Macbeth* into the shape of a feminist text, with the witches as radical separatists undermining the repressive patriarchy of the Scottish kingdom.

William Shakespeare is thus the most coherent realization of Eagleton's Azdakian criticism, a work that cheerfully raids the techniques of post-structuralism, slyly using the plays of Shakespeare and the deconstructive impulse as the material to carry a radical political polemic. It is a work that shows the strength and strategic possibilities of this mode of criticism, delighting in the ability to read the plays of Shakespeare in provocative ways and to rub the Bard 'against the grain'. But it also again asks how far the subversive 'rat' can indeed go, in the face of the actual demands of critical intervention. If everything can indeed be turned into everything else, is there actually any positive value that the radical critic can claim, as historical materialism had usually claimed for its philosophy? Or is the text now simply a discursive battleground to be fought over with no end, but instead constantly shifting in every reading? This is a point that Eagleton draws direct attention to, with the final appeal to the 'real material conditions' given at the conclusion of the work. Quoting from the Marxist historian Christopher Hill's work on the malnutrition of the lower half of the population during Shakespeare's historical period, Eagleton holds this as the fundamental human conditions that the unstable semiotics of Shakespeare obscures:

These were the real material conditions endured by a great many of Shakespeare's fellow countrypeople, while Hamlet was sliding the signifier, Timon slinging around his gold, and Antony and Cleopatra savouring the fleshpots. It was not Lear's 'superflux' which was shaken to the exploited and dispossessed, but the burden of a class society in crisis. To that extent, there is an identity between Shakespeare's period and our own; the difference is that the exploited and dispossessed have now become an historical force to be reckoned with. (*WS* 103–4)

The appeal to the historical real, the actual economic circumstances, as a counter to the sliding and indeterminacy that Eagleton has previously just located, suggests the final irony of the work. In *William Shakespeare*, Eagleton has offered an excoriating performance, ingeniously harnessing the methods outlined in *Literary Theory*, showing him as capable a deconstructive critic as any of the Yale-ilk. But, in the end, in holding the 'real material conditions' as a final anchor against the free-play of endless textuality, it also deconstructs its own deconstruction, pointing to a political reality that the Azdakian criticism finally must confront.

4

The Ideology of the Postmodern

The 1980s, as was argued in the previous chapter, saw Eagleton undertaking a twin engagement with poststructuralism, on the one hand attacking the political underpinning of Derridian deconstruction and its major Anglo-American derivatives, while on the other experimenting with forms of criticism that sought to appropriate the subversive methods and impulses of poststructuralism and rework them into a form of radical critical pluralism. The emergence of postmodernism as one of the dominant modes of cultural and intellectual expression, however, would force an alteration of Eagleton's strategic aims during the 1990s. Always an overdetermined concept, during the 1980s 'postmodernism' coalesced into a loose, sometimes contradictory, but nonetheless intellectually prominent grouping of theoretical concerns: the end of the 'enlightenment project' and the death of the 'grand narratives' as characterized by Jean François Lyotard; the rise of the simulacra and of hyperreality, as discussed in the work of Jean Baudrillard; the privileging of radical plurality, of the rhizomes and a thousand plateaus, as argued by Gilles Deleuze and Felix Guattari; the era of blank parody, where pastiche and reproduction are the dominant modes of artistic expression, as theorized by Fredric Jameson.[1] Whereas Fredric Jameson could claim in 1982 that the 'concept of postmodernism is not widely accepted or even understood today',[2] by 1987 Ihab Hassan could remark that the term postmodern 'had become a shibboleth for tendencies in film, theatre, dance, music, art, and architecture [. . .] in philosophy, theology, psychoanalysis, and historiography; in new sciences, cybernetic technologies, and various cultural lifestyles', indicative of the rapid emergence of the post-modern as a hybrid, diffuse, yet hegemonic intellectual horizon.[3] Over the coming years of the early 1990s, the prominence of post-modernism as the dominant intellectual formation seemed only to be entrenched by unfolding historical events: the collapse of the USSR and the (alleged) death of Marxism as a total system capable of contesting the ideology of liberal capitalism; the seemingly inex-tricable mutations and progress of advanced consumer society; the United States standing in an unrivalled position of cultural and military dominance; and the logic of late capitalism now the wall-to-wall value system of this new epoch.

Eagleton's writing of this decade was thus marked by a response to this intellectual conjecture, seeking both to theorize the condi-tions of the postmodern's rise, and unequivocally critique the fal-lacies that had arisen as a result of the Left's widespread adoption of postmodernism as an intellectual paradigm.[4] Yet it was equally characterized by the problem of the theoretical base from which to launch this critique. As will be traced through this chapter, Eagleton's writing was increasingly marked with the question of the basis of a Marxist (or even socialist) political and critical pro-gramme, in light of the historical and intellectual circumstances which threatened not so much to discredit it as to sideline social-ism as an active intellectual horizon. As Eagleton would ruefully note in 1996, postmodernism did in fact have one major advantage that was difficult to overlook: 'Part of postmodernism's power is the fact that it exists, whereas how true that is of socialism these days is rather more debatable . . . It would be intellectual dishon-esty to pretend that Marxism is any longer a living political reality, or that the prospects for socialist change, for the moment at least, are anything but exceedingly remote' (*IP* ix). Despite this, Eagleton would still forcefully argue for the relevance of a Marxist criticism, and found in postmodernism an antagonism that was not reconcil-able with a radical critical practice (as his dealing with deconstruc-tion had been, as seen in the last chapter), but rather necessitating intellectual resistance and political critique. As Eagleton would state in his 1996 introduction to a collected reader of Marxist liter-ary theory:

> If postmodernism is right, then Marxism is wrong – *pace* those brands
> of postmodern Marxism which bear about the same relation to the
> classical tradition as guitar-toting vicars do to the Desert Fathers. But
> in another sense the proposition is misleading. For it is not as though

one is being asked choose between Marx and, say, Lyotard or Baudrillard. The very idea of such a choice involves, for a Marxist at least, a grotesque kind of category mistake . . . Marxism is not the body of work of an individual; it belongs to a much wider movement, that of socialism, which has in its time involved some millions of men and women across the nations and the centuries. . . . The practical transformations socialism envisages . . . would no doubt take several centuries to complete, though certain other vital changes would need to be carried though in a much shorter period. However much one might admire the ideas of Lyotard or Baudrillard, one is discussing an essentially different kind of reality, as only intellectuals could fail to realize.[5]

As a consequence, a major undercurrent of Eagleton's writing through this decade was the attempt to revitalize the possibilities for a radical politics through a return to the human body as material grounds for a humanist solidarity, seeing it as offering a fundamental guarantor against the excesses of postmodernism doubt and scepticism – a move that offers both a reorientation of critical method from the previous highpoint of politicized deconstruction, and a subtle but important re-engagement with the questions of bodily politics first articulated in the context of his writings on the Catholic Left, as seen in chapter 1.

Aesthetics, Postmodernism, and the Body

The Ideology of the Aesthetic (1990) stands as one of Eagleton's major works. In scope, it is one of Eagleton's most ambitious studies, ranging over an array of major figures in the history of aesthetic thought, contributing both a tour through, and an argument with, key developments in the history of the aesthetic. While by no means in the same popularizing form, it is in many ways a fulfilment of the project begun in *Literary Theory* and *The Function of Criticism*: to trace the contemporary situations of criticism and theory back through their historical roots, and to account for the possible future role of these intellectual discourses, by assessing the genealogy from which we inherit them.

A basic but nonetheless crucial question to be asked from the outset is what Eagleton actually means when he deploys the term 'aesthetic'. In its most conventional sense in contemporary discourse, 'aesthetics' is a term usually limited to only one of the definitions given by the OED, that of 'The philosophy or theory of taste, or of the perception of the beautiful in nature and art' (OED, definition B. 2). As a term used in Eagleton's work, however, the use of the word challenges the idea of the aesthetic as being a philosophical system concerned purely with art or beauty. Instead, Eagleton uses the category of the aesthetic in a broader way, reinscribing it as a concept of wider relevance to social understanding. As Raymond Williams had noted in his *Keywords*, these previous definitions of the aesthetic were not a neutral shift, but rather indicative of a broader intellectual separation:

> It is an element in the divided modern consciousness of *art* and *society*: a reference beyond social use and social valuation which . . . is intended to express a human dimension which the dominant version of *society* appears to exclude. The emphasis is understandable but the isolation can be damaging, for there is something irresistibly displaced and marginal about the now common and limiting phrase 'aesthetic considerations', especially when contrasted with *practical* or *utilitarian* considerations, which are elements of the same basic division.[6]

In a similar vein, Eagleton's aim is to trace the origin and legacy of this division, expanding even further beyond Williams's account by arguing that the aesthetic was not simply symptomatic of a conceptual split of art from society, but a new mode for political power. In the eighteenth century the aesthetic, as Eagleton states in his opening, was initiated as a 'discourse of the body' – 'the business of affections and aversions, of how the world strikes the body on its sensory surfaces . . . and all that arises from our most banal, biological insertion into the world' (*IA* 13). This 'discourse of the body' (a term that comes closest to defining Eagleton's conception of the aesthetic) became implicated in a hegemonic projection of the rising bourgeois society which, with the decline of the coercive apparatus of the absolutist state, required some form of mechanism to bind together a society that threatened to fracture into individualism: 'The ultimate binding force of the bourgeois social order, in contrast to the coercive apparatus of absolutism, will be habits, pieties, sentiments and affections. And this is equivalent to saying that power in such an order has become *aestheticized*' (*IA* 20). While thus clearly linking the rise of the aesthetic as the mode of asserting social control, Eagleton marks that this development of the aesthetic was always a double-edged concept: in one way as a 'genuinely emancipatory force' that links a community of subjects 'by sensuous impulse and fellow-feeling rather than by heteronomous law'; and in another way as a new mode of repression 'inserting social power more deeply into the very bodies of those it subjugates, and so operating as a supremely effective mode of political hegemony' (*IA* 28). It is this dialectical movement – of both the coercive and emancipatory elements operating within the aesthetic – that Eagleton seeks to trace; finding what can be seized and what can be criticized in the history of this discourse. The investigation is thus not just in the realm of standard figures of 'aesthetic philosophy' from Baumgarten through to Kant and Hegel, but also philosophers such as Marx, Nietzsche and Freud – who Eagleton nominates as the three major aestheticians of the modern period – with their concern to think the aesthetic through again from the ground up, retracing the fundamental of the 'bodily foundations': 'Marx with the labouring body, Nietzsche with the body as power, Freud with the body of desire' (*IA*, 197).

It is far beyond the scope of this present study to consider the entirety of *The Ideology of the Aesthetic* in any detail, and I will thus make no pretence of addressing Eagleton's discussions and characterizations of each of the individual figures he covers through the study. Instead, I want to pause and consider the specific political project that Eagleton undertakes – in other words, how this monumental study of the development of the aesthetic functions is an engagement with, and critique of, the politics of late twentieth-century culture. In one sense, Eagleton is quite open about the fact that he did not see the focus on aesthetics as 'somehow prototypical of what radical critics should now most importantly be doing' (*IA* 11). But in another sense, the aesthetic presents a category to contest dialectically, both to draw out the politically progressive elements of the bourgeois tradition – the 'great revolutionary heritage' (*IA* 8), as Eagleton describes – and, by doing so, recuperate the aesthetic as category to counter the prevailing postmodernist orthodoxy. Eagleton describes, in reference to this trend, how 'a certain style of meditation on the body, on pleasures and surfaces, zones and techniques, has acted among other things as a convenient displacement of a less immediately corporeal politics, and acted also as an *ersatz* kind of ethics' (*IA* 7), and it is his purpose to contest this discourse of the body, to find a deeper purpose to which the tradition of understanding the aesthetic can be put.

The concern comes most explicitly to the fore in the concluding chapter, 'From the Polis to Postmodernism', which in tracing the development of art into the avant-garde and modernism, and the challenge presented by postmodernism, offers one of the most important lines of argument stemming from the work. Tracing the shift from the supposedly ideal time when 'the three mighty regions of the cognitive, the ethico-political and the libidinal-aesthetic were still to a large extent intermeshed' (*IA* 366) to the time when cultural, political, and economic systems separated into distinct fields (which is described as the time of modernity), Eagleton characterizes the period as one in which art achieved a relative autonomy while at the same time as rendering it increasingly socially peripheral: 'Indeed one might risk the rather exaggerated formulation that aesthetics is born at the moment of art's effective demise as a political force . . .' (*IA* 368).

Postmodernism is thus characterized as the aestheticization of culture in late capitalism, with its 'fetishism of style and surface' and 'its reifying of the signifier and displacement of discursive meaning with random intensities' (*IA* 373). Postmodernism is described by Eagleton in a twin move, representing on the one hand a radical subversive impulse, being the last 'upsurge of the avant garde, with its demotic confounding of hierarchies, its self-reflexive subversion of ideological closure, its populist debunking of intellectualism and elitism'; while on the other offering a political conservatism and celebration of the late capitalist status quo, with its 'wholesale abandonment of critique and commitment, its cynical erasure of truth, meaning and subjectivity, its blank, reified technologism' (*IA* 373). This conservatism and complicity is the thread that Eagleton attempts to draw out, suggesting that, for example, to be constantly sceptical of the notion of truth is not inherently radical but rather a reproduction of the debased political reality of an advanced capitalist society: at a time when media spin, government scandal, and brazen deception are fundamental norms of political life, holding forth the 'true facts' against power structures that function through suppression of knowledge is surely one of the most crucial tasks of a progressive politics (*IA* 379). Similarly, the revelling in the value of pastiche and historical eclecticism often glibly surrenders crucial tools for conceptualizing present struggles: if tradition and history can mean stagnant rituals such as the Changing of the Guards, it can also mean the radical heritage of pioneering movements such as the Suffragists (*IA* 378). Postmodernism thus suffers from the same cynicism that had characterized the avant-garde:

> The avant garde's response to the cognitive, ethical and aesthetic is quite unequivocal. Truth is a lie; morality stinks; beauty is shit. And

of course they are absolutely right. Truth is a White House communiqué; morality is the Moral Majority; beauty is a naked women advertising perfume. Equally, of course, they are wrong. Truth, morality and beauty are too important to be handed contemptuously over to the political enemy. (*IA* 372)

This concern, with recapturing the means to speak of 'truth, morality and beauty', establishes the basis for what is probably Eagleton's most detailed direct engagement with the works of Michel Foucault: a thinker whom Eagleton characterizes as representative of the key strains of postmodern ethics. Foucault, whose ideas on the function of power and discourse in society as developed in works such as *Discipline and Punish*, had long occupied an uneasy relationship in Eagleton's theoretical matrix. In *Literary Theory*, Eagleton had paid a very brief, cautious tribute to Foucault, citing him as a post-structuralist who offered a problematic but still 'positive direction', in contrast to the wilder flights of deconstruction, and whose ideas of discursive practices pervasively shaped Eagleton's conclusion. Over the coming years Eagleton's view would harden, as he criticized the 'wretched political reaction' of Foucault's 'defence of NATO and the "free world"' (*AG* 4), while also acknowledging that 'if anyone has presented traditional Marxism with a powerful challenge . . . with immense influence upon a whole younger generation of radicals . . . it is precisely Foucault' (*AG* 95). By the time of *Ideology of the Aesthetic*, however, Eagleton had firmly placed Foucault in what he considered to be the postmodernist tradition, as a theorist whose undoubted innovation in understanding the functioning of power on the human body (the aesthetic of power) comes at the cost of retaining an ethical basis from which to enact a social critique. Again, Eagleton locates a political contradiction at the level of Foucault's style. For Eagleton, Foucault is undoubtedly opposed to the many forms of oppression that he outlines in such meticulous detail in his work; yet his own scepticism towards universal political-ethical positions precludes the necessary basis from which to launch such a critique. This forces Foucault to adopt what Eagleton nominates as a libertarian pessimism, for which it is 'the system', in any variety, which becomes the point of oppression: a situation which fails to differentiate between the societal structures of liberal-capitalism and those of a fascist dictatorship. Foucault's description of power thus comes to have 'much in common with the classical aesthetic artefact, self-grounding, self-generative and self-delighting, without origin or end, an elusive blending of

governance and pleasure which is thus a kind of subject all in itself'
(*IA* 388).[7]

How, then, can a space be found to escape this aesthetic of postmodernism, a vantage point to resist the system while retaining a
hierarchy of values with which to order such concerns? The basis
from which a materialist counter-aesthetic must be built, Eagleton
suggests, is the fundamental and common basis of human body –
not the decentred body of postmodernity, but rather in the human
body whose common vulnerability dictates a ground for a universal
human nature:

> All human beings are frail, mortal and needy, vulnerable to suffering
> and death. The fact that these transhistorical truths are always cultur-
> ally specific, always variably instantiated, is no argument against
> their transhistoricality. For a materialist, it is these particular biologi-
> cally determined facts which have so far bulked largest in the course
> of human history, and have set their imprint upon what, in a nar-
> rower sense, we call culture. (*IA* 410)

Offering what would seem to be the sentiments of Herbert McCabe,
Eagleton holds love as the embodiment of the ultimate human
values of 'free reciprocal self-fulfilment', and suggests that, while
we already recognize the value of love as the highest human value
in our personal life, the task of the radical is to extend this idea of
love to the structure of society as a whole (*IA* 413) – a conclusion
that would seem to tie interestingly with Eagleton's earlier lauding
of the community formed in the Christian sacrament as representative of the non-reified community, opposed to the alienated relationships of capitalism, as argued in *The Body as Language*.

The Ideology of the Aesthetic stands as a marking point in Eagleton's career for a number of reasons. For one, after the rise to prominence as the popularizer of literary theory in the 1980s, it marked
out what has been called Eagleton's 'philosophical turn', intersecting Eagleton's literary-critical concerns with the wider traditions of
aesthetic philosophy. Indeed, many reviewers from the field of
philosophical aesthetics, who admitted being initially sceptical about
Eagleton's bold entrance to the field, nonetheless confessed a grudg-
ing admiration at the breadth and depth of his case, and his recon-
necting the idea of the aesthetic with wider political discourses. For
example, the review by Richard Schusterman, a prominent philosopher of aesthetics, saluted it as a 'bold and admirable attempt',
praising Eagleton's willingness to press discussion of the aesthetic

into new engagements beyond the 'disembodied' aetheticizing of Kant and Hegel (while also maintaining strong reservations about Eagleton's lack of specificity in the definition of the 'aesthetic').[8] On a more specific level, it was also a work that again marked a development in the question of Eagleton's mode of cultural criticism. Chapter 3 highlighted Eagleton's move into an Azdakian critical moment, with Eagleton deploying forms of poststructuralism, as most prominently manifested in *William Shakespeare*, with the comic and subversive central to his critical method. *Ideology of the Aesthetic* offers a departure from the highpoint of this radical pluralism, showing a willingness to contest the site of the human body as a foundation for truth, morality, and love in the face of a postmodern discourse that would shy away from such deployments of the term.

The relevance of ideology: *Ideology: An Introduction*

If the *Ideology of the Aesthetic* thus saw aesthetics as one of the dominant forms through which bourgeois ideology was expressed and perpetuated, Eagleton's next work *Ideology: An Introduction*, attempted an interrogation of the concept of ideology itself, providing both a wide-ranging and incisive introduction to the contentious range of debates surrounding the term. Like *Literary Theory*, its declared status as 'an introduction' does not indicate a work of simple exegesis, for underlying Eagleton's manifest explanations is an intervention into both wider concepts of 'ideology' at a time when ideology itself was being announced as an outdated or irrelevant category, and the specific contemporary theoretical debates concerning postmodernism and post-Marxism; and for such reasons it is, I would hold, one of Eagleton's most effective publications.

In 1991, the year *Ideology* was published, the very question of the relevance of 'ideology' as a critical concept was undergoing acute and important debate throughout the world. The most obvious historical case was the situation of the decline in world communism: with the removal of the Berlin wall in 1989, and the dramatic break up of the USSR occurring through the first years of the 1990s, it became possible, according to certain concepts of ideology, to argue that major ideological conflict in the world had now ceased, and thus that ideology was no longer a driving force in human affairs or history, with liberal democracy remaining as the only living and credible belief system. The most prominent case of such a view occurred in 1989, when the neo-liberal intellectual Francis Fukuyama published the article 'The End of History', in the conservative magazine *The National Interest* – an article that would go on to form the basis of his famous 1992 work, *The End of History and the Last Man.*[9] Fukuyama's thesis was that we had now reached a time at the end of history, with the ideological struggle that had previously driven history now resolved in favour of the liberal democratic ideal. As he sought to explain, 'What we may be witnessing is not just the end of the Cold War, or the passing of a particular period of postwar history, but the end of history as such: that is, the end point of mankind's ideological evolution and the universalization of Western liberal democracy as the final form of human government.' Fukuyama did not so much announce the end of ideology as proclaim the fact that humanity was now entering an era where ideology was irrelevant: with the death of Marxist-Leninism 'as a living ideology of world historical significance', we are entering a 'very sad time' where we will no longer be faced with struggles of an ideological nature, but only with the solution of the practical problems of mere technical importance.[10] Fukuyama's view of history has been proven astonishingly wrong on almost all levels, and drew a storm of criticism (not least of all being the argument that would finally provoke Jacques Derrida's most explicit engagement with Marxism and the declaration that he had always worked with a 'certain spirit of Marx'). Yet that a triumphant right would seize on these historical circumstances as evidence of the end of ideology was not particularly surprising. Perhaps more surprising were the remarkably similar opinions that would circulate among those who could be broadly characterized as belonging to the post-Marxist Left. Notable among these were those of Jean Baudrillard, the prominent theorist of the postmodern, who announced a similar concern with the end of history and the collapse of 'strong' events – describing history itself as a 'dustbin', cluttered with old ideologies and values.[11]

In such a context, Eagleton's point of intervention becomes apparent. On the most obvious level, *Ideology* is an argument against this sudden rush to declare ideology as obsolete: that ideology, in the sense of being large-scale systems of belief, had finally been resolved in the wake of the collapse of the USSR, or that 'ideology' could even be defined in such neat terms as 'Western Liberal Democracy' versus 'Marxist-Leninism'. The book's twin epigraph, taken from Richard Rorty (the first where Rorty states that ideology is a 'useless' concept, and the second where Rorty states that the national claim of someone as an American overrides any form of solidarity on the basis of a shared humanity), provides Eagleton with a specific polemical target. The announcements of the end of ideology, Eagleton argues, had come at a time when the 'last decade has witnessed a remarkable resurgence of ideological movements throughout the world', in the form of the rise of Islamic and Christian fundamentalism, the ongoing conflict in Northern Ireland, and the years of Thatcherism in Britain, which stand in direct contradiction to any attempts to argue that ideology is now a discredited concept (*I* xi). The challenge that Eagleton attempts is to reargue the importance of ideology as a theoretical tool, to reassess the long and often conflicting evolution of concepts of ideology, as a means of recuperating a politics on the 'most difficult' territory, for 'The most efficient oppressor is the one who persuades his underlings to love, desire and identify with his power; and any practice of political emancipation thus involves that most difficult of all forms of liberation, freeing ourselves from ourselves' (*I* xiii–xiv).

The result is a work less intent on coming to some overarching new definition of ideology (as was, say, *Criticism and Ideology*) than of assessing which of the various concepts of ideology are useful in contributing towards this understanding. The 'roughly' six definitions that Eagleton offers – ranging from the wide notion of 'the general material process of production of ideas, beliefs, and values in social life' (*I* 28), down to the very specific case of 'false or deceptive beliefs . . . [generated] from the material structure of society as a whole', as described by Marx's theory of the commodity fetish (*I* 30) – are not synthesized into a unified theory, but rather approached as an active resource to be explored: 'All of these perspectives contain a kernel of truth; but taken in isolation they show up as partial and flawed' (*I* 222).

While the student-aimed explanations of definitions and modes of ideology thus provide the manifest content in the work, Eagleton also undertakes a continued thread of argument with contemporary directions in theories of ideology. The debunking of the 'man in the street' definitions of ideology (for whom ideology is synonymous with the idea of 'the rigid belief of other people who I don't agree with') is an important but relatively straightforward component of Eagleton's critique, withering in the light of Eagletonian quips. The more difficult territory that Eagleton tries to account for and analyse is the challenge that postmodernism presents to the understanding of received definitions of ideology – the fact that ideology is no longer a central theoretical concept addressed in the writing of postmodernists and post-structuralists – whom he states in the introduction are the main driving force behind the claims of a 'post-ideological' era (see *I* xi–xii). The specific political derivation that Eagleton undertakes considerable engagement with is the development of 'post-Marxism', which received its most confident articulation in the influential 1985 manifesto by Ernesto Laclau and Chantal Mouffe, *Hegemony and Socialist Strategy*. The contemporary Left, Laclau and Mouffe had argued, was undergoing a mutation, with an explosion of new forms of struggle based on areas such as gender, race, and sexuality, and the result that 'all these imply an extension of social conflictuality to a wide range of areas, which creates the potential, but no more than the potential, for an advance towards more free, democratic and egalitarian societies'.[12] The challenge Laclau and Mouffe argued in light of this was for a fundamental reorganization of socialist methods and theory, resisting the Marxist emphasis on the centrality of class-position and instead basing a political project on a wider coalition:

> What is now in crisis is a whole conception of socialism which rests upon the ontological centrality of the working class, upon the role of Revolution, with a capital 'r', as the founding moment in the transition from one type of society to another, and upon the illusory prospect of a perfectly unitary and homogeneous collective will that will render pointless the moment of politics. The plural and multifarious character of contemporary social struggles has finally dissolved the last foundation for that political imaginary.[13]

Central to the investigation undertaken throughout *Ideology* is Eagleton's contention that, *pace* this post-Marxist tendency to distrust the privileging of specific areas of struggle, and its support for 'multifarious' modes of political activism, there must be a continued hierarchy of values for consequent definitions of ideology to hold any political use. For Eagleton, 'If someone actually believes that a squabble between two children over a ball is as important as the El Salvador liberation movement, then you simply have to ask them whether they are joking' (*I* 8). The twin aim that Eagleton attempts to balance in this engagement is thus, on the one hand, maintaining the existence and validity of ideology as a concept for understanding the complexity of contemporary political and cultural organizations (contra 'end-of-history' version of postmodernism) while, on the other hand, not sliding into the post-Marxist position where ideology is inflated into a category of an all-pervading mode of 'discourse'. This latter charge is one that Eagleton levels against a number of theorists, ranging from accusing the Foucaultian views of all-pervading power, and the substitution of 'discourse' for 'ideology', as a move that leaves the terms 'an empty sound' (*I* 7); to the work of self-identified post-Marxists such as Paul Hirst and Barry Hindess, whom Eagleton characterizes as having undertaken 'the steady trek from erstwhile revolutionary political positions to left reformist ones' (*I* 203). The point of such critique is an assertion of the continued relevance of Marxian categories that emphasize the role of class in the formation of ideology. In a quintessential Eagletonian move, he offers the example of how social position can contribute to the 'objective interests' by giving us the description of the 'third galley slave from the front on the starboard side':

> This location brings along with it certain responsibilities, such as rowing non-stop for fifteen hours at a stretch and sending up a feeble chant of praise to the Emperor on the hour. To say that this social location comes readily inscribed with a set of interests is just to say that anyone who found himself occupying it would do well to get out of it, and that this would be no mere whim or quirk on his part. (*I* 206)

The manifest humour here also carries with it the implications of a more urgent problem that Eagleton attempts to highlight – if the idea of 'objective interest' is surrendered in a postmodernist revulsion against the very notion of the objective, then one also loses the ability to speak of a mode of politics on the basis that it is actually intrinsically more desirable, whether it is for galley-slaves to become free, workers to become socialists, or women to become feminists (see esp. *I* 213–15). *Ideology*, just like *Literary Theory*, is thus more than an introduction: it is also a work of provocation that sets its task as 'helping to illuminate the processes by which such liberation from death-dealing beliefs may be practically effected' (*I* 224).

Shattering the mirage: *Illusions of Postmodernism*

This chapter has so far characterized the critique of the postmodern as the central thematic concern in Eagleton's writing of the decade, and I will now turn to *The Illusions of Postmodernism*, Eagleton's most sustained polemic directed at this conjecture. If the critique of postmodernism offered in *Ideology of the Aesthetic* and *Ideology: An Introduction* was given a degree of clarity due to the specific concepts of ideology or aesthetics providing a clear thematic focal point, *Illusions of Postmodernism* is a far more diffuse engagement. It deliberately sets itself not as an attempt to define and understand the postmodern in a philosophical context (as we have seen *The Ideology of the Aesthetic* achieve in closely argued detail), but rather shifts its grounds of argument and attack to the mode of a form of radical common sense. Eagleton attempts a critique that at once debunks much of the frequently repeated doxa of postmodernism and, from this, strives to create a position within which to recuperate a progressive politics that can overcome the limitations of postmodernism's privileging of fragmentation and subsequent political complicity with capitalism. As Eagleton explained his motivation, in an attempt to forestall criticism of his approach, 'I have in mind less the higher philosophical flights of the subject than what a particular kind of student today is likely to believe; and though I consider quite a lot of what they believe to be false, I have tried to say so in a way which might persuade them that they never believed it in the first place' (*IP* viii). The result is a work that sacrifices the philosophical ground of argument in order to derive a polemical immediacy, differentiating Eagleton's mode of approach from the critiques of postmodernism undertaken by other prominent Marxists, such as Fredric Jameson and David Harvey.

Eagleton's criticism of the postmodern occurs on several levels. On the first is the historical condition from which postmodernism has derived. Eagleton puts postmodernism as the direct product of the political disillusionment of the Left, after a supposed defeat which destroyed all faith in the possibility of launching a challenge to the totality of capitalism. In such circumstances of the Left shying away from confronting a political totality, the intellectual climate of postmodernity formulates: the marginal and subordinate are increasingly seen as the valuable areas of inquiry and struggle, total concepts such as truth and history are cast into radical question, theoretical investigations increasingly turn inwards on the questions of the body and subjectivity, and the political progress stagnates into a celebration of the status quo. The point of this account, Eagleton contends, is that while the intellectual climate may indeed exist, the fundamental rationale behind it – that of a political defeat creating the conditions where capitalism is supreme – is manifestly false: 'What if it were less a matter of the Left rising up and being forced back, than of a steady disintegration, a gradual failure of nerve?' or, as he colourfully puts it 'as though someone were to display all the symptoms of rabies, but had never been within biting distance of a mad dog' (*IP* 19).

This opening, with its deft narrative, caustic humour, and final sudden reversal, is one of Eagleton's great ironic performances. It is, also, a curiously problematic account. One of the most obvious critiques is the time frame: linking the rise of the postmodern so neatly to the rollback of the Left ignores the fact that postmodernism, as an intellectual concept, had a far more difficult genealogy.[14] But perhaps a more problematic factor is that in characterizing postmodernism as the product of a loss of nerves, Eagleton lapses into a surprisingly thin narrative, ignoring the rich body of Marxist work that sought to link postmodernity to a definite shift in wider material circumstances. For example, David Harvey, in one of the most commanding Marxist theorizations and critiques of the post-modern, convincingly argues that postmodernism was not so much illusions generated by an intellectual cadre of society in the wake of an imagined defeat, but instead the product of a real material history, generated from the shift of productive organization from 'Fordist modernism' to 'flexible accumulation' in the 1970s, combined with fundamental changes in 'time-space' perceptions due to the advance in travel and communication technology. As Harvey argued:

> The intensity of time-space compression in Western capitalism since the 1960s . . . does seem to indicate an experiential context that makes the condition of postmodernity somewhat special. But by putting this condition into its historical context, as part of a history of successive waves of time-space compression generated out of the pressures of capital accumulation with its perpetual search to annihilate space through time and reduce turnover time, we can at least pull the condition of postmodernity into the range of a condition accessible to historical materialist analysis and interpretation.[15]

Eagleton does cursorily gesture towards this case in the preface, acknowledging that 'this way of seeing, so some would claim, has real material conditions: it springs from an historic shift in the west to a new form of capitalism . . .' (*IP* vii), but this case fails to intersect fully with the narrative offered in the subsequent chapter, leaving an apparent and uneasy gap in these two modes of understanding.

On the second level of Eagleton's critique is the assertion of the positive grounds for a political solidarity, to stand in contrast to the currents of contemporary political organization that structured themselves around the privileging of the minority and peripheral. As was seen in the case of *The Ideology of the Aesthetic*, Eagleton's counter to the shallowness of postmodernism was a recourse to the material human body, and this concept is reargued in *The Illusions of Postmodernism*, and is indeed the constant thread woven through the argument – the fact that Eagleton confidently 'Speak[s] as a hierarchical, essentialistic, teleological, metahistorical, universalist humanist' (*IP* 93). For instance, chapter 3, 'Histories', is dedicated to attacking postmodern modes of historicization, which 'views history as a matter of constant mutability, exhilaratingly multiple and open-ended, a set of conjunctures or discontinuities which only some theoretical violence could hammer into the unity of a single narrative' (*IP* 46); which Eagleton resists by offering the biological certainty of a commonality of the human as a deeper mode of historicization: 'If another creature is able in principle to speak to us, engage in material labour alongside us, sexually interact with us . . . suffer, joke and die, then we can deduce from these biological facts a huge number of moral and even political consequences' (*IP* 47). Thus the final test that is proposed for the postmodern, then, is not on its philosophical merits, but rather on its ability to take a corporal form – how it would 'shape up to' fascism (*IP* 134) – and on this level is Eagleton's judgement of its ultimate poverty: 'in confronting its political antagonists, the Left, now more than ever, has need of strong ethical and even anthropological foundations; nothing short of this is likely to furnish us with the political resources we require. And on this score, postmodernism is in the end part of the problem rather than of the solution' (*IP* 134–5).

The Illusions of Postmodernism presented itself as unequivocal polemic, and not surprisingly proved to be a highly contentious work. Michael Ryan, for example, writing in *The Year's Work in Critical and Cultural Theory*, offered a savage criticism of what he saw as Eagleton's blurring of the diverse issues of poststructuralism and postmodernism into one indistinguishable intellectual category. Ryan characterized the work as one that offered 'fundamental slander' concerning the politics of postmodernism, and described it as a work in which 'Eagleton tries to convince an imaginary undergraduate that he never even had the dirty thoughts of postmodernism in his head in the first place.'[16] This blurring of modes is indeed true, with Eagleton attacking an ill-defined formation of postmodern concerns – but this was also the major motivation behind the work. As Perry Anderson suggested, while the ideological doxa of postmodernism that Eagleton attacks may be hazy and intellectually weak, consisting of little more than 'an undemanding medley of notions, whose upshot is little more than a slack-jawed conventionalism', the need for contestation of such intellectual formations is still acutely necessary, as 'since the circulation of ideas in the social body does not typically depend on their coherence, but their congruence with material interests, the influence of this ideology remains considerable – by no means confined to campus life alone, but pervasive in popular culture at large'.[17] *The Illusions of the Postmodern* lacked the level of comprehensiveness and detail that rendered *Ideology: An Introduction* such a success as both introduction and extensive intervention; it also lacked the historical and philosophical sweep which rendered the history of the postmodern in *The Ideology of the Aesthetic* as far more compelling. But, as Anderson suggests, it contested an equally important node of 'street-level' postmodernist debate, and its sheer polemical force achieved something more important than the specificity of detail.

Return of the common culture: *The Idea of Culture*

Eagleton's project of reconceptualizing modes of solidarity, in the face of the emphasis placed by many postmodern thinkers on cultural plurality and the politics of unique identity, in many ways reached its culmination with the publication of *The Idea of Culture*. It is a work that, while firmly aimed at contemporary debates concerning the postmodern, also intersects with a long tradition of English critical thought, ranging from works such as Matthew Arnold's *Culture and Anarchy* (1869), T. S. Eliot's *Notes Towards the Definition of Culture* (1948), F. R. Leavis's *Mass Civilization and Minority Culture* (1930), and almost the entire span of Raymond Williams's output. Thus, before turning to Eagleton's work, I will pause to set out some of the levels of Williams's concern with 'culture', to see how *The Idea of Culture* is implicated in this wider debate.

In *Keywords*, Williams had highlighted the shifts in definition that culture had undergone, for 'in all its early uses was a noun of process: the tending of something, basically crops or animals'. Despite the weight that subsequent intellectuals would place on the term, it was not until the mid nineteenth century that the word 'culture' became commonly used as an independent noun describing something approximating 'civilization', and not until the late nineteenth and early twentieth centuries that 'culture' was understood to be 'the independent and abstract noun which describes the works and practices of intellectual and especially artistic activity' in the sense of 'music, literature, painting and sculpture, theatre and film'.[18] Williams's long project was to resist such a fragmentation, in particular the propositions argued by critics such as T. S. Eliot, in whose definition culture was conceptualized in terms of a rarified pursuit: 'Culture may even be described simply as that which makes life worth living.'[19] In one of his crucial early essays, 'Culture is Ordinary', Williams had contested the legacy of such cultural thought, outlining the basis on which he considered a socialist should define culture. The title itself, with the assertion of the ordinary *as* culture, set itself as a manifest challenge, one that was followed through in the detail of his argument. Williams insisted that culture must be understood as a dialectical process: 'the known meanings and directions, which [society's] members are trained to; the new observations and meanings, which are offered and tested' – a process in which ordinary life and experimental creations are not conceived as separately existing spheres, but rather as areas always feeding into one another.[20] The point of Williams's assertion of this twin definition was to resist the deformation of what Williams described as the 'teashop' understanding of culture – 'the outward and emphatically visible sign of a special kind of people, cultivated people', where decisions are made 'to call certain things culture and then to separate them, as with a park wall, from ordinary people and ordinary work'.[21] In his account, Williams offered a qualified agreement with the Leavisite concern that advancing industrialism had brought with it a culture characterized by a crass commercialism ('the strip newspaper, the multiplying cheapjacks, the raucous triviality'), but the challenge that Williams proposed was not a retreat into high culture as a bastion against the world's ills, but rather to deploy the 'new resources [of industrialism] to make a good common culture',[22] by extending modes of education and cultural funding so as to allow the whole society to participate in fashioning this culture in common.

Williams's concerns had provided a direct influence over Eagleton in his earliest meditations on culture in the 1960s, and thus *The Idea of Culture* is both representative of a continuation of Eagleton's debates with the politics of postmodernism, as well as a relinking with an issue that had occupied Eagleton's attention in the earlier stages of his career. The opening sentence of *The Idea of Culture* –

'"Culture" is said to be one of the two or three most complex words in the English language' (*IC* 1) – is taken almost directly from the opening sentence of Williams's entry on 'Culture' in *Keywords* ('Culture is one of the two or three most complicated words in the English language'), indicating how closely Eagleton's study is linked to Williams's work on the same topic. While Eagleton's account is indebted to Williams's in many places (the first chapter, for example, draws heavily on Williams's *Keywords* account in tracing the shifts in definitions of culture), Eagleton's aim is to pick up where Williams's arguments left off, reasserting the possibility and value of a 'common culture' at a time when politics based on difference have come to the fore.

Throughout *The Idea of Culture*, Eagleton reiterates objections to the Eliot-modes of elitist culture, but the specific development undertaken is linking the development of postmodern culturalism as part of this wider, historical, debate. The target that Eagleton aims for throughout *The Idea of Culture* is the political movement of 'identity politics', extending the critique begun in *Ideology: An Introduction* concerning the post-Marxist shift towards modes of political organization based on affirmation of separate identity and difference, abrasively described here by Eagleton as 'one of the most uselessly amorphous of all political categories, including as it does those who wish to liberate themselves from tribal patriarchs along with those who wish to exterminate them' (*IC* 86). Eagleton reiterates that traditional understandings proposed culture as some unifying meta-discourse 'in which we could sink our petty particularisms in some more capacious, all-inclusive medium', whether this be Eliot's conservative vision or Raymond Williams's radical socialist. However, in recent decades Eagleton alleges that such an understanding has undergone a substantial alteration beyond the realm of the Arnold–Leavis–Eliot–Williams paradigm, where instead of a concept of unity, culture 'now means the affirmation of a specific identity – national, sexual, ethnic, regional – rather than the transcendence of it'. Essentially, culture is no longer seen as a form of solidarity, but rather the means of one subcultural group to distinguish itself from the others: 'what was once conceived of as a realm of consensus has been transformed into a terrain of conflict' (*IC* 38).

There is an obvious counter to this – why is this conflict a bad thing, if it manifests real political tensions rather than being a false provision of an imagined unity? Eagleton's answer to this lies in an argument that carries over from *Ideology: An Introduction*:

> But once one begins, in a spirit of generous pluralism, to break down
> the idea of culture to cover, say, 'police canteen culture', 'sexual-
> psychopath culture' or 'Mafia culture', then it is less evident that
> these are cultural forms to be approved simply because they are cul-
> tural forms. Or, indeed, simply because they are part of a rich diver-
> sity of such forms. (*IC* 15)

If such pluralism thus presents an essential political contradiction,
forcing it to support the radical and reactionary in equal and incom-
patible ways, Eagleton also suggests a more pragmatic reason why
such plurality should be resisted: 'the ruling political system may
take heart from the fact that it has not just one opponent, but a
motley collection of disunited foes' (*IC* 43).

The overriding call of *The Idea of Culture*, therefore, is again for a
reconsideration of some of the basic principles of a common culture,
as both a cure for the illness of postmodernism and identity politics,
and as a basis for a political solidarity. The main problem with
postmodern identity politics, Eagleton suggests in an argument
carried over from *The Illusions of Postmodernism*, is that in turning
the human body into a site of conflict, it effectively surrenders the
greatest potential form of solidarity that humans possess: 'the suffering, mortal, needy, desiring body which links us fundamentally
with our historical ancestors, as well as with our fellow beings from
other cultures, has been converted into a principle of cultural difference and division'. Thus, any possibility for a truly common
culture must acknowledge this basic humanist fact, as Eagleton
describes (in a way that offers faint but nonetheless significant
echoes of a community linked in the Christian sacrament):

> A common culture can be fashioned only because our bodies are
> of broadly the same kind, so that the one universal rests upon the
> other . . . Of course human bodies differ, in their history, gender eth-
> nicity, physical capacities and the like. But they do not differ in those
> capacities – language, labour, sexuality – which enable them to enter
> into potentially universal relationships with one another in the first
> place. The postmodern cult of the socially constructed body, for all
> its resourceful critique of naturalism, has been closely linked with
> the abandonment of the very idea of a politics of global resistance –
> and this in an age when the politics of global domination are more
> importunate than ever. (*IC* 111)

Eagleton concludes *The Idea of Culture* with a chapter devoted to
examining how such a common culture could be established, exam-

ining the previous models of T. S Eliot, F. R. Leavis, and Raymond Williams; a chapter that is a reappraisal and extension of his earlier work. In a 1967 essay, 'The Idea of a Common Culture', Eagleton had drawn an explicit link with the Williams position:

> For the socialist, belief in the possibility of a common culture is belief in the capacity of 'high' culture, when shared and re-made by a whole community, to be enriched rather than destroyed . . . Part of the difference [between the socialist position and that of the conservative and liberal], perhaps, lies in whether society is seen as static or moving, as a finished structure or ongoing human creation. The socialist belief in the possibility of a common culture is grounded in a recognition that the growth of literacy, industrialism and democracy in Britain has been a growth towards total control by a whole society over its own experience, a reaching for full collective responsibility through the struggles of a long revolution still far from finished.[23]

In the concluding sections of *The Idea of Culture*, Eagleton traces out an almost identical debate, reiterating a vision of a genuine common culture in the way Williams has envisioned it, as the result of radical socialist change: 'It requires an ethic of common responsibility, full democratic participation at all levels of social life, including material production, and egalitarian access to the culture-fashioning process' (*IC* 119). The point of re-emphasizing Williams's position now, Eagleton holds, is not simply as a throwback to an earlier debate, but as a resource that speaks to the heart of contemporary debates:

> Only through a fully participatory democracy, including one which regulated material production, could the channels of access be fully opened to give vent to this cultural diversity. To establish genuine cultural pluralism, in brief, requires concerted socialist action. It is precisely this that contemporary culturalism fails to see. Williams's position would no doubt seem to it quaintly residual, not to say positively archaic; the problem in fact is that we have yet to catch up with it. (*IC* 122)

Thus, the return to Raymond Williams's idea of a 'common culture' at the conclusion of *The Idea of Culture*, in effect, completes the full circle of Eagleton's career, with Eagleton returning to the subject that occupied his earliest publications, and explicitly aligning his work with the intellectual lineage of Raymond Williams, moving back into forms of a socialist humanism as resistance to the discourse of the postmodern Left – something that will be seen to come to its fullest head in the later discussions of tragedy in *Sweet Violence*. Perhaps the most intriguing aspect of *The Idea of Culture*, then, is what it reveals about Eagleton himself as a critic and commentator, and his own position in the English cultural tradition. Colin MacCabe, reviewing *The Idea of Culture*, astutely remarked that the critic Eagleton now 'most closely resembles is Samuel Johnson', an issue to which, to conclude this chapter, I will now turn.[24]

Eagleton and the public sphere

So far, this chapter has traced Eagleton's work in the 1990s though four of his major publications concerning aesthetics, ideology, postmodernism, and culture; and in the next chapter I will move to discuss one of the other major concerns of Eagleton's writing at this time, that of the question of Ireland. However, this positioning of Eagleton as a 'man of letters' in *The Idea of Culture* is indicative of an important wider development in his career that had occurred across previous decade. For one of the most decisive shifts that would occur at this point was not so much in the books that he would write and publish, but in the public position that he upheld. As detailed in the introduction, the controversy surrounding the election of Eagleton as Warton Professor at Oxford in 1991 was a symptomatic moment: the mere fact that such hostility could be generated by the faculty promotion of the most influential literary critic in Oxford indicated that Eagleton's position *meant* something in the wider cultural discourses, far beyond the specific scholarly merits of his individual publications. Furthermore, coinciding with this institutional prominence was his shift into new modes and forms of writing, attempting to connect with the 'public sphere' that had formed such a central part of his vision of the critical in *The Function of Criticism*. One example of this was Eagleton's increasing turn to forms of 'creative' writing as modes of exploring figures and debates in literary and cultural traditions (a selection of which I will look at in the next chapter). Across a ten-year period Eagleton would produce a rich seam of such works, writing a novel on Ludwig Wittgenstein and James Connolly, *Saints and Scholars* (1987); plays on the topics of Oscar Wilde (*Saint Oscar*, first produced 1989), the Easter Rising (*The White, the Gold and the Gangrene*, first produced 1993), the Irish Famine (*God's Locusts*, first produced 1995), and post-colonial intellectuals (*Disappearances*, first produced 1997); and, perhaps most ambitiously, a film script concerning the life of Ludwig Wittgenstein, which, in the process of being adapted by the director Derek Jarman, mutated into a work almost unrecognizable from that of Eagleton's script, leading to Eagleton's agent advising him to remove his name from the film, in the end only remaining associated through the persuasion of the BFI.[25]

If the form of 'creative writing' was thus providing Eagleton with an expanded public arena for the exploration of issues and debates, the modes of much of his 'critical' writing would similarly shift across this period. While Eagleton had always produced a prolific output of reviews, the forums that these had predominately found were in the realms of specialized journals: in the 1960s and 1970s it was *Slant* and *New Blackfriars*, in the 1980s it was *New Left Review* and *Diacritics*. Eagleton's earlier collection of his essays, *Against the Grain*, is symptomatic of this fact, with the pieces within it reprinted mainly from such journals as *New Left Review* and *Diacritics* – incisive and important essays, but works with a distinct, professionalized audience both targeted and reached. Through the 1990s, however, the outlets for Eagleton's writing had begun to shift fundamentally. Although still producing a range of academic monographs, another large proportion of his publications now eschewed the standard format of the academic article, and instead deliberately adapted a form for distribution through non-specialized cultural organs. While these essays found outlets in numerous newspapers and periodicals, including *The Times Literary Supplement* and the *Guardian*, by far the most frequent was the *London Review of Books*, the bi-weekly literary magazine founded in 1979, 'dedicated to carrying on the tradition of the English essay', in the conscious form of 'one of the great 19th-century periodicals' (as described on its website).[26] With a circulation of over 40,000 copies (and numerous more readers of the essays since the digitalization of *LRB* and resultant availability of much of Eagleton's writing for free online), it provided for Eagleton what he would subsequently describe as 'a kind of public sphere', which 'lingers on among us in however vestigial a form', and a forum 'in which one can try to write companionably about complex matters' (*FD* ix). Over the course of the 1990s this would be the venue for wide-ranging aspects of Eagleton's writing (the majority of which now form the basis of *Figures of Dissent*), such as incisive review articles on contemporary critics such as Harold Bloom, Stanley Fish, Gayatri Spivak, and Slavoj Zizek; as well as on wider historical topics and movements such as the Frankfurt School, T. S. Eliot, and *The Criterion*; Romanticism, and even David Beckham.

In many ways these works present a direct continuation of the spirit of *Literary Theory*, with the essays designed to incisively explain and critique key areas of cultural theory, offering concise deployments of the polemic and satirical modes of criticism that characterized his concerns in the 1980s. But on a wider level, they mark out a project by Eagleton to keep the democratic impulse of critical theory alive, in the face of the absorption of theory into the academic institutional mainstream over the course of the 1980s and 1990s, and the subsequent professionalization of this discourse into the specialist languages of theoretical sub-specialities, unintelligible to society at large. This was a concern brought into particularly stark relief in his highly controversial review of Spivak's *A Critique of Postcolonial Reason* where, while paying tribute to the 'long-term good' that Spivak had accomplished in feminist and post-colonial studies, he rebuked her over her failing of responsibility as a socialist intellectual:

> Radical academics, one might have naively imagined, have a certain political responsibility to ensure that their ideas win an audience outside senior common rooms. In US academia, however, such popularizing or *plumpes Denken* is unlikely to win you much in the way of posh chairs and prestigious awards, so that left-wingers like Spivak, for all their stock-in-trade scorn for academia, can churn out writing far more inaccessible to the public than the literary elitists who so heartily despise them. (*FD* 159)

This characterization of Spivak's discourse did not pass without strong challenge,[27] but the general contention offered here by Eagleton is suggestive of the key responsibility and task that Eagleton saw his public prominence – his position as socialist 'man of letters' – as requiring. Eagleton's writing of the 1990s sought not only to contest the intellectual validity of the postmodern but also, through this, to show the possibility of a public socialist critical project at a time of widespread doubt, with Eagleton remaining one of the most prominent British intellectuals who still keep the socialist horizon alive in the face of scepticism and disillusionment.

5

Nationalism, Socialism, and Ireland

In the spring 1994 edition of the *Irish Studies Review*, Eagleton offered a short, savage assessment of the historian Roy Foster, who was the recently appointed Carroll Professor of Irish History at Oxford, the author of several seminal works of modern Irish cultural history, and who would go on to write (in the years after Eagleton's piece initially appeared) the multi-volume biography of W. B Yeats. While in parts praising 'the imaginative flair, enviable erudition and authoritative ease of judgement . . . of our finest Irish historian', Eagleton argued that Foster's surface appearance of 'scholarly even-handedness' masked a revisionist agenda and an implicit political sympathy for upper-class Irish liberalism, where his 'yuppie contempt for fusty old Irish nationalism would come rather better from a man who gave some sense that he had ever been spiritually at home anywhere but in Big Houses and corridors of power'. Central to Eagleton's critique was Foster's choice of 'high-class Irish fallen on hard times', and the allegation that, by focusing on 'the Yeatses and Synges and Bowens, those poor dispossessed souls', Foster's work displayed the ability to be 'challengingly heterodox, breaking with the dreary grand narratives of the great majority of the Irish people, while being, politically speaking, as welcome to the Establishment as it is possible to be'.[1] Not surprisingly, Eagleton's attack caused significant controversy, including being denounced in a feature article in *The Times* with the title 'Irish History Deserves Better than This'.[2] Yet it also forcefully marked out the urgency of Eagleton's engagement with Irish cultural politics in this period, and his concerns with generating

debate over the compatibility between national history and socialist politics.

Ireland had long occupied an important place within the range
of Eagleton's interests. *The Gatekeeper* offered Eagleton's unsenti-
mental explanation of his situation as a third-generation Irish immi-
grant, stating that, while almost the entire population of his grammar
school 'were Irish . . . we did not know we were' (*G* 38), and describing how his grandfather 'could be dewy-eyed about Ireland . . . yet
his memories of the place seemed blurred and probably for the most
part thoroughly unpleasant' (*G* 120). Equally, the culture of Ireland
has been present as a concern through his later career, ranging from
his early essay on Yeats and the Easter Rising, through the 'unwrit-
ten' component of *The Ideology of the Aesthetic* consisting of a 'doubled
text, in which an account of European aesthetic theory would be
coupled at every point to a consideration of the literary culture of
Ireland' (*IA* 11), to Eagleton's recent physical relocation to become
a resident of Dublin. These interests, however, came into the most
acute manifestation during a decade-long period of Eagleton's
career, which saw a major sequence of works in which Irish cultural
and political questions formed the direct focus. While these works
cross conventional boundaries of academic form – ranging from his
novel, *Saint and Scholars* (1987), a sequence of plays, the most notable
of which include *Saint Oscar* (1989) and *The White, The Gold and the
Gangrene* (1993); and a trilogy of works on Irish cultural history –
what unifies this sequence is Eagleton's preoccupation with rubbing
Irish history against the grain, to see how figures and debates could
be drawn into a new light, by deploying the resources of cultural
theory on to the site of direct contemporary cultural and political
dispute.

There is a danger that Eagleton's 'Irish' writing can be seen as
some sort of idiosyncratic sideline from his real 'speciality' of
Marxist literary criticism, or that Eagleton's position as a Marxist
writing on nationalism and nationalist debates presents an irreconcilable contradiction, and indeed this later point has been a charge
frequently brought against Eagleton. Willy Maley, for example, was
prompted to question the political result of Eagleton's apparent
Irish shift, asking 'What will Eagleton's newfound Irishness do to
his Marxism? Will it shorten his left-wing span? Might it decon-
struct it?'[3] While Maley's speculation was as to whether this 'Irish'
Eagleton would dilute the 'Marxist' one, others would see the
process occurring in the opposite way. Thus Martin McQuillan, in
an article which provided a sustained critique of Eagleton's concern

with Ireland, saw Eagleton's turn to Ireland as an attempt to annex Irish history into a simplified Marxian mode:

> Eagleton's Irish adventures could be read as a repositioning of the verities of Marxism into a context which seems much more black and white, or at least green and orange. Given that history has been so undialectical as to produce Tony Blair and New Labour, Eagleton's search for the New Jerusalem has taken him to the satanic mills of Irish history. It is easier to tell the goodies from the baddies in a post-colonial struggle, and the binary of colonizer and colonized bears a reassuring similarity to Hegel's master/slave dialectic. In such a scenario the colonized Irish (Eagleton has never equivocated about whose 'side' he is on) become a substitute for the lost working class dispersed by the neo-liberalism of Mrs Thatcher.[4]

For McQuillan, much of Eagleton's writing has thus been characterized by its 'incorporative logic' (36), viewing figures such as Oscar Wilde through the reductive lens of a narrow Marxist concern.

These particular criticisms of Eagleton's position appear odd in many ways. As one writer concerning on this debate between McQuillan and Eagleton noted, 'As England's first colony and as the site of some of the worst horrors of English imperialism (which is saying something), Ireland *ought* to concern a Marxist critic working in England.'[5] Moreover, as Eagleton himself stressed, the issue of Irish cultural and intellectual history provided a direct and important test, for 'if the theory may illuminate Ireland in unaccustomed ways, the reverse is also the case', with the ambivalence of postmodernism towards questions of 'class, state, revolution, ideology, [and] material production' standing in stark contrast to the fact that these categories 'have been on any estimate central to Irish experience. In seeking to insert Irish history into cultural theory, then, I am also aiming to challenge the current repressions and evasions of the latter' (*HGH* x). In other words, the turn to Ireland at this stage of Eagleton's critical and creative work was not some sort of turn away from the demands of high theory, into some merry celebration of Gaelic culture, but instead the direct testing ground of the demands: the claims cultural theory, Eagleton contends, stand or fall on their ability to shape and inform a critical engagement with one of the most acute sites of cultural and political tension generated by the legacy of British colonialism.

Consequently, the idea that Eagleton had given over into a simplistic, 'goodies versus baddies', support of Irish nationalism seems to ignore much of what actually concerned Eagleton in his writing during this period. For one, Eagleton had anticipated such assumptions by critics, and prefaced 'Heathcliff and the Great Hunger' with a sly dig at this inevitable preconception by critics: 'They will know [without reading the work] that the book will be embarrassingly sentimental about Ireland; that it will romanticize its political conflicts with all the privileged fantasizing of radicals marooned in a more tranquillized culture and spoiling for a fight, and that it will take an unequivocally affirmative line on nationalism' (*HGH* x). Moreover, the position of nationalism within socialism was an issue that Eagleton had actively dwelt upon and interrogated. In 1988, Eagleton published the essay 'Nationalism: Irony and Commitment' as a pamphlet in a series organized by the Field Day Theatre Company (later published with essays by Fredric Jameson and Edward Said in the volume *Nationalism, Colonialism, and Literature*), and this is an essay that provides a key to understanding Eagleton's points of engagement with this field – or, as he put it, the seemingly 'impossible irony' that must be worked through. Eagleton recalls the fact that, for Marx, the affirmation of a 'working-class' identity was far from the end point of political action, as belonging to a social class 'is itself a form of alienation, cancelling the particularity of an individual life into collective anonymity'. Similarly, Eagleton held that any form of nationalism itself embodies a form of alienation, which must not be ignored, but rather worked through:

> [T]o attempt to bypass the specificity of one's identity in the name of freedom will always be perilously abstract, even once one has recognized that such an identity is as much a construct of the oppressor as one's 'authentic' sense of oneself. Any emancipatory politics must begin with the specific, then, but must in the same gesture leave it behind. For the freedom in question is not the freedom to 'be Irish' or 'be a woman,' whatever that might mean, but simply the freedom now enjoyed by certain other groups to determine their identity as they may wish.[6]

Therefore, one of the constant threads in this period of Eagleton's writing is a negotiation of these concerns, and this chapter will examine how Eagleton focuses upon areas of these debates through these works, starting by briefly looking at his Irish trilogy, with particular focus on the controversial essay 'Heathcliff and the Great Hunger'; before moving to more detailed examinations of the novel *Saints and Scholars*, and the dramas *The White, the Gold and the Gangrene* and *Saint Oscar*, where these concerns are embodied and worked over in a particularly intense and engaging form.

Rubbing Irish history against the grain

Eagleton's Irish trilogy is, in many ways, most closely akin to the project of *Walter Benjamin*: a seemingly diffuse series of essays, covering a range of figures and debates in the fields of Irish cultural history, many times resisting conventional academic forms of engagement. Nonetheless, within this range of essays a number of central trajectories are present. On the direct level, as his critique of Foster's 'Great House' canon of Irish culture would suggest, a predominant concern of Eagleton's intervention is a question of canonical politics. As he noted in the preface to *Crazy John*: 'Scanning the bibliographies, an outsider might be forgiven for concluding that the Irish literary pantheon was populated more or less exclusively by Yeats, Synge, Joyce, Beckett, Flann O'Brien and Northern Irish poetry' (*CJ* ix); and thus Eagleton gives substantial critical space in an attempt to expand this roll – whether it be examining the eighteenth century poet William Dunkin whom Eagleton holds as 'at least as fine a poet' as many of those English poets safely installed in the canon ('The Hidden Dunkin' *CJ* 1–16); the almost-forgotten playwright and journalist Frederick Ryan (1873–1913) whose writing, Eagleton suggests, offers a powerful challenge to contemporary revisionist and anti-revisionist historical debates ('The Ryan Line' *CJ* 249–72); or wider investigations of the intellectual culture that flourished in the city of Cork in the early nineteenth century, before an economic collapse prompted a dispersal of the intelligentsia ('Cork and the Carnivalesque', *CJ* 158–211). This project is most clearly at work in *Scholars and Rebels*, with its investigation into the development of the intellectual in nineteenth-century Ireland, drawing on Gramsci's theories of concerning the organic and traditional intellectual, in an investigation that parallels Eagleton's earlier concern with the development of the 'public sphere' in *The Function of Criticism*. Eagleton draws attention to groupings such as those around the *Dublin University Magazine* as a form of 'Irish Bloomsbury', and how this intellectual formation was intimately involved in the ideological shaping of Irish society in debates concerning nationalism and the national revival.

If this represents Eagleton's major concern with canonical politics, reinscribing lesser-known writers and movements in a wider Irish cultural tradition, other essays take a far more provocative approach, resisting the pretence of scholarly disinterest and instead flaunting their own 'literariness', and by doing so, attempt to open new modes of intervention in the contested arena of Irish history. Such was most prominently the case in the essay 'Heathcliff and the Great Hunger', one of Eagleton's most imaginative and controversial critical engagements, and one on which I want to pause to examine in further detail. It is an article that, through providing an account of the effaced Irish origins of the Brontë family, and a deliberately provocative reading of Emily Brontë's great novel alongside the history of the Irish famine, attempts to blast open *Wuthering Heights* as a space to metaphorically read a history of Anglo-Irish relations, teasing out a colonial subconscious in the work that would seem manifestly to resist such appropriation.

Eagleton begins with an account of the often overlooked 'fourth' Brontë, Patrick Branwell, the only brother, who had dabbled as a painter and a writer but, unable to hold down a steady position as a tutor, became an alcoholic and laudanum addict before dying of tuberculosis when only thirty-one years old. The specific point that Eagleton fastens upon is a trip he made in August 1845 to Liverpool, a city at that point teeming with hundreds of thousands of Irish fleeing the great famine:

> A few months after Branwell's visit to Liverpool, Emily began writing *Wuthering Heights* – a novel whose male protagonist, Heathcliff, is picked up starving off the streets of Liverpool by old Earnshaw. Earnshaw unwraps his greatcoat to reveal to his family a 'dirty, ragged, black-haired child' who speaks a kind of 'gibberish', and who will later be variously labelled beast, savage, lunatic and demon. It is clear that this little Caliban has a nature on which nurture will never stick; and that is simply an English way of saying that he is quite possibly Irish. (*HGH* 3)

Having dangled this possibility in front of us, Eagleton immediately retreats: it is not at all certain that Heathcliff's description matches a physical Irish child, and the dates of the composition of the novel do not comfortably match the dates of the composition of Emily's novel. Nonetheless, the space it creates serves as a speculative basis for an investigation of the wider position of Ireland in the consciousness of England. Examining the relation between Nature and Culture embodied within the novel in the figures of Heathcliff and that of Thrushcross Grange, for example, leads into comparisons of aestheticization of land in the English and Irish traditions, with Eagleton suggesting that, while land in the English literary tradition has been effectively aestheticized and 'cultured' ('Jane Austen tends to look at a piece of land and see its price and proprietor but nobody actually working there', *HGH* 4), the position of land in Irish literature refused such assimilation. Instead, Eagleton suggests that ideas of land and nature are still seen as a site of material struggle: 'Nature in Ireland is too stubbornly social and material a category, too much a matter of rent, conacre, pigs and potatoes for it to be distanced, stylized and subjectivated . . .' (*HGH* 8). This mediation, on Nature and Culture, serves as a debate around which the subsequent investigation by Eagleton is entwined. For one, Eagleton draws attention to the nature of Ireland as an untamed 'natural' site in the unconsciousness of 'civilized' English colonialism: the 'biological time-bomb which can be heard ticking softly away beneath the civilized superstructures of the Pall Mall clubs' (*HGH* 9), which finally explodes forth in the response to the Famine. From here Eagleton turns to the position of the Famine itself in the consciousness of Irish history – the fact that the defining event in modern Irish history is almost non-existent in subsequent Irish literature suggesting a 'repression or evasion' (*HGH* 12), an unrepresentability that Eagleton then links back to the 'Chinese box structure' of *Wuthering Heights*, where the 'modern period in Ireland flows from an origin which is also an end, an abyss into which one quarter of the population disappears' (*HGH* 14). And from here Eagleton turns to the question of the causes of the Famine itself, advocating neither the overreaction in accusing the British of 'calculated genocide', nor crediting the revisionist position of tolerantly judging the Famine as handled by the British to the best of their ability as could have been expected at the time. Instead, Eagleton asserts the importance of stating a 'utopian' position of the root cause, rather than debating the adequateness of the response: the agrarian capitalism implemented by the British, which, if abolished, would have prevented any famine in the first place. Again, Eagleton acknowledges the speculation of this reading: 'Such a revolution could not have conceivably happened at the time; neither the political will nor the political muscle for it were available.' Instead, it is an act of bearing witness, undercutting contemporary debates by remembering the conditions that actually made such a tragedy possible: 'the point of such subjective or counterfactual speculation is to place the ultimate responsibility for the disaster where it belongs – which is to say, not with the "landlords" or "the British", but with the system they sustained' (*HGH* 25).

Not surprisingly, given the provocative nature of the reading, *Heathcliff and the Great Hunger* generated considerable criticism from reviewers of the work. Edna Longley, while offering cautious praise of Eagleton's 'literary readings', was also highly sceptical of this lack of historical seriousness, stating of the title essay that 'Such Humpty-Dumpty Hibernianism is Eagleton at his worst'.[7] Denis Donoghue reacted in a similar light, nominating the reading as 'interesting to begin with, but daft in the end',[8] while many other reviewers were simply angered that Eagleton could deal with a historical calamity in such an apparently flippant way, blending history and speculative fiction together in a way that seemed not to attach due seriousness to the issue. Indeed, Eagleton is open to this charge, but this would also seem to miss much of the purpose of his provocation. In a later essay concerned with the intellectual conflict surrounding Irish history, Eagleton points to the fact that ongoing political and power struggle, combined with the still-open wounds of recent history, had left a deep mark on subsequent historiography, that was not open to a disinterested resolution:

> The constant misreadings on both sides; the quickness with which the discourses of academics pledged to a sober disinterestedness moves into rhetorical overdrive when these questions come up; the Pavlovian response produced in otherwise judicious men and women by certain taboo words or key phrases: all this is a sign that we are in the presence of the kind of rhetorical conflict which, as Wittgenstein might have said, can finally be resolved only by changing the forms of life which give birth to it. (*CJ* 311)

Thus, by foregrounding the provocative textuality of this reading of history, dwelling on the unrepresentability of the famine, and trying to pick apart the unconsciousness of these debates, 'Heathcliff and the Great Hunger' offered both a deliberately outrageous, but also very serious, point: that 'it is unlikely that any historical account will be entirely free of either sectarianism or sanitizing until the problems in the North are somehow resolved' (*CJ* 312), and that apportioning or excusing 'national' blame for the Famine remains an obfuscation of the real economic cause.

'Heathcliff and the Great Hunger' thus used the text of Brontë as a narrative with which to speculatively read Irish history, moving between the boundaries of the imaginative and the historical as a means of symptomatically reading that which otherwise remained unsaid. I will now turn to another mode employed by Eagleton, which explored similar debates in a particularly developed form: his novel and dramas focusing on the figures of James Connolly and Oscar Wilde, and their position within the political and cultural debates in Irish history.

Revolution, mythology, and James Connolly: *Saints and Scholars* and *The White, the Gold and the Gangrene*

If the negotiation between the demands of nationalism and social-ism was a key concern for Eagleton in his examination of Irish history, it is little wonder that the figure of James Connolly would become a central figure and reccurring point of meditation in his novel and dramatic works. A Scottish-born socialist who became one of the leading Marxist theorists of the early twentieth century, and who would work as a socialist leader and organizer in Scotland, America, and Ireland, Connolly was also a key figure in the Easter Rising, as one of the seven signatories to the Proclamation, and commander of the forces in the General Post Office. More than simply his actions, it has been the manner of his death that has contributed to much of the paradoxical symbolism surrounding the Easter Rising. Hastily executed by the British while still suffering from the wounds sustained in the rebellion, Connolly was tied to a chair and shot by a firing squad where he sat: an image that was seemingly symbolic of the doom of the wider rising, which had sought to overthrow the British occupation with a force of scarcely over one thousand men, and which had been quickly isolated by the British garrison and eventually backed into an unconditional surrender. Yet, paradoxically, out of this vulnerability and defeat came a victory far greater than any militarily feasible, with the swift and uncompromising brutality of the British response stripping away the legitimacy that (to borrow from Althusser) the ideological state apparatus had provided the British occupation, laying the coercive powers of the repressive state apparatus bare.

It is this image that Eagleton's novel *Saints and Scholars* meditates upon, as he speculatively sends Connolly to a small cottage on the west coast of Ireland where he encounters the unlikely occupants of Wittgenstein, Nikolai Bakhtin (the brother of the more famous literary theorist Mikhail Bakhtin), and Leopold Bloom. The novel is framed on both sides by the scene of James Connolly's execution in Kilmainhan prison, yet Eagleton interrupts this narrative of history to seize the figure of Connolly in a deliberately Benjaminesque way:

> Seven bullets flew towards Connolly's chest, but they did not reach it, at least not here they didn't. Let us arrest those bullets in mid air, prise open a space in these close-packed events through which Jimmy may scamper, blast him out of the dreary continuum of history into a different place altogether. (*SSch* 10)

What Eagleton creates though this fantastical blasting of the continuum of history is a personified clash of political and philosophical positions, weaving Wittgenstein and Connolly, as they debate with each other in this hiding place, as the embodiments of conflicting modes of theoretical discourse, a literary reworking of the arguments for the position of critic presented in *Literary Criticism* and the *Function of Criticism*. Wittgenstein, through the debates of the novel, is depicted as an intellectual whose theoretical insight is shorn of social function, who is on the run from the 'dons' of Cambridge and suffering from the self-diagnosed sickness of a Nietzschian 'will to knowledge'. As a consequence, he envies the common people who, he imagines, simply do what they do in the unreflective life of the organic community, and live 'in the innocent self-evidence of their gestures' (*SSch* 19), free from the uncertainty of reflective philosophical insight. Philosophy, for Wittgenstein, is a prison-house that can never get beyond the surface and into a deeper critique, reducing him to a suicidal despair due to the fact that 'Everything is the way it is and not some other way' (*SSch* 18). Wittgenstein can declare that 'Philosophy has nothing to do with life' (*SSch* 18), and inform Connolly that revolution 'is the dream of the metaphysician', and an ultimately futile act, 'like trying to use language to speak of what lies beyond it' (*SSch* 112, 113). His companion Bakhtin takes this position further, and indeed comes to symbolize a deconstructive critic *par excellence*. Instead of despair at this prison house of language, he instead revels in a post-structural joy at this lack of linguistic closure, a man who chooses his words 'more for music than for meaning, producing great arpeggios of gripping nonsense' (*SSch* 34), and where the Easter Rising becomes a joyous symbolic affirmation, removed from any actual 'goals' (*SSch* 1) of lasting political liberation or change: 'You rise up, though you know you can't win. You fight, but you don't hope to succeed. You're on the run, but not running away. That strikes me as magnificent. I find its incoherence quite entrancing. It's a kind of theatre – a charade. To know that death is inevitable yet still to dance, still to revolt, still to give bread to a beggar. That is the purest freedom possible. I bow to your uprising' (*SSch* 100–1).

But, in contrast to the depoliticized evasions of Wittgenstein's and Nikolai Bakhtin's language-philosophy, Eagleton depicts the question of language as a crucial wider issue to the activity of society. In strong contrast to the sterile academic debates in Cambridge undertaken by the tormented Wittgenstein are the passages of the novel devoted to descriptions of Dublin, which is in the grips of both famine and the Irish nationalist revolutionary movement. Indeed, in these circumstances 'cultural theory' has been infused with a new political urgency, as the nationalists and revolutionaries link the question of a revolution on the level of language as part of their wider project:

> Everyone in Dublin was an expert on the language question. The city was a cacophony of tongues, from the mincing vowels of West Britain to the thick slurred growling of the docklands, the chronically surprised shrillness of the North and the shoneens who aped Dublin Castle dialect. Some of the literati would write only in Gaelic, frightened of becoming European lest they be thought English. Others maintained that the Gaelic revival would simply make their fellow countrymen illiterate in two languages rather than in one. (*SSch* 50)

James Connolly himself is presented as a language philosopher – as Wittgenstein recognizes, Connolly is a 'fellow philosopher', albeit 'more lethal than any of the old men' in Cambridge (*SSch* 114). For Connolly, however, language was not a disconnected system of signs divorced from societal implications, to be revelled in purely as a self-referential system of free-play, but rather a dangerous and powerful tool that may be seized for political ends:

> Meanwhile, you talked, in the bars and pulpits and political meetings, at the race track and in bed and the back pews. Talk came out and drink went in, both dream machines, both devices for doing nothing century after century. Yet talk was a kind of action, unlike drink. Discourse was something you did: it could gather ten thousand armed men on the streets, unionize dockers, convert an aristocrat to a Fenian. The Irish had never fallen for the English myth that language was a second-hand reflection of reality. Laurence Sterne had exploded that fallacy in an orgy of laughter. For Swift and Burke

and O'Connell rhetoric was as real as a rifle: it could clothe children and console the dying, banish typhoid and purify the coinage. Language was both sickness and cure, the last freedom left to a demoralized land. (*SSch* 104–5)

Connolly is shown as the consummate revolutionary rhetorician, able to manipulate 'the words directly with his fingers, pressing them home into their trim ranks, as later he would reach through them to manipulate the admiring crowds, setting a hall alight with a well slotted phrase, ranking his points on the back of an envelope for rhetorical effect' (*SSch* 109). Yet, even more than mastering the spoken revolutionary rhetoric, Connolly also understands and controls the wider symbolic language surrounding the Irish revolution, and is willing to give his life as a symbolic act in order to enter into the larger signifying process of a cause that he describes as 'no more than a piece of language' (*SSch* 110). The novel concludes by returning to the beginning, showing Connolly's execution – but his physical death facilitates his final release to a higher existence, fusing the physical and the linguistic in the birth of a new history: 'When the bullets reached him he would disappear entirely into myth, his body nothing but a piece of language, the first cry of the new republic' (*SSch* 145).

This concern with the figure of Connolly, then, presents a forerunner of the concerns of the subsequent play, *The White, the Gold and the Gangrene*. A play described by one critic as 'a kind of Brechtian burlesquing of Beckett's *Waiting for Godot*',[9] it is a work that dwells on Connolly's death as a means to interrogate further the struggle for control over the signification, mythology, and history of the Irish Easter Rising. The play echoes concerns first iterated by Marx for, as Marx well understood, a political revolution such as this cannot simply be reduced to a struggle in the material realm, but is always matched by a corresponding struggle in the realm of history, mythology, and symbolism. Marx noted, in the famous passage of *The Eighteenth Brumaire of Louis Bonaparte*, that while humans may make their own history, they do so only in circumstances 'found, given and transmitted from the past':

And just when they seem engaged in revolutionising themselves and things, in creating something entirely new, precisely in such epochs of revolutionary crisis they anxiously conjure up the spirits of the past to their service and borrow from them names, battle slogans and costumes in order to present the new scene of world history in this time-honoured disguise and the borrowed language.[10]

It is only the proletarian revolution, Marx went on to write, that could escape such a nightmare, and forge something new beyond the horror of history, not drawing its 'poetry from the past, but only from the future', and letting 'the dead bury the dead'. Reflecting on these ambiguous comments, Eagleton, in an article discussing the revolutionary symbolism of Milton's *Paradise Lost*, offers what could be called a post-structuralist account of 'revolutionary mythology':

> The task of the revolutionary mythologer is to furnish the political process with a set of efficacious symbols, universalise its meanings by inscribing them within a global drama, unify its disparate forces by the power of the image, and summon the past into a metaphorical compact with the present. At stake in such revolutionary mythologizing is a struggle over the signifier, a fight for the hegemonic symbol, which is appropriated now this way, now that, depending on the balance of discursive forces.[11]

It is this struggle for the control of the revolutionary symbolism of Connolly's execution that Eagleton depicts in *The White, the Gold and the Gangrene*. Eagleton balances two complex levels of signification in the work: a directly tragi-comic drama, concerning the physical suffering and execution of Connolly, juxtaposed with the quick-fire Beckettian exchanges of the guards; and an allegorical debate, between the personification of revolutionary and reactionary history, with a struggle over the signified content of the Easter Rising and Connolly's own death at the hands of the British. On the immediate level, Eagleton constructs a work of brilliantly dark humour: a performance that constantly prevaricates between menace and farce, with the guards cheerfully upholding the prison regulations while acknowledging their absurdity, attempting to console Connolly while in the same breath tormenting him with his impeding execution. The irony of this is that Eagleton was not the author of the ultimate farce that the play dwells upon – that a crippled man could be tied to a chair and shot in the name of justice.

On the wider level, however, the play concerns itself with the issue of historical interpretation, a meditation on Walter Benjamin's cryptic point made in the *Theses on the Philosophy of History* that 'In every era the attempt must be made anew to wrest tradition away from a conformism that is about to overpower it . . . Only that historian will have the gift of fanning the spark of hope in the past who is firmly convinced that *even the dead* will not be safe from the enemy if he wins.'[12] McDaid and Mather are not only there to guard and execute Connolly in a physical sense, but also to attempt to control the symbolic signification of the event. The purpose of their torment is an attempt to reinscribe the uprising and Connolly's death as a pathetic rebellion followed by lawful punishment, rather than a defiant uprising brutally suppressed by a colonial power. This is borne out in the bureaucratic farce concerning the required consent for the execution, as the wardens wave paperwork in front of the incredulous Connolly:

> MCDAID   (*Pulling a form from his pocket*) Government issue C-stroke-8295-Stroke-BW; Consent to be Executed. You have to sign it, it's regulations. (*Takes out pen and hands it with form to Connolly.*) Here you are, scrawl your X on the bottom of this; press hard now, it has to come through underneath.

As McDaid explains, the symbolic purpose of execution is not just to punish an offender, but also to usurp them into a complicit understanding: 'It doesn't like having to wave a big stick; if it does, it's failed, people lose faith in it. The law wants your allegiance, Jim, it wants you to look it in the eyes and whisper that you've understood' (*SO* 71). This attempt to secure Connolly's complicity with their actions stems from their fundamental inability to comprehend the nature of his historical intervention. Their only mode for understanding Connolly is as a romantic Irish nationalist; yet in this mode Connolly's motivations and actions seem to the guards to be nothing more than an embarrassing failure: 'It wasn't spectacular, it wasn't sublime, it wasn't even bloody *tragic*. It was just embarrassing. And when the dust cleared, there was a solitary plaque on the wall: "On this day, in Dublin 1916, Commandant-General James Connolly shot himself in the foot"' (*SO* 86). Their 'present' to Connolly in the form of Liam, a living Irish caricature, is a particular acute instance of this disjunction. A 'tiny wizened man with a fixed inane grin, dressed like a caricature of an Irish peasant' who the warders proudly carry onto stage and reveal to Connolly, embodies every cliché of a romantic Irish nationalism. As McDaid announces him, 'You're looking at a sliver of the purest Gaelic stock to be found throughout the length and breadth of Connemara' (*SO* 108), and the list of Liam's supposed life achievements reads like a roll-call of heroic historic moments: 'Liam narrowly survived the Famine by holding up an Ascendancy dining club at pistol point and later refused a landlord's bribe to emigrate.

He acted as Parnell's personal interpreter in the Land League, and would probably be in the next cell to yourself right now if he hadn't been at the races during the rising' (*SO* 109).

The point of this fantasy is, of course, that it does not exist. Liam's abrupt switch, from a lilting flow of clichéd Gaelic sentiment, to a working-class Dublin accent when he requests payment at the end, is indicative of the extent of this constructed identity, a persona commercially adopted for the entertainment of others, which serves to perpetuate a mythology that has only a tenuous tie to actual history. Nonetheless, for McDaid and Mather, Liam is presented as the embodiment of the Easter Rising's purpose: 'If ever you're tempted to forget what you're fighting for, just call to mind that wise and simple visage' (*SO* 111). Romantic nationalism is, for these representatives of Imperial Britain, an understandable and containable political force – a mode of rebellion that can be assimilated into a present logic, that does not present it with any form of fundamental challenge. This is borne out in the close detail of Liam's narration, as he attempts to console Connolly:

> And isn't it only a small while now you'll be lost in the great wind that blows from beyond time and us destroyed and heart-sore with the fearfulness of it and it'll be weeping there'll be on the black rocks of Aran and under the cold stones of Ballincree and we'll be praying there for your soul James Connolly and it going up in glory to the soul of God. (*SO* 110)

In Liam's telling – a version that is acceptable to, and indeed encouraged by, the guards – Connolly becomes a hero fallen in the national cause, to be revered and lamented for his sacrifice, safely added to the pantheon of Irish heroes, another casualty added to the long list of wrongs. His death is greeted with a mournful resignation, mixed with a religious consolation that justice will be achieved in the afterlife – but with precisely no sense that the wider revolution he sacrificed himself for must now be carried forward in direct contemporary action.

The crucial intervention that Eagleton seeks to make in *The White, The Gold and the Gangrene* is to resist such a nationalist seizure of Connolly, and instead to inscribe his struggle in the Easter Rising as part of a wider socialist vision. Connolly's aims were not directed towards this romantic past, trying to forge a country from the stuff of national myth. Instead, he adheres to the form of ironic nationalism similar to that which Eagleton had outlined in his Field Day pamphlet, seeing the nationalist cause as a necessary but not final stage in the longer process of historical struggle towards a socialist society – a society in which all people could obtain a genuine freedom, not just the notional freedom of switching one flag for another. This is by no means a dramatic invention by Eagleton, but rather a retelling of Connolly's own historical position. As Connolly himself argued passionately in a 1897 article, 'If the national movement of our day is not merely to re-enact the old sad tragedies of our past history, it must show itself capable of rising to the exigencies of the moment', with the political movement not being 'merely a morbid idealizing of the past', but also capable of engaging with 'the problems of the present' and the 'adjustment to the wants of the future'. In Connolly's view, socialism was not just an optional political element that could be adopted or forgotten by a nationalist movement depending on historical circumstances, but rather the only way that a nationalist revolution could actually be successful in more than a form of token imagery. As he described:

> If you remove the English army to-morrow and hoist the green flag over Dublin Castle, unless you set about the organization of the Socialist Republic your efforts would be in vain. England would still rule you. She would rule you through her capitalists, through her landlords, through her financiers, through the whole array of commercial and individualist institutions she has planted in this country and watered with the tears of our mothers and the blood of our martyrs. England would still rule you to your ruin, even while your lips offered hypocritical homage at the shrine of that Freedom whose cause you had betrayed. Nationalism without Socialism – without a reorganisation of society on the basis of a broader and more developed form of that common property which underlay the social structure of Ancient Erin – is only national recreancy.[13]

It is this position that Eagleton draws out in the play. In response to McDaid's and Mather's increasingly frustrated attempts to drag his reasoning out, Connolly finally speaks; but the prophetic experience of which he speaks stands in stark contrast to the cheerful and pragmatic cynicism of his captors. As he describes

> I heard a sound once that broke the silence. It was in the countryside, in Donegal; I was just standing there in the darkness. The hills stunned, holding their breath, attending to their own stillness. And then suddenly, imprinting the silence like the quick press of a bird's claw, a sound: eerie, unblemished, utterly inhuman. A momentary

wailing, like the bleat of some fabulous beast, so pure and unfractured that the blood stood still. I knew then that I'd strive to imitate that sound – cup the words in my palms and let it resonate through them. (*SO* 112)

For Connolly, it is the sound of the future – 'the murmuring of a world where we might speak otherwise' – which drives his present actions, giving him 'faith that there's something beyond the human which isn't against the human' (*SO* 113), and functioning as a harbinger of a new order and system that will justify his logic and struggles in a way that the mocking of the history cannot.

It is this – Connolly's struggle to realize this order of the future, not fulfil the legends of the past – that represents the ultimate threat to the guards, and one that cannot be assimilated or suppressed by their logic or laws. By answering to the future, and not the present, Connolly has situated his actions beyond the grasp of the present narratives of reaction; by being willing to sacrifice his body to realize this new order, he has taken away the last mode of control that the present order has over him. In a move that echoes the ideas of Herbert McCabe, Connolly, by embracing his death, has achieved the ultimate freedom in his life to live without fear and live without compromise: he is the embodiment of the 'intense' individual that Eagleton would theorize in *The New Left Church*. As McDaid notes with alarm, 'He's glimpsed the emperor without his clothes . . . So he's free – that's why we've got to keep him locked up . . . We've got to send him on his way before he slips through our fingers entirely. We're holding on to him by a hair as it is' (*SO* 115). The guards rush to complete their execution of Connolly but history has already escaped them: shedding the body of the present is again the final step to joining the poetry of the future.

A double monument to Oscar Wilde: *Saint Oscar*

The White, the Gold and the Gangrene thus, in a particularly intense way, dramatizes the tensions between the demands of a nationalist and socialist revolution, as first worked over in *Saints and Scholars* and also theorized in 'Nationalism: Irony and Commitment'. In a related but substantially different way, the concern with ironic interrogation of political and national identity infuses the dramatic action in *Saint Oscar*. As Eagleton explained his rationale for the play, 'Several of the characteristics which make Wilde himself appear most typically upper-class English – the scorn for bourgeois normality, the flamboyant self-display, the verbal *brio* and icono-clasm – are also, interestingly enough, stereotypical Irish traits; and pondering this odd paradox was one point of origin of *Saint Oscar'* (*SO* 2), with the 'paradoxes of [Wilde's] sexual, social and national identities [lying] somewhere near the heart of the play' (*SO* 5).[14] First produced in 1989 by Field Day Theatre Company in Dublin, and adapted by the Tall Tales Theatre Company in 2003 into a one-actor show, *Saint Oscar* centres on the life of Wilde around the time of his trial on charges of sodomy, and depicts Wilde debating the merits of socialism with his friend Richard Wallace, and arguing about Irish nationalism with his mother, Lady Wilde. Despite the scintillating defence that Wilde offers of himself in the courtroom, he is tried and condemned to gaol, where his lovers and previous friends gradually abandon him, until he ends up broke and dying in Paris at the play's conclusion. Counterbalanced against this nar-rative is an Eagletonian rendition of Wilde's ironic wit, integrating the thematic strands through displays of Wilde's intellectual flair and humour. While the biographical details around Wilde's life have long been a highly contentious area,[15] Eagleton's play offers less an attempt to polemically seize Wilde for a particular sectarian perspective, than a work deploying a recognizably Brechtian method, presenting us with a version of Wilde which constantly interrupts and challenges our perceptions. This is not to say that Eagleton's play is a work that delights in a liberal ambiguity or paradox. Rather, it is an active attempt to investigate the complexi-ties of Wilde, to fasten on the contradictions and see what elements can be drawn out into the present.

The first area of interrogation that *Saint Oscar* undertakes is the question of Wilde's politics, and Eagleton states in the introduction to *Saint Oscar* that a large part of his interest in Wilde stems from Wilde's socialist political affiliations, for Wilde 'wrote finely about socialism, [and] spoke up for Irish republicanism when the British sneered at it . . .' (*SO* 4). Wilde's own political essay, *The Soul of Man under Socialism*, set out an eloquent and idiosyncratic argument for socialism, attacking those who simply saw altruism and charity as a cure for the dispossessed of society, and instead advocating the abolishment of private property and the creation of an 'Individual-ist Socialism' that would allow the 'true personality of man' to flourish and grow to its full potential. As Wilde argued, the 'chief advantage that would result from the establishment of Socialism is, undoubtedly, the fact that Socialism would relieve us from that sordid necessity of living for others which, in the present condition of things, presses so hardly upon almost everybody'. The political task that Eagleton undertakes in *Saint Oscar* is not one of political seizure, but rather one of Brechtian alienation, foregrounding the contradictions between Wilde's professed socialist political beliefs and his aristocratic upbringing and mannerism. Instead of appropriating Wilde as a trenchant socialist *Saint Oscar* Eagleton, following a similar strategy to that undertaken in *Brecht and Company*, instead zeros in on Wilde's political ambivalence, to examine both how Wilde represented a definite challenge to the late Victorian English value system, and how the utopian socialism of Wilde, while failing to link with a directly political outlet or form a solidarity with a working-class movement, nonetheless still represents a horizon for socialist hope for the future.[16]

From the opening of the play, Eagleton generates a comic *Verfremdung*, foregrounding the faultlines that the work sets out to analyse, presenting a Wilde that directly invites the audience to critically and not passively engage with the material presented on the stage. The opening, with a Brechtian Chorus singing 'The Ballad of Oscar Wilde', immediately creates this ironic and satirical distance, where Wilde is described as a 'fat foreign ponce' who 'kissed the fine arses of titled buffoons' (*SO* 15–16), and throughout the play, the tensions between the socialist and socialite Wilde are constantly invoked, creating a shifting ironic undercurrent that constantly interrupts our attempts to position Wilde neatly within political categories. Wilde himself explains to the audience that 'I was a socially disadvantaged child: public school, Trinity College, Dublin, Magdalen College, Oxford' (*SO* 18): rhetoric that at once invokes the educational lineage of the upper-class, while deriding the very privileges that such education is meant to convey. Eagleton thus sets two understandings of Wilde into direct examination: the satirical mocker of Establishment preoccupations and values who, at the same time, is desperate to adhere to the very system he mocks.

This clash between the socialist and socialite is brought into a manifest exposure in the debate between Wilde and his socialist friend Richard Wallace. Wallace attempts to rouse Wilde to action with news of the rise of the worker's movement, but finds Wilde's response less than he had hoped for, with Wilde greeting this news with indifference, and actively mocking the workers for whom Wallace is trying to gain Wilde's solidarity. Wilde at once declares a socialist politics, 'Of course I'm a socialist: haven't you read my fairy stories for children? They're all revolutionary tracts' (*SO* 30). However, the rhetoric of revolution is unrealized in his conception of praxis. The Wilde depicted by Eagleton seems content to view politics as essentially a personal matter on a similar level of importance to his choice of attire: when Wallace informs him that 'All this concerns you Oscar; your cause and workers' struggle are the same', Wilde responds with the equivocal statement: 'But I don't have any cause . . . The only struggle I have is how to get out of bed without rupturing myself, which is hardly of interest to the proletariat' (*SO* 29). For Eagleton's Wilde, this refusal of solidarity is not a cynical betrayal of his ideas so much as it is their actual enactment; for as he states: 'I'm a socialist *because* I'm an individualist. How can anyone be an individual in this cesspit of a society?' (*SO* 31) – a rendering of socialism that, in refusing to commit to a 'cause', risks ending up as little more than an idealist vision.

Yet, having thus drawn out the ambivalences of Wilde's position, Eagleton promptly and deftly upends the debate, forcing a reconsideration of Wilde's socialist politics in the light of the tendency of more 'orthodox' socialism to slide into reaction. In Act 2, Wallace again meets with Wilde, but now the roles are reversed: Wallace is a capitalist himself, who has surrendered to a form of pragmatic reformism, where the 'most we can hope for is a rather more humane form of capitalism' (*SO* 56). It is now Wilde who rebukes Wallace, and speaks glowingly of the rise of socialism, claiming that: 'In a century from now everyone will be androgynous, the workers will run society, and the government will be paying Ireland a million pounds' reparation a year' (*SO* 56). For the contemporary audience of Eagleton's play, there is an ironic tension between this mix of the fantastic, the now commonplace, and the still-hoped for Utopia. Wilde's utopian socialism, on the one hand, refuses to be drawn into a commitment of the sort that Wallace desired, but on the other, it is this very refusal to be tied down that allows it to survive as a horizon of hope for a better society. As he rebukes Wallace, a pessimistic reformist hope is 'not worth hoping for at all. That's like saying the most you can hope for is to get the pox in one ball only. If you're going to hope, do it on a grand scale' (*SO* 56): a hope that Eagleton dialectically draws out of Wilde in *Saint Oscar*, showing Wilde's aesthetic of a socialist future as a promise still alive.[17]

In a concurrent debate, *Saint Oscar* also explores the question of Wilde's Irishness, and his position, as he puts it, of 'speak[ing] for Ireland in an English accent' (*SO* 59). Again, the desire to seize

Wilde as a defiant Irish nationalist is resisted, and instead Eagleton focuses on the tension of Wilde's position, depicting him as a figure prevaricating between patriotic sentiments and an inner sense of cultural inadequacy, whose ability to serve the nationalist cause of Ireland was compromised by his desire to uphold his reputation and class-position among the British Establishment.

This tension is drawn out most explicitly through depictions of the debates between Wilde and his mother, over the questions of the responsibility that Wilde holds towards the nationalist cause. Eagleton depicts Wilde as refusing to credit the situation in Ireland or lend his support to any attempts at change, instead content to hide in his eccentric aristocratic exile, mocking the Irish and English alike, with his wit serving as a tool for political evasion. Wilde at once claims that he speaks up for Ireland 'whenever the God-forsaken English scoff at it' (*SO* 21), while at the same time still refusing the possibility of using his wit and writing towards a political end for Ireland: 'A writer has no people. The least whiff of an audience is fatal to art; it's almost as disastrous as the truth.' (*SO* 21).

The crux of this relationship comes to the fore in rendering Wilde's famous courtroom scene, which has been subject to many retellings by subsequent authors. In an article examining the historical evidence for Wilde's behaviour during his court case, McDiarmid argued that the 'Irish rebel paradigm is the wrong paradigm' in which to view Wilde's speech from the dock in his trial for sodomy, and cites Eagleton's *Saint Oscar* as the foremost example of a work written in this 'wrong paradigm'. Eagleton is described as providing Wilde with a 'self-consciously traditional speech from the dock, one closer in its staginess, if not in its diction, to those in the Sullivan collection' of Irish patriotic speeches, with the implication being that Eagleton's play has merely repeated the 'traditional' depiction of Oscar Wilde as a defiant nationalist at his trial, and is thus at odds with the historical record.[18] McDiarmid's criticism is curious, for it seems Eagleton deliberately refuses to portray Wilde in the mode of the fearless Irish hero, but instead consciously parodies this very patriotic depiction of Wilde's courtroom behaviour. Wilde is urged to adopt the mythology of a defiant Irish nationalist – as his mother pleads with him: 'Stand up in court and defy them. Stand up and exult in your own being – in your own difference' (*SO* 25) – but Wilde is conscious of this mythology, and in a metatheatrical speech derides such forms of romantic nationalist seizure:

> Oh, I see. Your final chance to turn me into one of your Celtic heroes.
> The Cuchulain of the Old Bailey . . . No, mother, I refuse this last
> theatre of yours. I'll answer to the charges in my own way, with wit
> and cunning . . . (*SO* 25)

Instead of defiance, Wilde's demeanour throughout most of the trial
is sly and sarcastic, as he attempts to refute the charges against him
not with confrontation, but rather with his mocking wit – an Irish
precursor to Brecht confronting HUAC, embarking on a slyly ironi-
cal description of his actions with the rent boys, with *double enten-
dres* in almost every line:

> Oh indeed; we passed many an hour analysing the structure of
> [Shakespeare's] sonnets. I'm glad to say that many of these youths
> developed quite remarkably under my tutelage. Some came on apace;
> absolutely none of them failed to put forth a frail bud. It was an
> experiment in the crossing of class barriers. (*SO* 39)

It is only in the final moments of the trial, when Wilde is faced
with the real prospect of a prison sentence with hard labour, that
he comes to resemble anything approximating the defiant Irish
patriot. Manoeuvred into a corner from which his wit can no
longer free him by the aggressive prosecutor Edward Carson,
Wilde offers a tirade against British justice, argued not in terms of
guilt or innocence, but rather of the position of the British to judge
the Irish:

> My lord, I object to this trial on the grounds of a fundamental incom-
> patibility between the English and Irish notions of truth . . . I object
> to this trial on the grounds that no Irishman can receive a fair hearing
> in an English court, because the Irish are figments of the English
> imagination. (*SO* 46–7)

It is in these moments, therefore, that Wilde approaches the image
of being 'Cuchulain of the Old Bailey', and his rhetoric moves from
witty word-games to proud defiance of the British Establishment in
the name of the oppressed Irish. But, equally, the very suddenness
of the shift, after Wilde's previous sarcastic refusal to portray himself
as an Irish nationalist, is an alienating one, which does not under-
mine his logic so much as raise questions as to Wilde's position as
a committed nationalist. We are thus left, at the end of the play,
with a Wilde that is not seamlessly reconciled to an ideological
position, but rather thrown open:

I want them to write on my tombstone: 'Here lies Oscar Wilde, poet and patriot.' No, that's a bit terse; not true either. How about: 'Here lie the two Oscar Wildes: socialite and sodomite, Thames and Liffey, Jekyll and Hyde, aristocrat and underdog.' I could have a double grave and a double monument; friends could choose which one to mourn at, or alternate between the two. (*SO* 61)

In *Saint Oscar* Eagleton has sought to fashion such a double monument, and created a work that does not so much comfortably assimilate Wilde to a historical cause, than depict him as a figure that still interrogates the borders of Irish and socialist identity.

Conclusion

This chapter has traced a route through Eagleton's writing on Ireland, and has tried to foreground some of the major engagements that recur in both his critical and creative modes. By way of a conclusion to this section, I want to return briefly to a wider question which arose earlier in this study, but which seems to achieve an acute relevance here. In chapter 3, I examined Eagleton's concern with the development of rhetoric and cultural studies as critical fields to replace the previous modes of literary study, and noted that this had been a direction that Eagleton himself, for the most part, had not pursued. I now want to complicate that statement by suggesting that the works that I have addressed in this chapter seem to offer perhaps the most coherent example of this form of criticism in action. A critical method that works in both fictional and non-fictional forms, ranging from polemics and essays to novels and drama; addressing figures and issues in literature, history, politics, and culture; intersecting with both contemporary and historical debates: Eagleton's Irish writing is not an interesting periphery to his wider cultural theory project, but rather one of its most dynamic fulfilments.

6

The Full Circle?

In the preface to his recent study of the concept of terrorism, *Holy Terror*, Eagleton remarked about the return of his recent writing to the topics that had occupied his thoughts four decades ago. Stating that the book 'belongs to the metaphysical or theological turn (or full circle) which my work seems to have taken in recent years', he equally set forth a strong political claim for his return: 'the politics implicit in this rather exotic talk of Satan and Dionysus, scapegoats and demons, are more, not less radical than much that is to be found in the more orthodox discourses of Leftism today' (*HT* vi). I have traced out in previous chapters Eagleton's gradual shift back into a rapprochement with the positions of his earlier work, with *Ideology of the Aesthetic*, for example, returning to the human body as a foundation to counter the self-referential discourse of the postmodern, while *The Idea of Culture* signalled a reconsideration of the Williams-inspired notions of a 'common culture' as a means of resisting the fragmentations of identity politics. It would be with the new millennia, however, with the prospects of any sort of socialism seemingly more remote than anytime in recent history, and the rise of fundamentalist tensions as one of the driving forces in international and domestic politics, that Eagleton would explicitly return to the discourse of theology, not as a substitution for political concerns, but rather as an avenue for expanding the scope of radical cultural criticism. Eagleton was by no means the only figure of the Left to return, at this historical point, to reconsider the radical implications in theological discourse and the Christian tradition, with prominent theorists such as Slavoj Žižek, Jacques Derrida, and Alain Badiou being three of the most significant examples.[1] Yet Eagleton's own position, echoing as it does his earlier writings from his *Slant* phase in the 1960s, brings with it its own unique problematic. This chapter will explore the question of the 'full circle' in this latest phase of Eagleton's writing, and will trace how these works connect with the debates from earlier incarnations in Eagleton's career, and by doing so attempt to highlight some of the wider theoretical issues that such a return prompts about Eagleton's current critical position.

Prominent signals of Eagleton's renewed interest in his theological roots can be found in his 2001 memoir, *The Gatekeeper*, with Eagleton foregrounding his Catholic upbringing to the extent that, in this account, it becomes the key structuring principle in the development of his later political concerns. The title of the memoir itself refers to his position as a ten-year-old altar server at a convent, where Eagleton participated in the rituals which would commit young women to a life of confinement in the service of their religious faith. Eagleton also stressed his own brush with the priestly vocation, when he briefly attended a seminary, but decided to forgo co-option on the prudent grounds that pledging celibacy at such an age might be cutting himself off from a wider range of life experiences. More than interesting biographical facts, Eagleton is keen to stress the continuum between his early engagement in Catholicism and his later theoretical positions. The nuns, for instance, were at once depicted by Eagleton as naive sacrifices trapped in an otherworldly existence, but also, in their own ways, portrayed as powerful symbols of a radical approach to the world, in their refusal to live a compromised existence, and instead wilfully embrace an alternative mode of existence: 'these women . . . acknowledged in their own eccentric way the wretchedness of human history, which they would no doubt have called the sinfulness of the world, and were thus the reverse of the bright-eyed liberal modernizers' (G 14). *The Gatekeeper* thus functions as, among others things, an explicit foregrounding of Eagleton's conception of religion as a resource for political discourse, setting out the intellectual grounds for the subsequent direct return to these issues as a prominent factor in his critical work.

Reclaiming Tragedy: *Sweet Violence*

It is such an understanding that would underpin Eagleton's next major work, *Sweet Violence*, in which he undertakes a grand tour of the span of Western art and philosophy, speaking as easily of Aristotle and Aeschylus as it does of Žižek and Lacan, in an attempt to interrogate the idea of tragedy and the debates surrounding the genre. It is a work that frustrates easy engagement, and is in many ways Eagleton's most elusive work, due to the sheer range of material from which it draws. But, throughout the diffuse trajectories of *Sweet Violence*, Eagleton's engagement concerns several distinct problematics within the contested field of 'tragedy', and this is what I now will seek to draw out.

The major issue with which Eagleton engages in *Sweet Violence* is a problematic first outlined by Raymond Williams in his work *Modern Tragedy* (1966),[2] and one to which Eagleton's account is in many places directly indebted. The relationship with *Modern Tragedy* is perhaps the crucial unconscious running underneath *Sweet Violence*, in that Williams's work provides both the basic theoretical foundations and points of political engagement, as well as highlighting a fundamental theoretical crux that Eagleton's account tries to surmount. Williams's account had aimed at providing an emphasis on the presence of authentic tragedy in the physical world and day-to-day life of the mid-twentieth century, in a rebuttal to the prominent critic George Steiner and his 1961 work, *The Death of Tragedy*. In this influential account, Steiner had attempted to establish a distinction between two understandings of tragedy: the 'high' form of tragedy, embodied mainly in drama, and the 'popular' form of tragedy in life, as it is used in daily discourse; and having made this distinction, proceeded to ignore the latter understanding for the former. Steiner had asserted that from 'antiquity until the age of Shakespeare and Racine', the possibility of writing great tragedy 'seemed within the reach of talent', but since that time, 'the tragic voice in drama is blurred or still.'[3] As a result, the problems of modernity are supposedly to be viewed as mere social problems, not the stuff of 'proper' tragedy. As Steiner commented: 'Where the causes of disaster are temporal, where the conflict can be resolved through technical or social means, we may have serious drama, but not tragedy. More pliant divorce laws could not alter the fate of Agamemnon; social psychiatry is no answer to *Oedipus*. But saner economic relations or better plumbing *can* resolve some of the graver crises in the dramas of Ibsen.'[4]

How did Williams seek to counter such a case, which would seem to steer tragedy far away from being a concept that could be used to understand contemporary conflict and suffering? Tragedy, for Williams, was not some mystical experience missing from the world since the seventeenth century, nor was it just the death of princes. Rather, it is part of the texture of the 'ordinary life'. It is a man driven to silence in an 'unregarded working life', it is the 'terrifying loss of connection between men', it is the 'action of war and social revolution', it is 'a mining disaster, a burned-out family, a broken career, a smash on the road'. Williams notes, in an ironic voice, the objections often raised to such a conception: 'Tragedy, we are told, is not simply death and suffering, and it is certainly not accident . . . It is, rather, a particular kind of event, and kind of response, which are genuinely tragic, and which the long tradition embodies' (*MT* 13–14). But what Williams sought to contest is exactly the meaning of this 'long tradition', questioning whether 'it is really the case that what is called the tradition carries so clear and single a meaning' (*MT* 14). Williams argued that a powerful ideological effect of inherited understanding of tragedy is to reduce the understanding of tragedy to 'a crisis of personal belief', resulting in a situation where it can be 'taken for granted that modern tragedy can be discussed without reference to the deep social crisis, of war and revolution, through which we have all been living' (*MT* 62) and where the 'idea of tragedy, in its ordinary form, excludes especially that tragic experience which is social, and the idea of revolution, again in its ordinary form, excludes especially that social experience which is tragic' (*MT* 64). As he declares with heavy irony, 'War, revolution, poverty, hunger; men reduced to objects and killed from lists; persecution and torture; the many kinds of contemporary martyrdom: however close and insistent the facts, we are not moved, in a context of tragedy. Tragedy, we know, is about something else' (*MT* 62).

It is this separation that Williams contests, as he sought to recuperate the tradition of tragic theory that he associates with Marx, where 'Social development was seen as necessarily contradictory in character, and tragedy occurs at those points where the conflicting forces must, by their inner nature, take action, and carry the conflict through to a transformation' (*MT* 35). Williams was not simply proposing that tragedy could be used as a descriptive term for categorizing historical phenomena, but rather that understanding revolution in a tragic perspective would allow a genuine political insight and resolution. Williams attempts to move beyond what he perceives as a deadlock in thought about political revolution. He is clear in his belief of the necessity of revolutionary change in social relationships, arguing that 'A society in which revolution is necessary is a society in which the incorporation of all its people, *as whole human beings*, is in practice impossible without a change in its fundamental form of relationships' (*MT* 76, emphasis in original), which can only by truly achieved with the 'end of classes' (*MT* 77). But neither is he convinced by what he considers to be the orthodox Marxist line that advocates an uncritically positive understanding of revolutions, arguing that it is incorrect simply to 'interpret revolution as only constructive and liberating', for the 'more general and abstract, the more truly mechanical, the process of human liberation is ordinarily conceived to be, the less any actual suffering really counts, until even death is a paper currency' (*MT* 75).

Williams advocates negotiating this problem by using the concept of tragedy as a means of understanding the action of political revolution, for it is in this view that the upheaval and disorder of revolution can be faced, without passing glibly over the violence on the one hand, or lapsing into a reactionary refusal of the possibility of political change on the other. As he explains:

> The tragic action, in its deepest sense, is not the confirmation of disorder, but its experience, its comprehension and its resolution. In our own time, this action is general, and its common name is revolution. We have to see the evil and the suffering, in the factual disorder that makes revolution necessary, and in the disordered struggle against the disorder. We have to recognize this suffering in a close and immediate experience, and not cover it with names. But we follow the whole action: not only the evil, but the men who fought against the evil; not only the crisis, but the energy released by it, the spirit learned in it. (*MT* 83)

Although works that are fundamentally different in timbre and structure, the influence of Williams's position in *Modern Tragedy* on that of Eagleton in *Sweet Violence* is important and pervasive. Both studies hover around the same problematic: how can the understanding of tragedy be seized from reactionary and reductive definitions, and be put to use for political radicals as a concept of direct aid to their struggles?

Eagleton, following Williams, resists distinction between artistic and 'real-world' forms of tragedy, and the politics behind the move to define and limit tragedy according to a narrow conception of literary conventions. In this direct way, *Sweet Violence* offers something of a settling of old, personal scores, in that it addresses the ideological understandings of tragedy first encountered by Eagleton as an undergraduate at Cambridge. Eagleton detailed such a personal account in *The Gatekeeper*, describing how as a student he 'came to conceptual blows . . . almost from the outset' with his tutor, Dr Greenway [Redpath], over the lauding of such an art form as the embodiment of the highest human values. Greenway had held 'that tragedy was a rare, quasi-religious ritual which could no longer exist in the modern world', whereas Eagleton thought there was 'excellent reason for believing that there was still more than enough of it about' (*G* 170). Greenway in this account seems to function for Eagleton as a personification of what could broadly be termed the 'Death of Tragedy' school championed by Steiner, and signals the continuation of an argument stemming from Eagleton's Cambridge Tragedy days.

It is this view that Eagleton spends the first chapter (and indeed many other later sections) addressing and rebutting, as he traces out various theories of tragedy that have been offered, noting that 'Few artistic forms have inspired such extraordinarily pious waffle' (*SV* 16), and arguing against the idea that 'all-out nuclear warfare would not be tragic, but a certain way of representing it in art might well be' (*SV* 15). C. S. Lewis, A. C. Bradley, and I. A. Richards, among others, are all summoned and given short treatment; as are more recent post-structuralist critics who rely on a similarly restricted conception of the tragic, with Eagleton charging both modes of understanding, although theoretically antithetical, of coming to a similar dismissal of tragedy as a relevant contemporary concern: 'some conservative critics have thus decided that tragedy is no longer possible, while some radicals have concluded that it is no longer desirable' (*SV* 21). In response to this, Eagleton offers the proposition that 'there are other understandings of it, not least of those aspects of tragedy which seem most alien and obsolete, which . . . are surprisingly close to contemporary radical concerns' (*SV* 22), thus setting up Eagleton's point of intervention in the genre.

This sets the theoretical ground for Eagleton's engagement in the second major problematic: the continued validity of concepts of the tragic for discourse today, and specifically the discourse of political progressives. This is an argument that Eagleton holds out as being contrary to the dominant contemporary modes of Leftist discourse, those forms of postmodernism for which the instability of human subjectivity preclude the ability of engaging with tragedy as a trans-historical concern. Eagleton's specific target is what he terms 'left-historicism', a catch-all term that would seem predominantly to be aimed at modes of criticism and theory influenced by the new historicism of Greenblatt. Such criticism has revitalized many areas with its attention to the links between literary works and wider discourses of societal power, but at the same time marked by a certain Foucaultian pessimism concerning the ability of discourse to speak across historical moments. As Greenblatt had famously declared with regards to Shakespeare's *Henry the Fifth*: 'We are free to locate and pay homage to the play's doubts because they no longer threaten us. There is subversion, no end of subversion, only not for us.'[5]

As a counter to this Left-historicism, Eagleton asserts the tragic as offering strong grounds for forging a cross-historical solidarity. For, as he notes, 'suffering is a mighty powerful language to share in common, one in which many diverse life-forms can strike up a dialogue' (*SV* xvi), and one that links tragedy across time, from that of ancient Greece to that of late capitalism. Eagleton argues that a genuinely materialist understanding of the human, attending to the *longue durée* of the human species, will inevitably lead to something approximating a humanist position, for it is a material fact that humans share many biological characteristics that have survived unchanged over the millennia:

> But a genuine materialism, as opposed to an historical relativism or idealism, is also attentive to those aspects of our existence which are permanent structures of our species-being. It is concerned with the creaturely, ecological dimensions of our existence, not only with cultural value and historical agency ... However left-historicism may suspect that universals are governing-class conspiracies, the fact is that we die anyway. (*SV* xii, xiii)

It is from these 'permanent structures of our species-being', which serve as a common link between humans in different historical conjunctions, that Eagleton sees the grounds for constructing a radical-humanist aesthetic of tragedy. Tragedy, Eagleton argues, in its focus on the human body pushed to its limits and breaking points, is a particularly valuable mode of understanding as it allows us to establish a meta-historical solidarity on the basis of the common human capacity for pain and suffering:

> We feel sympathy for Philoctetes because he is in agonizing pain from his pus-swollen foot. There is no use in pretending that his foot is a realm of impenetrable otherness which our modern-day notions can only grasp at the cost of brutally colonizing the past ... But as far as his agony goes, we understand Philoctetes in much the same way as we understand the afflictions of those around us. (*SV* xiv)

Such an issue is brought directly to the fore, for example, in chapter 3, 'The Value of Agony', in which Eagleton meditates on the various forms of suffering depicted in tragic literature, ranging from figures such as Oedipus, Lear and Jesus, as a way of working out how the idea of suffering can be put towards a political use – in other words, examining how the structures of feeling captured in tragic literature can be seen to be replicated in wider historical forms. In seeing suffering as a value in itself as a kind of character-building exercise (the 'boy scout' view of suffering, as Eagleton derides it), as many theorists of the tragic do, they surrender to a highly reactionary, fatalist account; whereas to understand suffering as unbearable because it lies within our potential to overcome it is to unlock a radical potential. To make this point, Eagleton turns to the figure of Jesus, drawing on a theological discourse that serves as one of the major expansions beyond Williams's account. The importance of the case of Jesus is that, according to Eagleton, he did not revel in suffering: he cured the sick, he regarded his own impeding execution with trepidation, and begged for his father to spare his fate. The consideration of Jesus thus establishes that 'there is a difference between the belief that suffering is precious in itself, and the view that, though pain is generally to be avoided as an evil, there are kinds of affliction in which loss and gain go curiously together' (*SV* 36).

The invocation of Jesus at this point is not for the sudden purpose of advocating a Christian faith, but rather as representative of a model, or structure of feeling, concerning suffering that can then be used to illuminate the Marxist view of history. Marxism, by not simply holding out for some utopian future time when suffering may be abolished (which is contrary to the view attributed to it by Steiner, who claims that Marxism is anti-tragic due to its fundamentally optimistic world-view), but basing this hope for the future in an understanding of the corruption and suffering of the present, is ultimately a philosophy that embodies this tragic view of suffering. It is this that sets Marxism against liberal idealism, in that it sees 'exploitation as the definite condition of history', but which allows it to escape the pessimism or reactionary acceptance of the status quo of pragmaticism or conservatism, in that it carries a firm belief that 'men and women are both worthy and capable of much more than is currently apparent' (*SV* 40).

Tragedy, in other words, does not simply offer visions of despair but also the resources of hope, and it is by understanding this recurring structure of feeling – whether in religion, literature, or history

– that we can turn tragic perceptions into a political tool for the present. This is the strategy that underpins Eagleton's mission in the otherwise diffuse discussions, across the work as a whole. Such a concern with using the concepts of tragedy to assist in understanding capitalism is most forcefully carried through to the final chapter, ambiguously titled 'Thomas Mann's Hedgehog'. In this chapter, Eagleton reflects on the supposed religious origins of tragedy, and in particular the idea of the link between tragedy and sacrifice. As he notes, such a view of tragedy as sacrificial ritual is distrusted by Leftists, for it often means 'relinquishing one's own desires in the service of a master's', for sacrifice is 'what women do for men, infantrymen do for generals, or what the working class are expected to do for the benefit of all'. Yet, Eagleton argues, despite these negative connotations, the Left should not be too quick to surrender the concept of tragic sacrifice to its opponents, for sacrifice can also mean 'that there are times when something must be dismembered in order to be renewed' and that 'if a situation is dire enough, it must be broken to be repaired' (*SV* 275). In particular, what interests Eagleton is the idea of the scapegoat or *pharmakos,* an argument directly carried over from *The Body as Language* and its discussion of the idea of the *anawim.* As he explains, while Greek tragedy may or may not have its genesis in animal sacrifice, the 'figure of the scapegoat is clearly central to a certain strain of tragedy', with the rite of Thargelia in ancient Greece, where the pollution accumulated by the city during the previous year was expelled by selecting for purification two *pharmakoi* (*SV* 278). This *pharmakos* is thus 'symbolically loaded with the guilt of the community', and therefore serves both as a substitute and a displacement for the people of the *polis,* for in 'burdening it with their guilt, the people at once acknowledge their frailty and disavow it, project it violently outside themselves in the slaying of the sacrificial victim or its expulsion beyond their political frontiers' (*SV* 279). This figure of the *pharmakos,* as Eagleton recounts, is at the centre of a number of great tragic stories: Oedipus, Jesus, Lear, and the hedgehog of Thomas Mann's *The Holy Sinner* all offer reworkings of the image of the scapegoat. But, by understanding how the *pharmakos* has functioned throughout Western literature, we are able to grasp the central tragic moment of capitalist modernity. Whereas in most classical tragedy the tragic scapegoat is a single figure, deposed from society and forced to wander in exile, the tragic fact of capitalism is that in this system it is the majority who are the scapegoats:

In the current preoccupation with minorities, one vital insight is in danger of being obscured. The astonishing fact about global capitalism is that it is the *majority* who are dispossessed. There are, to be sure, degrees of dispossession, and shipyard workers are by no means destitute. But while the idea of a social order which excludes certain vilified minorities is familiar enough, and these expulsions are visibly on show, the mind shaking truth of a class analysis is that social orders have always invisibly shut out the majority . . . [T]he modern-day scapegoat is essential to the workings of the very *polis* which shuts it out. It is not a matter of a few hired beggars or gaol-birds, but of whole sweated, uprooted populations. (*SV* 296)

Given Eagleton's return to *The Body as Language* as, at crucial points, the source book for his later position, there is one final interesting issue to compare, between Eagleton's earlier and later dealing with the problem of tragedy. In *The Body as Language*, Eagleton had paid tribute to Williams's account of tragedy, but also seized upon an apparent contradiction. If, as Williams had held, tragedy was both a personal suffering common to all humans and a world-historical moment of tension that could be overcome, then the possibilities of overcoming tragedy would seem to be a task beyond the scope of a materialist theorization:

It *must* be true that irredeemable, local and personal breakdown is genuinely tragic, and it *must* be true that tragedy can be overcome. To deny either proposition is at the deepest level unthinkable, as *Modern Tragedy* brilliantly shows. But it is only by the self-transcendence of history itself that the *either/or* of this tragic contradiction can be converted into a *both/and*. The Jesus who confronted and conquered tragedy in the world-historical action of the cross was also the Jesus who wept over the death of an historically insignificant friend; it is only in the kingdom of heaven, where 'death shall be no more, neither shall there be mourning nor crying nor pain', that the redemptive power of that first tragic action will penetrate the darkness of the second with its own victory. (*BL* 113).

Sweet Violence, then, outlines the same problematic as Williams's *Modern Tragedy*, and indeed Eagleton's return to the theological discourse of his earlier Catholic Left positions allows a deepening of Williams's case. But having reiterated much of his earlier theological position from *The Body as Language*, Eagleton now retreats from the final step. Tragedy offers an arsenal of concepts to deepen Leftist discourse, but the resolution of this final contradiction, which Eagleton had previously held as unthinkable to ignore, quietly disappears from the account: a signal of both the extent of Eagleton's return to the theological mode, and the absence of the very religious certainty which once underpinned it.

After Theory: then what?

If one of the predominant themes in *Sweet Violence* was to issue a call for a reconsideration of unfashionable 'metaphysical' topics as a means of opening new modes of conceptualizing and articulating the facets of human struggle, *After Theory* represents the culmination of this turn. The dust jacket of the Allen Lane edition (but not, intriguingly, the Basic Book edition intended for the USA) of *After Theory* bears the simple silhouette of a passenger jet, an unmistakable symbol that suggests the thrust of Eagleton's book: that the modes of theoretical discourse developed by the wave of progressive thinkers through the 1960s were no longer sufficient for addressing an urgent, post-millennial political conjecture, and that new concepts must be employed by the Left in order to comprehend and critique these new circumstances. This basic proposition – as to whether the moment of theory had passed – was by no means a unique one, with the demise of theory predicted almost from the moment of its birth, acquiring an increased prominence as its rise progressed.[6] Yet Eagleton's position, as the critic who more than anyone else helped propagate theory in the literary-critical academy, assured his account a particular prominence and weight among this institutional debate. Indeed, *After Theory*, in many ways, could be subtitled *Literary Theory: A Conclusion*. Picking up where his 1983 account had left off, Eagleton traces the fate of literary and cultural theory over the past decades, from its highpoint in the seventies to the present time: a time in which, Eagleton argues, 'The golden age of cultural theory is long past' (*AT* 1). Eagleton's point is not to assert that we must now somehow adapt a wholly spontaneous existence, for he acknowledges that 'If theory means a reasonably systematic reflection on our guiding assumptions, it remains as indispensable as ever' (*AT* 2). Instead, Eagleton argues, the situation that we now face is the 'aftermath' of 'high theory', in which we have both 'grown rich on the insights of thinkers like Althusser, Barthes and Derrida,' but also, in some sense, 'moved beyond them' (*AT* 2).

The project of *After Theory* consists of two major trajectories: first, to take stock of the state of theory, to assess the gains and losses achieved since theory's rise to prominence on the back of 1960s' radicalism; and, second, from here to push critical discourse into new territory, into which previous modes of critical theory have been either unable or unwilling to enter. Eagleton's contention is that, while such theory may have originally offered itself as a radical critique, the critical edge has been lost. 'For the moment,' Eagleton claims, 'we are still trading on the past – and this in a world which has changed dramatically since Foucault and Lacan first settled to their typewriters' (*AT* 2). Instead, we now find ourselves in a situation in which 'Structuralism, Marxism [and] post-structuralism' are no longer cutting-edge, but instead ideas which have been safely co-opted into an institutional process. As a result, with the institutionalization of cultural studies in the academy, the political underpinning of this project has been displaced: 'what is sexy instead is sex,' with 'Quietly-spoken middle-class students huddle[d] diligently in libraries, at work on sensationalist subjects like vampirism and eye-gouging, cyborgs and porno movies' (*AT* 2–3). Eagleton is willing to give such a form of cultural studies its credit, admitting that it has established that 'popular culture is also worth studying', and refuted the tacit, long dominant academic assumption that 'human beings had no genitals' (*AT* 4). But the scales have tipped too far in the opposite direction: 'Intellectual matters are no longer an ivory-tower affair, but belong to the world of media and shopping malls, bedrooms and brothels. As such, they re-join everyday life – but only at the risk of losing their ability to subject it to critique' (*AT* 3).

If this is Eagleton's assessment of the current state of cultural theory, where did the rot set in? Eagleton locates the highpoint of cultural theory as having occurred in the years between 1965 and 1980, when thinkers such as Jacques Lacan, Claude Levi-Strauss, Louis Althusser, Roland Barthes, Michel Foucault, Raymond Williams, Julia Kristeva, and Jacques Derrida were at the peak of both their intellectual innovation and wider influence. This was not coincidence, but was 'the only period since the Second World War in which the political far left rose briefly to prominence', an era steeped in 'civil rights and student insurgency, national liberation fronts, anti-war and anti-nuclear campaigns, the emergence of the women's movement and the heyday of cultural liberation' (*AT* 24). If there was thus a direct tension on a historical level spawning the demand for new modes of thinking to inform the struggle, there equally was a tension on a theoretical level with how the dominant mode of Leftist thought – Marxism – could be modified to cope with these new demands. Eagleton points to the fact that much of the major wave of cultural theory of this period had initially functioned as an attempt to extend Marxism, but soon increasingly became seen as a way of moving beyond. Marxism, for the radicals of the 1960s, was at once tarnished by the long crimes of Stalin and specifically by the invasion of Czechoslovakia, but also by the changing economic and social circumstances with which it was unprepared to cope: 'It seemed ill-adapted to a new kind of capitalist system which revolved on consumption rather than production, image rather than reality, the media rather than cotton mills. Above all, it seemed ill-adapted to affluence' (*AT* 38). In other words, with much of the radical focus being placed on questions of culture, Marxism, with the theoretical primacy of the economic base, became sidelined from the debates. The decline of socialism as a political force in the 1980s and 1990s effectively completed this severance: 'Culture had been among other things a way of keeping radical politics warm, a continuation of it by other means. Increasingly, however, it was to become a substitute for it' (*AT* 45). Eagleton's essential case is thus one that has recurred across his career, from *Literary Theory* through to *The Idea of Culture*: critical theory has become severed from a practical politics, that must now be restored if it is to have a continued relevance.

Having registered these ambivalences towards the contemporary political function of theory, Eagleton also conceded that it has brought with it numerous gains, spending a whole chapter defending it against the most frequent charges, lest his apparent change of direction gives comfort for those traditionalists who had always distrusted theory as a necessary intellectual pursuit. The critical issue that Eagleton sees as lying at the basis of the contemporary position of theory is not so much what it has opened up for study, but rather in what it can only remain silent about:

> Cultural theory as we have it promises to grapple with some fundamental problems, but on the whole fails to deliver. It has been shamefaced about morality and metaphysics, embarrassed about love, biology, religion and revolution, largely silent about evil, reticent about death and suffering, dogmatic about essences, universals and foundations, and superficial about truth, objectivity and disinterestedness. This, on any estimate, is rather a large slice of human existence to fall down on. (*AT* 101–2)

The solution, Eagleton proposes, is for the Left to adapt a new discourse not afraid to talk of these topics, and it is in the closing chapters of *After Theory* that Eagleton embarks on this second, more prophetic, trajectory, addressing such issues as morality, death, ethics, and evil, again drawing heavily from his previous works in the *Slant* period and the ideas of Herbert McCabe. These are the most provoking sections of the work, but they are also the most fragile and difficult. On the one hand, Eagleton's chiding of cultural theory for its failure to address the topics that most acutely face humans, and his turn to issues such as love, death, suffering is a development, and his motivation behind this move is surely right:

> If it is to engage with an ambitious global history, it must have answerable resources of its own, equal in depth and scope to the situation it confronts. It cannot afford simply to keep recounting the same narratives of class, race and gender, indispensable as these topics are. It needs to chance its arm, break out of a rather stifling orthodoxy and explore new topics, not least of those of which it has so far been unreasonably shy. (*AT* 222)

The challenge to theory about its 'shyness' is a provocative one, but at the same time it raises a series of crucial questions as to Eagleton's own position for launching such a push, perhaps the most fundamental of which being that, if the position of the Catholic Left was problematic to the extent that by the 1970s it was wholly abandoned in lieu of developing new forms of 'theory', why is the solution to this theory now held to be a return to the discourse that it replaced in the first place? This is perhaps most evident in Eagleton's concluding visions, where he proposes that the current political order is based 'upon the non-being of human deprivation', but instead 'what we need to replace it with is a political order [based on] non-being as an awareness of human frailty and unfoundedness', as 'only this can stem the hubris to which fundamentalism is a desperate, diseased reaction' (*AT* 221) – a vision that resembles Eagleton's concern in *The New Left Church* with the ideas of vulnerability and meekness providing the basis for a socialist-Christian political programme (*NLC* 27). This is a challenging idea, but the difficulty lies in locating the specific site for such a struggle to take place. It is unlikely that anyone on the Left could disagree with such a statement – that it would be better if ruthlessness and deprivation were replaced with humility and compassion – but the more difficult question is, in the face of the seemingly all-pervasive system of advanced capitalism, to what conjecture Eagleton's new mode of discourse is to be put. During the 1960s, as was argued in chapter

1, Eagleton's writing was aimed towards a direct and specific political conjecture: the state of the Catholic Church, as it went through
a time of fundamental structural and political change, and an overall
political culture in which progressive politics was in the ascendancy. Eagleton's interventions at this point thus had a clear and
manifest political aim, that being forging a direct link between the
discourse of the Catholic Left and that of the wider New Left, and
his work had a defined audience, stemming from the *Slant* groups,
the December conference, and the other proliferation of progressive
political groupings. To put it in the terms of Eagleton's own argument from *The Function of Criticism*, it was a discourse that inter-
sected with an already existing counter-public sphere. In this second
incarnation, however, when such a specific counter-public sphere
is manifestly lacking, the question is as to whether this metaphysical discourse, as wide-ranging and provocative as it may be, will
inform a similar mode of practical politics (as Eagleton has always
insisted cultural criticism should do), or whether it will only serve
to further sever cultural theory from interventionist institutional
debates.

   This was a problem that, while present, was largely avoided by
Sweet Violence, with it being a work squarely situating itself as an
intervention within a cultural tradition, resisting conservative and
postmodernist dismissal of the genre to reinvigorate tragedy as a
political term; but a question that comes directly into the open when
considering two of his subsequent works working within this 'metaphysical' turn, *Holy Terror* and *The Meaning of Life*, in that one fas-
tened on a direct site of critical debate, while the other had a far
more ambiguous question as to the purpose of its intervention. Few
terms, over the past decade, have assumed the prominence in
Western discourse as that of terrorism. Invoked on a daily basis by
politicians and journalists, the rhetoric of terror and terrorism has
moved beyond the descriptor of specific atrocities and now serves
as a political clarion call evocative of pure evil, whether to justify
military intervention overseas in an oxymoronic 'War on Terror',
or as a nebulous threat dictating ever-increasing surveillance of
citizens in Western society. This is a debate that has equally per-
vaded the intellectual sphere, with fiercely contested debates over
definitions and deployment of the term. In a 2002 review-article in
the *Guardian*, Eagleton outlined the shape of this debate, contrasting
the book of the conservative orientalist Bernard Lewis, *The Crisis of
Islam*, against Noam Chomsky's *Power and Terror*. Eagleton characterized Lewis not simply as an apologist for the Iraq war, but rather

as providing an active intellectual legitimacy for the USA's actions. Lewis was described by Eagleton as the 'resident intellectual jester to the court of George Bush, a member of the scholarly wing of the occupation of Iraq', for whom terrorism is primarily a one-way process, the work of 'wickedness' to which the West is a passive victim. In contrast, Eagleton praised Chomsky's method of historical research, and his ability to counter his opponent through dispassionate and objective presentation of evidence.[7]

Holy Terror represents Eagleton's intersection into this debate, offering a case politically sympathetic to Chomsky's assertion that the only way to prevent terrorism is to stop participating in it, yet one conducted with a fundamentally different methodology. Eagleton sets out his terms in a way that positions itself against prevailing Leftist modes of debate almost as much as those of the Right, claiming that 'the left is at home with imperial power and guerrilla warfare, but embarrassed on the whole by the thought of death, evil, sacrifice, or the sublime' (*HT* vi) – thoughts that Eagleton proposes as nonetheless a crucial terrain of debate to contest in understanding contemporary debates concerning fundamentalism. The issue that Eagleton pursues in *Holy Terror* is not terrorism as such, but instead the much wider topic of terror, constructing a genealogy of a series of terms that have come to define the scope of contemporary politics, drawing on threads of argument from *Sweet Violence* and *After Theory* and weaving them into a focused investigation. The overarching point of intervention is to reinsert the concept of terror as a historical concept, not a fundamental new force that suddenly erupted on the world some time in the past decade. As Eagleton notes,

> [T]errorism runs all the way back to the pre-modern world. For it is there that the concept of the sacred first sees the light of day; and the idea of terror, implausibly enough, is closely bound up with this ambiguous notion. It is ambiguous because the word *sacer* can mean either blessed or cursed, holy or reviled; and there are kinds of terror in ancient civilization which are both creative and destructive, life-giving and death-dealing. (*HT* 2)

The immediate recourse is back to the literature of Ancient Greece and the cult of the Dionysus, and from here Eagleton teases out manifestations of terror in forms ranging from Shakespeare, the sublime aesthetic of Burke, and the psychoanalysis of Freud and Žižek. The span of Eagleton's investigation means that, at many points, *Holy Terror* threatens to erupt into an unruly enquiry, with the porous idea of 'terror' threatening to become too broad to cope with the specificity of the contemporary political phenomenon. Similarly, while Eagleton had praised Chomsky's reliance on 'facts' from historical and archival research, Eagleton's own account remains resolutely in the abstract, generating a certain looseness to Eagleton's approach as he ranges across philosophical, religious, and literary texts while making scarce use of the directly historical – a fact that raises the problem of this turn to metaphysics lurching into a mystification severed from a direct political reality.[8] But this is, in part, the point: terrorism is now a word in contemporary political and media discourse that is deployed as a synonym for 'mindless evil', and thus Eagleton's work is a struggle over the concept, designed to refuse this historical amnesia and instead reinscribe it as a process that has always haunted humanity. The purpose that Eagleton negotiates is not to retreat into a serene aesthetic pondering of a struggle that is always with us, but rather to goad us into recognizing that terrorism can only be defeated by understanding it in its full complexity: as Eagleton notes 'Genuinely believing that your enemy is irrational, as opposed to pretending to do so for propagandist reasons, will almost certainly ensure that you cannot defeat him. You can only defeat an antagonist whose way of seeing things you can make sense of' (*HT* 117).

Thus *Holy Terror* was a work that contested a particularly important and controversial ideological node: a result that was born out in the response to the work. For many conservative critics, *Holy Terror* represented a scandalous text, with Eagleton delving into a field that the cultural theorist had no business getting into. David Womersley, the inheritor of the Warton Chair at Oxford, provided a review for *The Social Affairs Unit* (a right-wing think-tank) in which he offered the dire warning that 'It is a dangerous thing to trifle with a serious subject; and Holy Terror is a dangerous, mischievous, book.'[9] This was not an isolated view, but one echoed in other prominent avenues of the mainstream conservative press. Noel Malcolm, writing in the *Sunday Telegraph*, for example, seemed offended by Eagleton's notion of even suggesting that there could be a continuum between the 'terrorism' of Al-Qaeda and Western 'state-terror', and gives apparently serious consideration as to whether or not *Holy Terror* is a work that supports the viewpoint of Al-Qaeda.[10] Such a view is plainly ridiculous, but the sheer blinkeredness of these responses, where alternative views of 'terrorism' are denounced as being treacherous, is symptomatic of exactly the point that is being contested: in circumstances where there is such poverty in understanding such a crucial concept, the role of the critic should be to rub these debates against their grain to provoke a deeper engagement, something that Eagleton's metaphysical turn directly enables.

If *Holy Terror* was thus a work of particularly acute ideological intervention, using Eagleton's 'metaphysical turn' towards extending a contemporary debate in a *Keywords*-like move, *The Meaning of Life* is a more difficult title to place. There is a certain irony in the title, both in the manifest boldness of its terms of investigation, and the fact that Eagleton's name will now forever be entwined in catalogues with Monty Python,[11] and indeed this is a tone that Eagleton constructs throughout the work, informing the reader that the 'meaning of life is a subject fit for either the crazed or the comic, and I hope I have fallen more into the latter camp than the former' (*ML* ix). What Eagleton offers is a short, popularizing engagement with this impossibly difficult question, pondering on what to ask the question actually means, with Wittgensteinian language-games, deconstruction, terrorism and postmodernism all picked up for pithy assessment in addressing questions of happiness, death, and love. Underneath Eagleton's account still remains a subtle but recognizable socialist politics: 'The capital which might be devoted to releasing men and women, at least to some moderate degree, from the exigencies of labour is dedicated instead to the task of amassing more capital' (*ML* 155). Consequently the meaning of the 'good life' that Eagleton advocates is one which resists being defined in individualistic terms, but instead one established in the dialectic between the individual and society, not far from Eagleton's suggestion in *The Body as Language*, that 'In the dance, man's fullest personal self-expression occurs in terms of his physical being-with-others: the community of the dance is the language of personal identity, so that for the dancer to be himself is to be in community with others, in a complex and changing action' (*BL* 9). The allegory that Eagleton now offers as a solution to the problem is similarly musical; that of a jazz group, which embodies a constant dialectic between the individual and the wider group:

A jazz group which is improvising obviously differs from a symphony orchestra, since to a large extent each member is free to express herself as she likes. But she does so with a receptive sensitivity to the self-expressive performances of the other musicians. The complex harmony they fashion comes not from playing from a collective

score, but from the free musical expression of each member acting as
the basis for the free expression of the others. (*ML* 171–3)

In the end, then, the meaning of life is not at all far from the 'spontaneous life' that Eagleton, in 1968, had argued was most fully and
positively depicted in *The Tempest*, where 'men are not wholly
active, shapers of their individual lives, nor wholly passive, parts
of a larger design in which they are merely manipulated objects;
human life is in someway an interpenetration of the two' (*SS* 156).

If *The Meaning of Life* therefore represents a retelling of many of
the major themes already developed in the 1960s (minus the vision
of the sacramental community, which Eagleton had presented as an
already-existing model of the kingdom of heaven), it provokes the
question of what Eagleton's purpose is now in reworking this into
coffee-table book form. In one way, it is an attempt to move cultural
theory into a popularized but still serious engagement with one of
the most difficult but still universal questions, and at a time when
bookshops are saturated with New Age guides and Oprah Winfrey
varieties of easily digestible affirmations, this is indeed no inconse-
quential project. This is a historic process that Eagleton traces as the
product of modernity, where 'Books with titles like *Metaphysics
for Merchant Bankers* were eagerly devoured' (*ML*, 48). Yet while
Eagleton is critical of the intellectual paucity that could spawn
this meaning-of-life 'lite' industry, it is possible to ask the question
whether Eagleton's cultural theory turning to popularizing metaphysics in this way negotiates a space to enact the function of
criticism that he deems necessary, or whether it will be absorbed
back into the industry it seeks to criticize. The challenge Eagleton
offered to cultural theory in *After Theory* was a far reaching and
necessary one: it must break forth from the narratives it has
relied on for the previous decades and chance its hand at something
new, a task that Eagleton identified as more urgent and radical
than those repeating only the discourses of class, race, and gender.
Eagleton's theological full circle is vulnerable to criticism on a
number of fronts: as Roland Boer has stated, in an article examining
Eagleton's theological return, 'For some, this is nothing other than
a return to mystification, a dangerous recourse to religion when
nothing else will do.'[12] I have registered a similar caution in this
section, seeing this turn as opening new opportunities for critical
engagement at a time when discourse of fundamentalism, terrorism
and evil have come to an urgent point of debate in contemporary
society; while also pointing to the possibility of such a return to

metaphysics, drawing on the work of the *Slant* period of the 1960s, as too easily gliding over the different political conjectures in which these two phases are situated. I will return to this question briefly at the conclusion of this chapter, but now I will move to the other aspect of the 'full circle' that Eagleton's career has made.

The return of literature?

If Eagleton's recent work has been marked by this re-engagement with a theological paradigm first addressed in the 1960s, with the consequential questions concerning the position of the 'metaphysical turn', Eagleton has also made a significant engagement with directly literary topics with the publication of *The English Novel* and *How to Read a Poem*; and these are again works that raise certain questions about Eagleton's current critical position. As has been traced in previous chapters of this book, Eagleton's earlier literary-critical works have been characterized by their adaptation and deployment of a series of theoretical models: with *William Shakespeare* offering a display of Eagleton's post-structural 'political semiotics'; *The Rape of Clarissa* forging a link between deconstructive and feminist critical modes; *Myths of Power* turning Lucien Goldmann's Marxian theories of 'Category Structures' towards the development of new modes of political criticism of the Brontës; *Shakespeare and Society* attempting to link between analysis of Shakespeare's plays and the ideas on culture and society developed in the work of Raymond Williams. In contrast, it is not clear that Eagleton's turn back to the novel or poetry at this stage of his career was marked by a similar desire to push criticism into new engagements, and instead presents a certain sense of uneasiness as to where his literary-critical project feels it should next move.

Such uneasiness is manifested from the preface of *The English Novel*, a wide-ranging study covering the historical development of the genre from Defoe through to Woolf. Eagleton briefly foregrounds the overriding canonical assumptions he is adopting in the work: 'I must apologize for confining myself so high-mindedly to the literary canon, but this was determined by the need to discuss authors whom students are at present most likely to encounter in their work. It should not, needless to say, be taken to imply that only those English novelists presented between these covers are worth reading' (*EN* ix). This slightly embarrassed preface is curious on a number of levels, not least because of the fact that, for much of his career, Eagleton considered such uncritical reproductions of inherited literary canons as deserving of stern attack. It raises the direct question of what Eagleton, in his turn back to the English novel, is seeking to achieve. Is this a work purely guided by a pragmatic urge, to provide the student with the most immediately useful material for their survey courses, putting to one side what Eagleton really thinks should be taught due to the 'need' of the classroom? Or is this actually the canon that Eagleton believes *should* be the substance of our study, but cannot quite bring himself to offer an explicit defence, instead content to tacitly leave the situation as it is? In either case, the result is a work that maintains a crucial silence when it comes to actually stating the grounds for its own assumptions – assumptions that appear to rearticulate previous critical positions and canonical selections from a variety of Eagletonian moments. One symptomatic example of this fact can be prominently found in the chapter on the Brontës. The opening to this chapter, discussing the 'fourth Brontë', Branwell, and the possible links between the character of Heathcliff and Ireland, echoes the earlier essay 'Heathcliff and the Great Hunger' from the 1995 book of the same name; while the later statement, that 'in the story of Catherine and Heathcliff, what one might roughly call Romance and realism meet only to collide' (*EN* 141), is a reiteration of one of the central theoretical arguments made in the 1975 *Myths of Power*. Similarly, the general concern with the central tradition of the English novel being dominated by writers who are not actually 'English' draws upon the arguments made in the 1970 work *Exiles and Émigrés*; while the discussion of Richardson's concern with letters and 'masculine' and 'feminine' writing reiterates the substance of much of the discussion from *The Rape of Clarissa*. What Eagleton offers is thus a fusion which, for all its many moments of insight, also feels like a work of stasis, repeating earlier points of discussion, but strangely unwilling to move them forward into distinct new critical ground or textual selection.

This stasis is perhaps not just attributable to the eclectic sources from which Eagleton draws his work, but also to a wider theoretical spectre that has haunted Eagleton's career. For all the numerous times Eagleton has polemicized against Leavis, it is telling that, even at this stage of his career, Eagleton is still working in many ways within a silently Leavisite canonical paradigm. In *Literary Theory*, as was seen in chapter 3, Eagleton had castigated the narrowness of the Leavisite canon, listing how the *Scrutiny* view of 'English Literature' consisted of a schematized road map, with

Austen, George Eliot, Joseph Conrad, and D. H. Lawrence forming the main tradition of the English novel, and with the 'B road' consisting of Defoe, Fielding, Richardson, Sterne, most of the Victorian novelists, Joyce, Woolf, Dickens, and Emily Brontë (See *LT* 33). Eagleton's parody in *Literary Theory* was a scathing and illuminating rendering of the limits of *Scrutiny's* literary discourse, especially in pointing out the fact that for Leavis it seemed that 'English Literature' merely contained all of 'two and a half women, counting Emily Brontë as a marginal case', while 'almost all of its authors were conservatives' (*LT* 33). Yet it is almost the identical narrative that Eagleton now traces through his own history of the English novel, save with token by-roads such as the inclusion of Swift as a partner to Defoe, and Walter Scott being paired with Austen. Similarly, both Leavis and Eagleton essentially hold Joyce as the last major point of the English novel, the difference being that for Leavis *Ulysses* represented a 'dead end', in which 'there is no organic principle determining, informing, and controlling into a vital whole, the elaborate analogical structure, the extraordinary variety of technical devices, the attempts at an exhaustive rendering of consciousness, for which *Ulysses* is remarkable';[13] while for Eagleton Joyce represents a writer for whom we are still now trying to find an equivalent. That is not to say that Eagleton has offered in *The English Novel* anything like a Leavisite critical practice; Eagleton's critical drive is still firmly political and underpinned by his command of a range of theoretical perspectives, unlike the nebulous Leavisite concerns that firmly resisted allowing themselves a theoretical or philosophical underpinning. But it also points to a curious reluctance for Eagleton, even at this stage, to move beyond a critical paradigm that he repeatedly criticized for its inherent limitations.

The fact that Eagleton *could* evidently have written a work that would break forth from the *Scrutiny* roads, and linked this tradition with a detailed account of developments in the post World War Two novel, is probably the most interesting point. The final chapter, 'Postscript: After the Wake', offers an almost impossibly brief (six pages which seek to cover the last 60-odd years of the English novel) but richly suggestive overview of the currents in the English novel since Joyce's final monumental work, touching on issues such as the work of the Angry Young Men in the late 1950s, the rise of the 'postimperial' writers in the 1960s and 1970s, the school and campus novels of J. K. Rowling and David Lodge, and the alternative universes of J. R. R. Tolkien and C. S. Lewis.

Having traced this out, Eagleton ends on a note of pessimism regarding the contemporary novel's ability to engage with the new political realities that we face. Liberal humanism, Eagleton holds, is still the dominant novelistic ideology: 'an honourable world view, humane, enlightened and morally serious', but whether 'it is adequate to a globalized world of terrorism and transnational corporations is a different question' (*EN* 337). It is this world that Eagleton charges the contemporary English novel with failing to address:

> But in a postsocialist, postfeminist world . . . the contemporary English novel is doing dismally little to disturb the reigning orthodoxies. So-called postmodernism has made significantly little difference to this situation; it has been, for the most part, liberal humanism in cooler clothing. We are still looking for a form of writing that would be equal to the world which has changed beyond recognition since James Joyce completed *Finnegans Wake*, or rather left its final sentence to circle back to its first. (*EN* 337)

This, then, would seem to be the area of the most vital need of a detailed contemporary political critique, wresting the canonical paradigm away from being another retelling of Leavis's A and B roads, pushing our understanding from this tradition into the interaction between the novel and society at this historical conjecture, rather than as a brief postscript to the highpoints achieved in 1939. Indeed, this is a fact that Eagleton would further lament in a prominent subsequent article in the *Guardian* where, while assessing the timid political state of contemporary British literature, he asserted that: 'Most British writers welcome migrants, dislike Tony Blair, and object to the war in Iraq. But scarcely a single major poet or novelist is willing to look beyond such issues to the global capitalism that underlies them.'[14]

The English Novel thus represents more the culmination of Eagleton's long interest in the novel in the English tradition – a synthesis of many of the positions he has developed through his career – but one he also marked by a certain theoretical indecision, working within a canonical politics rather than what Eagleton himself describes as the area of most pronounced critical urgency.

Similarly, *How to Read a Poem* seems to signal a return back into the modes of practical criticism, appearing at first glance an oddly conservative book. With a blurb claiming that the book is 'designed to banish the intimidation that too often attends the subject of poetry, and in doing so to bring it into the personal possession of the student and the general reader', and serialized in the weekend arts section of *The Times*,[15] it is again a work that takes a challenging position, both within Eagleton's corpus, and in terms of how Eagleton seeks to shift directions of institutional literary-critical orientation. As a guide, it achieves its manifest aims: with chapters devoted to topics such as 'What is Poetry?', 'In Pursuit of Form', and detailed readings of four examples of nature poetry, it offers a concise and lucid account of the key elements and concerns of the necessary critical modes with which to engage with poetry as a distinct literary form, rather than simply a form of discourse in which only the content is of relevance for examination.

What is of particular interest is Eagleton's choice for returning to the specific issue of the teaching of poetry. This is the issue that Eagleton pursues at length in the first chapter of the book, returning to the question of the 'function of criticism', and his explanation of the sudden necessity of this mission. Eagleton's concern is that students and teachers of literature are now predominantly engaging in techniques of content criticism: 'It would be hard to figure out, just by reading most of these content analyses, that they were supposed to be about poems or novels, rather than about some real-life happening. What gets left out is the *literariness* of the work' (*HRP* 3, emphasis in original). Eagleton spends substantial space defending against the charge that it was literary theory that allowed the formation of such circumstances, arguing that the 'truth is that almost all major literary theorists engage in scrupulously close reading' (*HRP* 2). A harsh critic might raise a sceptical eyebrow at aspects – not least of all considering that it was Eagleton himself who was probably the most influential critic to convince students that 'one can think of literature less as some inherent quality or set of qualities displayed by certain kinds of writing . . . than as a number of ways in which people *relate themselves* to writing' (*LT* 9, emphasis in original). What Eagleton does negotiate, however, is the fact that practical criticism is not alien to theory, nor is it alien to political reading. Consequently, Eagleton seeks to re-emphasise the role of close reading of literature, not as an elevation of a New Critical 'Verbal Icon' or escape from political and social considerations, but instead as a necessary (but not sufficient) condition for understanding the political functions of this writing. Poetry, in particular, compresses a unique form of experience:

> The modern age has been continually divided between a sober but rather bloodless rationalism on the one hand, and a number of enticing but dangerous forms of irrationalism on the other. Poetry, however, offers to bridge this gap. More than almost any other discourse, it deals in the finer nuances of meaning, and thus pays its dues to the value of reasoning and vigilant awareness. At its best, it is a supremely refined product of human consciousness. But it pursues this devotion to meaning in the context of the less rational or articulable dimensions of our existence, allowing the rhythms, images and impulses of our subterranean life to speak through its crisp exactitude. This is why it is the most complete sort of human language that one could imagine . . . (*HRP* 21–2)

In a position not totally dissimilar to the Eagleton of *The New Left Church*, where the value of literature was held in its ability to retain values and sensitivity in the face of a philistine capitalist consumer society, the skills of poetic close reading are proposed as an antagonistic force to the vulgarity of consumer capitalism: 'What threatens to scupper verbal sensitivity is the depthless, commodified, instantly legible world of advanced capitalism, with its unscrupulous way with signs, computerized communication and glossy packaging of "experience"' (*HRP* 17).

To be quite clear, Eagleton never dismissed the value of poetry as a part of the wider field of cultural studies, but rather offered an ambivalent sense of the importance of its role. As he stated in *Literary Theory*: 'Within all of this varied activity, the study of what is currently termed "literature" will have its place', but with 'its place' no longer having the assurance of being 'the most important focus of attention' in light of the new political demands of cultural studies. What *How to Read a Poem* offers, then, is not so much a contradiction of this position, but a removal of the ambiguity: the place of poetry is unequivocally described as 'a supremely refined product of human consciousness . . . the most complete sort of human language that one could imagine' (*HRP* 22). *How To Read a Poem* thus again repositions Eagleton as an oppositional critic, but now standing in opposition to the main emphasis of the movement that his own work has instigated, the defender of the radical legacy of the Cambridge School of practical criticism, a shift once more against the grain of contemporary literary-critical discourse.

Conclusion

In October 2006, Eagleton published a review of Richard Dawkins's atheistic polemic, *The God Delusion,* in the *London Review of Books.* Dawkins, Charles Simonyi Chair in the Public Understanding of Science at the University of Oxford, had long been among the world's most prominent atheist intellectuals, and *The God Delusion* offered an unequivocal critique of all forms of theistic faith, examining the scientific case against the existence of a god, as well as arguing that the perpetuation of religion had created the conditions for continued growth of bigotry and fanaticism. Not surprisingly, Dawkins's account quickly attracted significant media attention, featuring on best-seller lists around the world and attracting reviews in outlets across the political spectrum. Among the rush of media attention, both for and against Dawkins's account, Eagleton's review quickly stood forth as one of the most critical assessments of Dawkins's book (barring those from the Christian fundamentalist and creationist camps).

Eagleton praised Dawkins for his willingness to take the fight to religious fundamentalism, but offered scathing criticism on a number of grounds. He accused Dawkins of theological illiteracy: 'Imagine someone holding forth on biology whose only knowledge of the subject is the *Book of British Birds,* and you have a rough idea of what it feels like to read Richard Dawkins on theology.' In Eagleton's view, Dawkins was guilty of portraying all forms of religious belief as an undifferentiated mass, which failed to distinguish between the reactionary forms such as conservative Christian Creationists and Islamic fundamentalists, and the traditions of intelligent and philosophically sophisticated theology. For Eagleton, 'critics of the richest, most enduring form of popular culture in human history have a moral obligation to confront that case at its most persuasive, rather than grabbing themselves a victory on the cheap by savaging it as so much garbage and gobbledygook'. Eagleton's major point of critique was that Dawkins's stress on religion as the root cause of fundamentalism and intolerance, while seemingly progressive in holding out rational-liberal principles as a counter to mysticism and superstition, is actually politically counter-productive, in attributing violent fundamentalism to purely religious, rather than socio-economic, causes. As Eagleton described, 'Dawkins quite rightly detests fundamentalists; but as far as I know his anti-religious diatribes have never been matched in his work by a critique of the global capitalism that generates the hatred, anxiety, insecurity and sense of humiliation that breed fundamentalism. Instead, as the obtuse media chatter has it, it's all down to religion.'[16]

Not surprisingly, Eagleton's review prompted considerable debate in subsequent issues of the *London Review of Books*, with letters being published ranging from those deriding the philosophical underpinnings of Eagleton's account, to those praising Eagleton's willingness to tackle the difficult topic of holding up a progressive concept of religion in contrast to the burgeoning forms of fundamentalism gripping the world.[17] But perhaps more significant was the astonishing dissemination of the review across the internet, with hundreds of pages carrying links to Eagleton's review at the *LRB* site, and hundreds more posts quoting and discussing Eagleton's characterizations of Dawkins's book. Eagleton's review was quoted, praised, criticized, and attacked, in weblogs and forums, ranging from those of atheist socialists puzzled as to why Eagleton should be defending religion, to conservative creationists shocked to find a Marxist writing knowledgably on theological matters. The dissemination of the piece was so widespread that a Catholic Archbishop in Australia was accused of plagiarizing Eagleton's review while composing his own review of Dawkins's book – one of the most remarkable demonstrations of the scope of Eagleton's readership and influence.[18]

This chapter has registered a degree of ambivalence as to the recent directions of Eagleton's writing, seeing the full circle of Eagleton's career as both opening up the range of his critical engagements, while presenting a number of fundamental questions about his position as cultural critic, with the once *enfant terrible* of British literary criticism now occupying a strangely traditionalist position in the academy, calling students back to the close reading of poetry and canonical lists of novelists, with the radical theology of the 1960s' Catholic Left now redeployed as a counter to the excesses of the cultural theorists and the fodder to pocket-guides to the meaning of life. But the acute impact of this review, and the intellectual and political debates it managed to stimulate in a readership outside of a readily defined political spectrum, is perhaps the clearest possible example not only of Eagleton's continued ability to intervene politically at sites of critical tension, but also the fact that Eagleton's critical writing now probably achieves a prominence and audience far greater than at any previous point in his career – and this at a time when the general fortunes for socialist cultural criticism are at one of the lowest ebbs in their history. As Eagleton argued in a 2002 article, 'It's the survival of socialism, not Marxism, which is important; though it may turn out that Marxism has been such a major carrier of socialism that the survival of the one is impossible without the survival of the other.' In such circumstances, any resource which can nurture this socialist seed remains crucial: 'The role of socialist ideas is, in this sense, to protect the as-yet unborn future: to offer, not a storm, but a place of shelter in the tempest that is contemporary history.'[19] It is to this end that Eagleton's writing has constantly worked, and contributed, perhaps more than any other in the field, towards its fulfilment.

Notes

Introduction

1 Richard Aczel, 'Eagleton and English', *New Left Review* 154 (1985), pp. 113–23. Reference on p. 122.

2 Jeffrey J. Williams, 'Eagleton, the Wanderer', *The Chronicle Review*, 20 October 2006, 53: 9, p. B5.

3 Besides *The Gatekeeper*, Eagleton has been the subject of several profile articles in the mainstream press which provide relevant background interviews with Eagleton and his acquaintances, the most informative being Nicholas Wroe, 'High Priest of Lit Crit', *Guardian*, 2 February 2002 (available online at: http:// education.guardian.co.uk/academicexperts/story/0,1392,643458,00. html; and John Crace, 'Terry Eagleton: The Doctor of Dialectics', *Guardian*, 27 February 2007 (available online at: http://education.guardian. co.uk/academicexperts/story/0,2021894,00.html.) An interesting work that provides overview and interview material is Terry Eagleton and Michael Payne, *The Significance of Theory* (Oxford, Blackwell, 1990), and David Alderson, *Terry Eagleton* (Houndsmills: Palgrave Macmillan, 2004) offers what is to date the only other book-length treatment.

4 As cited in Wroe, 'High Priest of Lit Crit'.

5 Stephen Heath, quoted in Fred Inglis, *Raymond Williams* (London: Routledge, 1995), p. 188.

6 Terry Eagleton, quoted in Inglis, *Raymond Williams*, p. 199.

7 James Wood, 'Long Knives to Fish Knives', *Guardian*, 23 May 1991.

8 Catherine Bennett, 'A Cry from the Citadel', *Guardian*, 15 August 1991.

1 Eagleton and the Catholic Left

1   Anon, 'Disciples of Christ and Marx', *Time*, 10 March 1967. Available online at: www.time.com/time/magazine/article/0,9171,836776,00. html

2   Terry Eagleton (ed.), *Directions: Pointers for the Post-Conciliar Church* (London: Sheed and Ward, 1968), pp. vii, viii.

3   *The New Left Review* had been created by the merger of *The New Reasoner* and *The Universities and Left Review*, both of which had been founded in 1957.

4   Stuart Hall, Raymond Williams, and Edwards Thompson (eds), *The New Left May Day Manifesto* (London, 1967), p. 42.

5   Raymond Williams, 'Introductory Note', *Slant* 1:1, p. 2. The dialogue between *Slant* and figures in the wider, secular New Left was an exchange that occurred over the lifespan of *Slant*, as evidenced by the participation of Raymond Williams and Stuart Hall in the 1967 *Slant* symposium 'From Culture to Revolution', designed to create 'a dialogue between Christians and non-Christians who shared a common socialist commitment'. See Terry Eagleton and Brian Wicker (eds), *From Culture to Revolution: The Slant Symposium 1967* (London: Sheed and Ward, 1968), p. 1.

6   The *Slant* movement itself had evolved out of the earlier December Group, a yearly conference that ran from the early 1960s 'to discuss social problems from a Catholic point of view independent of any official organization'. See Adrian Cunningham, 'The December Group: Terry Eagleton and the New Left Church', *The Year's Work in Critical and Cultural Theory* 1:1 (1991), pp. 210–15. Reference on p. 211. This article provides details concerning the origins and activities of the December Group and the *Slant* movement, as well as detailing the roles and involvement of many individuals within the movement.

7   Herbert McCabe, *The New Creation: Studies on Living in the Church* (London: Sheed and Ward, 1964), pp. xi, xii.

8   Herbert McCabe, *Law, Love, and Language* (London: Sheed and Ward, 1968), p. 2.

9   Ibid., p. 99.

10   Ibid., pp. 158–9.

11   Ibid., 168.

12   Laurence Bright (ed.), *Christians and World Freedom* (London: Sheed and Ward, 1966), pp. 4–5.

13   Alexander Newman, 'The Status of Madness', *Slant* 4:2 (1968), pp. 10–13.

14   John Cumming, 'Real Ends: Brecht and Human Nature', *Slant* 2:3 (1966), pp. 3–9.

15   Terry Eagleton, 'Labour in the Vineyard', *Slant* 1:1 (1964), pp. 15–20. References on pp. 16, 19.

16 See Terry Eagleton, 'The Bending of a Twig', *Slant* 1:4 (1965), pp. 4–8; 'Parish and Politics', *Slant* 1:5 (1965), pp. 12–14; 'Mass and Media', *Slant* 1:2 (1964), pp. 12–14.

17 Terry Eagleton 'Politics and Benediction: Attack and Defences: Reply', *Slant* 2:4 (1966), pp. 24–5. Reference on p. 24.

18 Terry Eagleton, 'Politics and Benediction', *Slant* 2:3 (1966), pp. 16–20. Reference on p. 16.

19 Ibid.

20 Ibid.

21 Ibid., p. 19.

22 Edmund Hill, 'Politics and Benediction: Attack and Defences', *Slant* 2:4 (1966), pp. 21–4. Reference on p. 23.

23 Eagleton 'Politics and Benediction: Attack and Defences: Reply', p. 24.

24 Karl Marx, *Economic and Philosophical Manuscripts of 1844*, in Robert C. Tucker (ed.), *The Marx-Engels Reader*, 2nd edn (New York: Norton, 1978), p. 72.

25 Karl H. Hertz, 'The New Left Church' (review), *Journal for the Scientific Study of Religion*, 6:2 (1967) pp. 309–10. Reference on p. 310.

26 Adrian Cunningham and Terry Eagleton, 'Part 1: Christians Against Capitalism', in Adrian Cunningham et al., *Slant Manifesto* (London: Sheed and Ward, 1966), pp. 3–56. References on pp. 4, 14–15.

27 Ibid., pp. 49, 50, 51. Eagleton would also contribute a chapter to this work which traced the history of the relationship between the Catholic Church and the working class. See 'The Roots of the Christian Crisis', pp. 57–82.

28 See Terry Eagleton, 'The Idea of a Common Culture', in Terry Eagleton and Brian Wicker (eds), *From Culture to Revolution: The Slant Symposium 1967* (London: Sheed and Ward, 1968), pp. 35–57.

29 See McCabe, *Law, Love and Language*, especially chapter 2, pp. 35–67.

30 Terry Eagleton, 'Slant on Where We are at', *Slant* 25:5/6 (May 1969), p. 2.

31 See, for example among others, Terry Eagleton, 'Faith and Revolution', *New Blackfriars*, 52 (1971), pp. 158–63; 'William Hazlitt: An Empiricist Radical', *New Blackfriars*, 54 (1973), pp. 108–17; 'First-Class Fellow Travelling: The Poetry of W. H. Auden', *New Blackfriars*, 57 (1976), pp. 562–6; and 'Marx, Freud, and Morality', *New Blackfriars*, 58 (1977), pp. 21–9.

32 This was the view expressed by Denis Donoghue, in a prominent review of *Literary Theory*. See 'A Guide to the Revolution', *The New York Review of Books*, 8 December 1983, pp. 43–5.

33 'Priesthood and Paradox', *New Blackfriars*, 77:906 (1996), pp. 316–19. Reference on p. 319.

34 McCabe, *Law, Love and Language*, p. 21.

35 Willy Maley, 'Brother Tel: The Politics of Eagletonism', *The Year's Work in Critical and Cultural Theory*, 1:1 (1991), pp. 270–87. Reference on p. 273.

2 From Williams to Althusser: Eagleton's Early Literary Criticism

1 See John Higgins, *Raymond Williams: Literature, Marxism and Cultural Materialism* (London: Routledge, 1999), for a comprehensive critical overview of Williams's writing. Also see Andrew Milner, *Re-Imagining Cultural Studies: The Promise of Cultural Materialism* (London: Sage, 2002), for a wide-ranging study of how Williams's work has influenced subsequent movements in critical theory.

2 Williams sets out how his critical position developed in the essay 'Culture is Ordinary' (1958), reprinted in *The Raymond Williams Reader*, ed. John Higgins (Oxford: Blackwell, 2001), pp. 10–24.

3 Raymond Williams, *Marxism and Literature* (Oxford: Oxford University Press, 1977), p. 5.

4 Terry Eagleton, *Raymond Williams: Critical Perspectives* (Cambridge: Polity, 1989), p. 1.

5 See Raymond Williams, *The Long Revolution* (London: Chatto & Windus, 1961), p. 89. See also Williams's *Keywords: A Vocabulary of Culture and Society* (London: Fontana, 1976), pp. 133–6 and 243–7 where Williams offers concise entries on the concepts of the individual and society.

6 Williams, *The Long Revolution*, pp. 93–4.

7 Williams, *The Long Revolution*, p. 118.

8 Terence Eagleton, 'Nature and Spirit: A Study of Edward Carpenter in his Intellectual Context' (unpublished doctoral thesis, University of Cambridge, 1968). Eagleton's dissertation, which was supervised by Raymond Williams, offers both archival work concerning the correspondence of Carpenter and his relationship to a wider intellectual circle of political and social writers and activists, as well as a close reading of sections of Carpenter's poetry, concerned with linking the areas of Carpenter's poetic and political writing. The constraints of the degree are probably the reason for the formal, distinctly 'un-Eagletonian' nature of the dissertation – a work that Eagleton wryly admitted did not move his examiners enough 'to consider inflicting . . . on the world in the shape of the book' as it had 'caused quite enough suffering as it was' (*G* 97).

9 See Jean-Paul Sartre, *Being and Nothingness*, trans. Hazel E. Barnes (London: Methuen, 1957) esp. pp. 47–70, for Sartre's discussion on the concept of 'bad faith' and comments concerning authenticity as a 'self recovery' of being (p. 70).

10 In *Literary Theory* Eagleton would berate *Scrutiny* for its fetishization of the concept of 'Life', stating that it was a 'word that *Scrutiny* made a virtue out of not being able to define', which symbolized 'the enclosed coterie of the Leavisites themselves' (*LT* 42). While Eagleton was never what could be termed a mainstream Leavisite critic, it is interesting to note, despite Eagleton's criticism, the residual influence of Leavis and *Scrutiny* on Eagleton himself.

11 See, for example, 'Shakespeare's Society', *Times Literary Supplement*, 13 July 1967, p. 617; and Irving Wardle, 'Exploring Nine Plays', *The Times*, 26 January 1967, p. 14.

12 F. R. Leavis, *The Great Tradition: George Eliot, Henry James, Joseph Conrad* (London: Chatto and Windus, 1948), p. 2.

13 Raymond Williams, *The English Novel from Dickens to Lawrence* (London: Chatto and Windus, 1970).

14 Georg Lukács, *The Meaning of Contemporary Realism*, trans. John and Necke Mander (London: Merlin, 1963), p. 98.

15 This is not to say, by any means, that Eagleton was the only Anglo-American Marxist critic working at this time, with Fredric Jameson being another obvious example, having published important works such as *Marxism and Form* (Princeton, NJ: Princeton University Press, 1971), and *The Prison-House of Language* (Princeton, NJ: Princeton University Press, 1972) in the early 1970s.

16 The only substantive difference between the 1988 second edition and the first edition (published 1975) is an additional preface by Eagleton discussing the changes in literary theory since 1975, and the implications this has for *Myths of Power*.

17 Lucien Goldmann, 'The Sociology of Literature: Status and Problems of Method', *International Social Science Journal*, 19:4 (1967), pp. 493–516. Reference on p. 502.

18 Goldmann, 'The Sociology of Literature', p. 495.

19 See Lucien Goldmann, *The Hidden God: A Study of Tragic Vision in the Pensées of Pascal and the Tragedies of Racine*, trans. Philip Thody (London: Routledge, 1964).

20 The most famous example of this argument is probably Jacques Derrida, 'Structure, Sign, and Play in the Discourse of the Human Sciences', in his *Writing and Difference*, trans. Alan Bass (London: Routledge, 1978), pp. 278–94.

21 'Quick Guide', *The Times*, 6 February 1975, p. 8.

22 See Francis Mulhern, *The Moment of Scrutiny* (London: New Left Books, 1979), for a more detailed critique of the *Scrutiny* movement, to compliment Eagleton's brief but valuable analysis.

23 *The Marx-Engels Reader*, ed. Robert Tucker, 2nd edn (New York: Norton, 1978), p. 4.

24 Alick West, 'The "Poetry" in Poetry', *Left Review* 3:3 (1937), pp. 164–71. Reference on p. 167.

25 Louis Althusser, *For Marx*, trans. Ben Brewster (London: Allen Lane, 1969), p. 13.
26 Louis Althusser, *Lenin and Philosophy*, trans. Ben Brewster (London: New Left Books, 1971), pp. 127–86.
27 Althusser, *Lenin and Philosophy*, pp. 221–2.
28   Pierre Macherey, *A Theory of Literary Production*, trans. Geoffrey Wall (London: Routledge, 1978), p. 13.
29 Ibid., p. 149, emphasis in original.
30 Ibid., p. 155.
31 For early examples of this critical debate in *New Left Review* over Althusser, see Norman Geras, 'Althusser's Marxism: An Account and Assessment', *New Left Review* I/71, January–February 1972, pp. 57–86; Andre Glucksmann, 'A Ventriloquist Structuralism', *New Left Review* I/72, March–April 1972, pp. 68–92. For a direct example see also the exchange between Terry Eagleton and Francis Mulhern, occurring over a number of issues of *New Left Review*, concerning the article (and later a chapter in *Criticism and Ideology*) 'Ideology and Literary Form' (1975). Terry Eagleton, 'Ideology and Literary Form', *New Left Review* I/90, March–April 1975, pp. 81–109; Francis Mulhern, 'Comment on Ideology and Literary Form', *New Left Review*, I/91, May–June 1975, pp. 80–7; Terry Eagleton, 'Reply to Mulhern', *New Left Review*, I/92, July–August 1975, pp. 107–8.
32 For the most important critique of Althusser and his disciples from a member of the 'older' New Left, see E. P. Thompson, *The Poverty of Theory* (London: Merlin, 1978), which offers a scathing but brilliant assessment of the implications of Althusser's work.
33 Howard Felperin, *Beyond Deconstruction* (Oxford: Oxford University Press, 1986), p. 65.
34 The most notorious being 'A double-articulation GMP/GI-GI/AI LMP is, for example, possible, whereby a GI category, when transformed by AI into an ideological component of an LMP, may then enter into conflict with the GMP social relations it exists to reproduce' (p. 61). Such a formula may dazzle the eye with a seemingly scientific complexity, but simply abbreviating words does not actually make a statement 'scientific', as such.
35 See *Marx and Engels on Literature and Art: A Selection of Writings*, ed. by Lee Baxandall and Stefan Morawski (St Louis: Telos Press, 1973), pp. 134–6. Reference on p. 135.
36 Tony Bennett, *Formalism and Marxism* (London: Methuen, 1979), p. 154.
37 Francis Mulhern, 'Marxism in Literary Criticism', *New Left Review*, 108 (1978), pp. 77–87. Reference on p. 78.
38 Jacques Derrida, *Of Grammatology*, trans. Gayatri Spivak (Baltimore: Johns Hopkins University Press, 1976); Michel Foucault, *Discipline and Punish: The Birth of the Prison*, trans. Alan Sheridan (London: Allen

Lane, 1977); Jacques Lacan, *Écrits: A Selection*, trans. Alan Sheridan (London: Routledge, 1977).

39 James J. Paxson, 'The Green[blatt]ing of America: Some Thoughts on the Institutional Geneaology of Greenblatt's New Historicism', *Minnesota Review*, 41–42 (1995), pp. 221–35.

3 The Critic as Azdak: Eagleton in the 1980s

1 Terry Eagleton, 'Fredric Jameson: The Politics of Style', *Diacritics*, Vol. 12, No. 3. (Autumn, 1982), pp. 14–22. References on pp. 15, 17. Reprinted in *Against the Grain*.

2 Gerald M. Berkowitz, 'Theatre Reviews', *Shakespeare Quarterly*, 31:2 (1980), pp. 163–7. Reference on p. 167.

3 This play was recently the subject of an in-joke aside in *How to Read A Poem*, where Eagleton quoted a passage from the play as a 'rather mediocre piece of dramatic dialogue' (*HRP* 70). I would like to thank Terry Eagleton for very kindly making available his manuscript of this work.

4 These debates were republished in Ernest Bloch et al., *Aesthetics and Politics: Debates Between Bloch, Lukács, Brecht, Benjamin, Adorno* (London: Verso, 1977).

5 For the key collections of Brecht's writing, see John Willett (ed.), *Brecht on Theatre* (London: Methuen, 1964); and Willett (ed.), *The Messingkauf Dialogues* (London: Methuen, 1965).

6 These biographical questions surrounding Brecht would come under even more scrutiny with the publication of John Fuegi's highly controversial biography (of the same name as Eagleton's play) *Brecht and Company: Sex, Politics, and the Making of the Modern Drama* (New York: Grove, 1994), which, among other things, compared the personality of Brecht to those of Hitler and Stalin.

7 Walter Benjamin, 'Theses on the Philosophy of History', in *Illuminations: Essays and Reflections*, ed. Hannah Arendt, trans. Harry Zohn (New York: Schocken Books, 1968), p. 262.

8 See Susan Sontag's introduction to Walter Benjamin, *One Way Street and Other Writing*, trans. Edmund Jephcott and Kingsley Shorter (London: NLB, 1979), pp. 7–28.

9 For a concise comparison of Eagleton's book with others on Benjamin emerging at the same time, see Stanley Corngold and Michael Jennings, 'A Review Essay: Walter Benjamin in Recent Critical Perspective', *Modern Language Studies*, 16:3 (1986), pp. 367–73.

10 James H. Kavanagh, Thomas E. Lewis, Terry Eagleton, 'Interview: Terry Eagleton', *Diacritics*, 12:1 (1982), pp. 52–64. Reference on p. 63.

11 Harold Bloom et al. (eds), *Deconstruction and Criticism* (London: Routledge and Kegan Paul, 1979). It should be noted that, within this

collection, there was a considerable range of methods practised, with de Man and Hillis Miller being described in the preface as 'boa-deconstructors', while Harman and Bloom practised a less radical form.

12 This cautious hope taken from the political silence of Derrida at this point in the early 1980s stands in stark contrast to Eagleton's assessment of Derrida's later engagement with Marxism, *Specters of Marx: The State of Debt, The Work of Mourning, and the New International* (London: Routledge, 1994). As Eagleton wrote of *Specters*, 'there is something pretty rich, as well as movingly sincere, about this sudden dramatic somersault onto a stalled bandwagon' for, 'whatever Derrida himself may now like to think, deconstruction – he must surely know it – has in truth operated as nothing in the least like a radicalized Marxism, but rather as an ersatz form of textual politics in an era when, socialism being on the run, academic Leftists were grateful for a displaced brand of dissent which seemed to offer the twin benefits of at once outflanking Marxism . . . and generating a sceptical sensibility which pulled the rug out from under anything as drearily undeconstructed as solidarity, organization or calculated political action'. Terry Eagleton, 'Marxism without Marxism: Jacques Derrida and *Specters of Marx*', in Stephen Regan (ed.), *The Eagleton Reader* (Oxford: Blackwell, 1998), pp. 260–1.

13 See Eagleton, 'Liberality and Order: The Criticism of John Bayley', *New Left Review*, 110 (1978) pp. 29–40. Reprinted in *Against the Grain*.

14 Logan Speirs, 'Terry Eagleton and "The Function of Criticism"', *The Cambridge Review*, 15:1 (1986), pp. 57–63. Reference on p. 58.

15 Jürgen Habermas, *The Structural Transformation of the Public Sphere: An Inquiry into a Category of Bourgeois Society*, trans. Thomas Burger (Cambridge, MA: MIT Press, 1989), p. 27.

16 Richard Aczel, 'Eagleton and English', *New Left Review*, 154 (1985), pp. 113–23. Reference on p. 122.

17 See Jacques Derrida, *Of Grammatology*, trans. Gayatri Chakravorty Spivak (Baltimore: The Johns Hopkins University Press, 1976); Derrida, *Glas*, trans. John P. Leavey and Richard Rand (Lincoln: University of Nebraska Press, 1990).

18 Paul-Gabriel Boucé, *The Review of English Studies*, NS, 36:141 (1985), pp. 94–5. It is also interesting to note that Boucé saw a critical omission in Eagleton's text as being Eagleton's failure to recognize the 'Christian ethics' at work in Clarissa, and saw Eagleton as being 'at great pains to obfuscate the pervasive religious and spiritual dimensions of *Clarissa*', p. 95.

19 Elaine Showalter, 'Critical Cross-Dressing: Male Feminists and the Woman of the Year', in Alice Jardine and Paul Smith (eds), *Men in Feminism* (London: Methuen, 1987), pp. 116–32. References on pp. 127, 130.

20 Interestingly, one of the main responses to Showalter came not from Eagleton, but rather from Toril Moi (with whom Eagleton was in a relationship at the time and whose influence over *The Rape of Clarissa* was signalled in the preface as being 'deep and pervasive') who, in her important work *Sexual/Textual Politics* cited Showalter as one of the major Anglo-American figures practicing a 'reductive' mode of feminist criticism that placed too much emphasis on the category of 'woman', failing to address other political currents such as class the are equally important. See Toril Moi, *Sexual/Textual Politics: Feminist Literary Theory* (London: Methuen, 1985).

21 See Terry Eagleton, 'Response', in Jardine and Smith, *Men in Feminism*, pp. 133–5.

22 Elaine Showalter, 'Elaine Showalter Replies', in Jardine and Smith, *Men in Feminism*, p. 136.

23 The fact that Eagleton was taken to task for his appropriation of feminist discourse is particularly interesting in the light of one scene from *Brecht and Company*, where a 'Male Oppressor' persistently interrupts the women who sing 'The Women's Song', enthusiastically telling them how much he admires them, and that 'I wish I had the dignity and endurance of your sex, crushed as you've been by people like us' – a scene that would indicate Eagleton's acute consciousness of the risks of a masculine co-option of feminist struggle.

24 For example, see Jonathan Dollimore and Alan Sinfield (eds), *Political Shakespeare: New Essays in Cultural Materialism* (Manchester: Manchester University Press, 1985), for a highly influential collection of essays which developed new directions in Shakespeare studies by combining political commitment with new modes of theoretical engagement.

4 The Ideology of the Postmodern

1 See, for example, Jean François Lyotard, *The Postmodern Condition: A Report on Knowledge*, trans. Geoff Bennington and Brian Massumi (Manchester: Manchester University Press, 1984); Jean Baudrillard, *Simulacra and Simulation*, trans. by Sheila Faria Glaser (Ann Arbor: University of Michigan Press, 1985); Gilles Deleuze and Felix Guattari, *A Thousand Plateaus: Capitalism and Schizophrenia*, trans. Brian Massumi (Minneapolis: University of Minnesota Press, 1987); and Fredric Jameson, *Postmodernism, or, the Cultural Logic of Late Capitalism* (London: Verso, 1991).

2 Fredric Jameson, 'Postmodernism and Consumer Society', in Hal Foster (ed.), *Postmodern Culture* (London: Pluto, 1985), pp. 111–25. Reference on p. 111. This chapter was first given as a talk in 1982.

3 Ihab Hassan, *The Postmodern Turn: Essays in Postmodern Theory and Culture* (Columbus: Ohio State University Press, 1987), p. xi.

4 Eagleton would first engage with postmodernism in a substantive way as early as 1985, with an essay responding to Fredric Jameson's seminal article 'Postmodernism, or the Cultural Logic of Late Capitalism' (a work that is a precursor to Jameson's later book of the same name), which explored postmodern culture in relationship to the aesthetics of modernism and the radical avant garde. See 'Capitalism, Modernism and Postmodernism', in *Against the Grain*, pp. 131–47.

5 Terry Eagleton, 'Introduction: Part 1', in Terry Eagleton and Drew Milne (eds), *Marxist Literary Theory: A Reader* (Oxford: Blackwell, 1996), pp. 1–15. Reference on p. 15.

6 Raymond Williams, *Keywords: A Vocabulary of Culture and Society* (London: Fontana, 1976), p. 28. Emphasis in original.

7 For a more detailed critique of Eagleton's treatment of Foucault in *The Ideology of the Aesthetic*, see Dominic Paterson, 'Everything in its Right Place: Foucault and "The Ideology of the Aesthetic"', *Postgraduate Journal of Aesthetics* 1:3 (2004), pp. 111–23.

8 Schusterman's major criticism concerned Eagleton's lack of consistency in defining what he actually meant by employing the term 'aesthetic': 'Rather than helpfully trying to establish some [clarificatory ordering] of the most important meaning or dimension of the aesthetic, he simply takes advantage of whatever variant meaning happens to suit the vector of argumentation in which he is for the moment engaged.' See Richard Schusterman, review of Terry Eagleton, *The Ideology of the Aesthetic*, *The Journal of Aesthetics and Art Criticism*, 49:3 (1991), pp. 259–61.

9 Francis Fukuyama, *The End of History and the Last Man* (New York: Free Press, 1992). See also Jacques Derrida, *Specters of Marx* (London: Routledge, 1994).

10 See Francis Fukuyama, 'The End of History', *The National Interest*, Summer 1989, pp. 3–18.

11 See Jean Baudrillard, *The Illusion of the End*, trans. Chris Turner (Stanford: Stanford University Press, 1994).

12 Ernesto Laclau and Chantal Mouffe, *Hegemony and Socialist Strategy: Towards a Radical Democratic Politics* (London: Verso, 1985), p. 1.

13 Ibid. p. 2.

14 Charles Jencks, for example, traces the first appearance of the word 'postmodern' to the opening decades of the twentieth century, and shows the concept of 'postmodern' catching on in the early 1960s in the writing of Irving Howe, Harold Levine, and Leslie Fiedler. See Charles Jencks, *What is Post-Modernism?* (London: Academy Edn, 1986), p. 8.

15 David Harvey, *The Condition of Postmodernity: An Enquiry Into the Origins of Cultural Change* (Oxford: Blackwell, 1989), pp. 306–7.

16 Michael Ryan, 'Postmodernism', *The Year's Work in Critical and Cultural Theory* 5 (1995), pp. 147–50. Reference on p. 149. It should be noted that Ryan's hostile take on Eagleton's book was not the first

exchange between the two on this issue, for Eagleton had subjected Ryan's own work (which had attempted to re-read Marxism in a post-structuralist light), to an equally harsh treatment over a decade earlier. See Michael Ryan, *Marxism and Deconstruction: A Critical Articulation* (Baltimore: The Johns Hopkins University Press, 1982); and Terry Eagleton, 'Frère Jacques: the Politics of Deconstruction.' *Semiotica* 63 (1987), pp. 351–8. Reprinted in *Against the Grain*.

17 Perry Anderson, *The Origins of Postmodernity* (London: Verso, 1998), p. 115.

18 Raymond Williams, *Keywords: A Vocabulary of Culture and Society* (London: Fontana, 1976), pp. 77, 80.

19 T. S. Eliot, *Notes Towards the Definition of Culture* (London: Faber and Faber, 1948), p. 27.

20 Raymond Williams, 'Culture is Ordinary', in John Higgins (ed.), *The Raymond Williams Reader* (Oxford: Blackwell, 2001), pp. 10–24. Reference on p. 11.

21 Ibid., p. 12.

22 Ibid., p. 17.

23 Terry Eagleton, 'The Idea of a Common Culture' (1967), reprinted in Stephen Regan (ed.), *The Eagleton Reader* (Oxford: Blackwell, 1998), pp. 104–15. Reference on p. 115.

24 Colin MacCabe, 'After Ray', *Guardian*, 25 March, 2000. Available online at: http://books.guardian.co.uk/print/0,3858,3978085-99939,00.html

25 In 1990, Tariq Ali had begun work on a series of programmes for Channel 4, intended, as he explained, to be a 'set of one-hour dramas based on the lives, times and ideas of a set of philosophers from Ancient Greece to modern times'. Eagleton, as a result of his depiction of Wittgenstein in the novel *Saints and Scholars*, was asked to write a script for the programme on Wittgenstein. While most of the other programmes in the series were abandoned due to budget cuts, the Wittgenstein show grew in scope until it was turned into the full-length Derek Jarman film, funded by the British Film Commission. As Colin MacCabe explains in the preface to the BFI publication containing both Eagleton's and Jarman's scripts, 'It must be said that the transformations Jarman and Ken Butler brought to the original Eagleton screenplay are well in excess of the inevitable changes that attend any metamorphosis from script to screen', with the exact significance of these changes diplomatically designated by MacCabe for 'the reader to judge' (2). Colin MacCabe (ed.), *Wittgenstein: The Terry Eagleton Script/ The Derek Jarman Film* (London: British Film Institute, 1993). See also Terry Eagleton, 'My Wittgenstein' in *The Eagleton Reader* ed. Stephen Regan (Blackwell, Oxford, 1998), pp. 336–42, for Eagleton's own discussion of his impressions of the final film, which he describes as having 'some splendid moments', as well as some 'deeply embarrassing ones'.

26 See page at the *London Review of Books* website: www.lrb.co.uk/about/index.php

27 See, for example, Judith Butler's letter in response, *London Review of Books*, 1 July 1999, available online at: www.lrb.co.uk/v21/n13/letters. html where Butler at once defended Spivak and spoke of Eagleton's 'introductory primers' which 'spoon-fed' audiences – conveying the high theoretical disdain that seems to vindicate exactly Eagleton's point.

5 Nationalism, Socialism, and Ireland

1 Terry Eagleton, 'A Postmodern Punch', *Irish Studies Review*, 6 (1994), pp. 2–3.

2 Daniel Johnson, 'Irish History Deserves Better Than This', *The Times*, 23 April 1994.

3 Willy Maley, 'Brother Tel: The Politics of Eagletonism', in *The Year's Work in Critical and Cultural Theory*, 1:1 (1991), pp. 270–87. Reference on p. 282.

4 Martin McQuillan, 'Irish Eagleton: of Ontological Imperialism and Colonial Mimicry', *Irish Studies Review*, 10:1 (2002), pp. 29–38. Reference on p. 34.

5 Dougal McNeill, 'Sounding the Future: Marxism and the Plays of Terry Eagleton', *Cultural Logic* 8 (2005), paragraph 12. Available online at: http://clogic.eserver.org/2005/mcneill.html

6 Terry Eagleton, 'Nationalism: Irony and Commitment', *Nationalism, Colonialism, and Literature*, ed. by Eagleton et al. (Minneapolis: University of Minnesota Press, 1990), pp. 23–42. Reference on pp. 23, 30.

7 Edna Longley, 'Humpty-Dumpty Hibernianism', *The Times Higher Education Supplement*, 25 August 1995, p. 21.

8 Denis Donoghue, 'I am not Heathcliff', *New Republic*, 21 August, 1995, pp. 42–5

9 Steve Connor, 'Art, Criticism and Laughter: Terry Eagleton on Aesthetics', available at: www.bbk.ac.uk/english/skc/artlaugh.htm

10 Karl Marx, *The Eighteenth Brumaire of Louis Bonaparte*, in Robert C. Tucker (ed.), *The Marx-Engels Reader* (New York and London: Norton, 1978), p. 595.

11 Terry Eagleton, 'The God that Failed', *Re-membering Milton: Essays on theTexts and Traditions*, ed. Mary Nyquist and Margaret W. Ferguson (New York and London: Methuen, 1988), pp. 342–9. Reference on p. 342.

12 Walter Benjamin, 'Theses on the Philosophy of History,' in *Illuminations: Essays and Reflections*, trans. Harry Zohn, ed. Hannah Arendt (New York: Schocken Books, 1968), p. 257.

13 James Connolly, 'Socialism and Nationalism' (1897). Available online at the James Connolly Internet Archives. www.marxists.org/archive/connolly/1897/01/socnat.htm

14 See Eagleton's 'The Doubleness of Oscar Wilde' in *Wildean*, 19 (2001), pp. 2–9, for further discussion of what Eagleton terms as Wilde's 'Schizoid' personality.

15 Wilde's earliest biographers, for example, often gave highly distorted accounts and suppressed key facts, while even Richard Ellmann's magisterial biography, *Oscar Wilde* (Hamish Hamilton: London, 1987), has been criticized for its reproduction of a photograph which Ellmann incorrectly claimed was of a cross-dressing Wilde. See Merlin Holland, 'Biography and the Art of Lying', in Peter Raby (ed.), *The Cambridge Companion to Oscar Wilde* (Cambridge: Cambridge University Press, 1997), pp. 3–17, for a concise overview of the contentious area of Wilde's biographies.

16 Richard Ellmann offers a similar assessment of Wilde's relationship to socialism, noting that, while Wilde spoke approvingly of socialism, this stemmed from the belief in socialism 'on the grounds that it was so "beautiful" to do as one likes', which left Wilde, at many points, closer to 'advocating anarchism . . . than socialism' (pp. 309, 310).

17 In such circumstances, it is hard to credit Martin McQuillan's claim that Eagleton misrepresented Oscar Wilde by attempting to 'appropriate' him with a 'familiar incorporative logic' for the socialist tradition, and that many of the incidents in Eagleton's play are little more than 'flights of activist fancy', or that there 'may be some doubt as to the historical accuracy of the red, rather than pink, Oscar which Eagleton offers us in this play', for it would seem that Eagleton's concern in the play is exactly to examine how far Wilde resists any such appropriation. See Martin McQuillan, 'Irish Eagleton', p. 36.

18 Lucy McDiarmid, 'Oscar Wilde's Speech From the Dock', *Textual Practice* 15:3 (2001), pp. 447–66. References on pp. 448, 449.

6 The Full Circle?

1 See, for example, Slavoj Žižek, *On Belief* (London: Routledge, 2001); Jacques Derrida, *Acts of Religion* ed. Gil Anidjar (London: Routledge, 2002); Alain Badiou, *Saint Paul: The Foundation of Universalism*, trans. Ray Brassier (Stanford: Stanford University Press, 2003).

2 Raymond Williams, *Modern Tragedy* (London: Chatto and Windus, 1966). All further references will be given in body as *MT*.

3 George Steiner, *The Death of Tragedy* (London: Faber and Faber, 1961), p. 10.

4 Ibid. p. 8.

5 Stephen Greenblatt, *Shakespearean Negotiations. The Circulation of Social Energy in Renaissance England* (Berkeley: University of California Press, 1988), p. 65

6 For just one example, the cultural theory journal *Symploke* would dedicate its 2003 issue to the question of 'Theory Trouble', indicative of the wider debate around the position and role of theory occurring at the time of the publication of *After Theory*.

7 Terry Eagleton, 'Roots of Terror', *Guardian*, 6 September 2003. Available online at: http://books.guardian.co.uk/review/story/0,12084,1035753,00.html

8 One example of this comes when Eagleton contrasts the motives with suicide bombers and those of genuine religious martyrs, where he states that 'The suicide bomber . . . usually has one eye fixed firmly on his eternal rewards' (*HT* 94): a statement that would seem to treat suicide bombers as a largely homogenous, religiously motivated group, ignoring the fact that one of the most deadly suicide bombing campaigns over the past decades has been that conducted by the Tamil Tigers, a secessionist terrorist group motivated by secular-nationalist ideology.

9 Available online at: www.socialaffairsunit.org.uk/blog/archives/000713.php Womersley also remarkably claimed in this review that: 'Those of us who have battled through the joyless Marxism of the early writings would have found there little to suggest this eventual engagement with concepts and forms of belief which were once either brutally derided or coldly ignored.' Given the fact that, as outlined earlier in this study, Eagleton generated a prodigious output of theological writing early in his career, it is perhaps more appropriate to state that there is 'little to suggest' Womersley has actually read much of Eagleton at all.

10 Noel Malcolm, 'Terrorism? It's a form of primal scream therapy', *The Sunday Telegraph*, 11 September 2005, Reviews, p. 13.

11 Indeed, this may well be a deliberate sly point, given that Eagleton has previously remarked on the fact that he has sometimes been mistaken for Terry Jones of the Python's troupe, and that he included several stills taken from the Monty Python film *The Meaning of Life*.

12 Roland Boer, 'Terry Eagleton and the Vicissitudes of Christology', *Cultural Logic* 2005. Available online at: http://clogic.eserver.org/2005/boer.html

13 F. R. Leavis, *The Great Tradition* (London: Chatto and Windus, 1948), pp. 25–6.

14 Terry Eagleton, 'Only Pinter Remains', *Guardian*, 7 July 2007. Available online at: www.guardian.co.uk/comment/story/0,,2120880,00.html This article would also see Eagleton instigating significant controversy when criticizing the knighting of Salman Rushdie as being 'the establishment's reward for a man who moved from being a remorseless

satirist of the west to cheering on its criminal adventures in Iraq and Afghanistan'. This prompted Rushdie, among all the international furore which erupted over the acceptance of the award, to single out Eagleton for response, in a letter in the 9 July 2007 edition of the *Guardian*, where Rushdie denied the charge he supported the invasion of Iraq and highlighted his activities in opposing the war, prompting an apology from Eagleton in the 12 July issue.

15 This series ran over six weeks in *The Times*, from 20 January to 24 February 2007.

16 Terry Eagleton, 'Lunging, Flailing, Mispunching', *London Review of Books*, 19 October 2006. Available online at: www.lrb.co.uk/v28/n20/eagl01_.html

17 See, for example, letters published in the subsequent edition of the *London Review of Books*, 16 November, 2006, available online at: www.lrb.co.uk/v28/n22/letters.html which covered this spectrum of responses.

18 See discussion of this incident in Jack Malvern, 'The Archbishop whose words came from same hymnsheet as a Marxist', *The Times*, 10 March 2007. Available online at: www.timesonline.co.uk/tol/comment/faith/article1494951.ece

19 Terry Eagleton, 'A Shelter in the Tempest of History', *Red Pepper*, February 2002, Available online at: www.redpepper.org.uk/arts/x-feb02-eagleton.htm

Index